HOW CHURCHILL WAGED WAR

THE MOST CHALLENGING DECISIONS
of the SECOND WORLD WAR

FRONTLINE
BOOKS

www.frontline-books.com

ISBN: 978 1 52677 109 4

CIP data records for this title are available from the British Library

For more information on our books, please visit
www.frontline-books.com, email info@frontline-books.com
or write to us at the above address.

Printed and bound by CPI Group (UK) Ltd, Croydon, CR0 4YY

Pen & Sword Books Ltd incorporates the imprints of Pen & Sword
Archaeology, Atlas, Aviation, Battleground, Discovery,
Family History, History, Maritime, Military, Naval, Politics,
Social History, Transport, True Crime, Claymore Press,
Frontline Books, Praetorian Press,
Seaforth Publishing and White Owl

For a complete list of Pen and Sword titles please contact
PEN & SWORD LTD
47 Church Street, Barnsley, South Yorkshire, S70 2AS, England
E-mail: enquiries@pen-and-sword.co.uk

Or

PEN AND SWORD BOOKS
1950 Lawrence Rd, Havertown, PA 19083, USA
E-mail: Uspen-and-sword@casematepublishers.com

Contents

For Andrea, Amy and Isobel (and Tommy the black dog)

Whilst writing, a book is an adventure. To begin with it is a toy, then an amusement, then it becomes a mistress and then it becomes a master and then it becomes a tyrant and, in the last stage, just as you are about to be reconciled to your servitude, you kill the monster and fling him to the public.

Speech by Churchill at Sunday Times Book Prize, 2 November 1949
(Churchill Papers, CHUR 5/28A/7)

Acknowledgements

It has been my great good fortune to work at the Churchill Archives Centre and be a part of Churchill College, Cambridge. I hope the reader will feel that this book proves that I have benefitted from these connections. While all errors and opinions are my own, I am grateful to all my colleagues for supporting and encouraging me. This book only exists because of the College's generosity in granting me a sabbatical, and I owe a huge debt to Natalie Adams, Adrian Crisp, Sarah Lewery and Andrew Riley for covering my duties during my absence.

Professor David Reynolds had been an inspiration and a mentor, and his willingness to discuss my ideas has saved me from many mistakes and pitfalls. To quote his own phrase, he has proved himself an invaluable 'critical friend'. Needless to say, I am grateful to John Grehan and all at Pen & Sword for embracing the concept of this book.

The exercise of writing has allowed me to experience the other side of the reading room desk, and I want to thank all those who looked after me, in the Churchill Archives Centre, the National Archives, Cambridge University Library, Nuffield College and the Royal Archives. While I am naturally biased, this exercise has confirmed my conviction that archivists and librarians are the unsung heroes of the research world. Heidi Egginton, Gurnee Hart, Fiona Isles, Michael Norwich, Tony Wild and Professor David Woolner all read sections of the text and provided most useful feedback.

My thanks also to all the Churchill family, who have trusted me to write what I believe to be true, and especially to Randolph and Catherine Churchill and to Celia Sandys, who have always been supportive of this project. Material in the personal copyright of Sir Winston Churchill is reproduced with the permission of Curtis Brown, London, on behalf of the Estate of Winston S. Churchill, © The Estate of Winston S. Churchill. Quotations from The Fringes of Power are reproduced by permission of Hodder & Stoughton Limited, © 1985 Sir

John Colville. Acknowledgements are also due to the Trustees of Lord Alanbrooke, Lord Attlee, Patrick Alymer, Anthony Bonner, Churchill College, Ian Jacob, Victoria Kelly, Lord Moran, Debbie Schlosser and Charles Tilbury. This work contains public sector information licensed under the Open Government Licence V.3.0.

My parents, Tim and Anne, set me upon this course and have never wavered in their support. This book is quite rightly dedicated to my wife Andrea and my daughters Amy and Isobel. Churchill has dominated our family life for some time, and I hope they enjoy the final text.

Introduction

At 14.54 on Monday, 13 May 1940, Winston Churchill stood before the House of Commons and delivered his first address as Prime Minister. In his remarks, which took less than six minutes, he famously declared that, 'I have nothing to offer but blood, toil, tears and sweat' and spoke of his policy to wage war 'by sea, land and air' with the single aim of victory: 'victory at all costs, victory in spite of all terror, victory, however hard and long the road may be'.[1]

This moment was later beautifully captured by Sir Edward Spears, the member of parliament for Carlisle, who recalled Churchill calmly standing, 'in the queer light of the House, which so often seems to trail a veil of last winter's fog across the beams of the ceiling, he seemed rather white, but his jaw was set'.[2] As a Churchill supporter, Spears may not have been the most impartial witness, and by the time he was writing in the 1950s, secure in the warm glow of victory, this speech had already assumed a truly iconic status. It is now commemorated in cash on the British £5 note, which features the blood, toil, tears and sweat quote alongside the illustrated clock of Big Ben, set to 15.00 hours to mark the moment when Churchill finished speaking.

Churchill normally prepared extremely thoroughly for his great speeches. It is not unusual to find in his papers several drafts of an important address, culminating in the final blank verse speaking notes referred to by his private office as 'speech form'. Yet, for this most important of speeches, delivered only three days after taking high office, and critical in setting the tone for his new administration, only a single page survives in his files. It begins in typescript but then, after just a handful of lines, degenerates into a hand-written scrawl that itself peters out before reaching the most famous lines.[3] The accompanying

---

[1] CAC, Churchill Papers, CHAR 9/139B/194.
[2] Spears, E., *Assignment to Catastrophe*, Vol I, (Heinemann, 1954), p.138.
[3] CAC, Churchill Papers, CHAR 9/139B/192.

envelope suggests that other pages may have been passed at a later date to his private secretary, Anthony Bevir.[4] These may have included a complete final version that has since been misplaced or destroyed, or which is awaiting a triumphal rediscovery. Or perhaps Churchill was simply overtaken by events and forced to deliver the speech without having completed his notes. Either way, it is still a page that captures something of the immediacy and drama of that moment. For his words, which are only rendered more dramatic if adlibbed, marked a beginning, a statement of intent, and a declaration that Winston would wage war.

To his audience, that resolve and determination would not have been in doubt. His fellow parliamentarians knew him well enough, and had heard him often enough, to be assured of his bellicosity. What may have interested them more is what the speech did not contain; namely any detail or substance on exactly how the new Prime Minister would deliver victory. With the benefit of hindsight we know that it was achieved, and that, with it, Winston Churchill secured his place in history as an iconic figure and famous orator. Today his name is inseparable from his inspirational phrases and pugnacious image, complete with bulldog expression, omnipresent cigar and two fingered V for Victory salute. This transition from human politician to famous figurehead happened very quickly, in part encouraged by wartime propaganda. Yet, much as he enjoyed his celebrity status, it is clear that Churchill wanted to be remembered for what he did as much as how he looked or what he said.

When it was finally all over, in September 1945, he flew to Lake Como in northern Italy. As reading matter, the now former Prime Minister took with him specially printed volumes of his own, still secret, official minutes. Here on green paper in blue-bound volumes, marked as the property of His Majesty's Britannic Government, were the instructions, statements and questions with which he had continuously bombarded all those around him during the course of his premiership.

According to his doctor, Lord Moran, Churchill 'remained buried' in these documents for the entire five-and-a-half-hour journey (one hour for each year), 'only taking his eyes from the script to light a cigar'. This was about more than reliving past glories and seeking reassurance in the aftermath of his defeat in the 1945 general election. Churchill's thoughts were already turning to the future, and to the possibility of publishing his personal account of the conflict; his own multi-volume history of *The Second World War*. In part, his motivation

---

[4] CAC, Churchill Papers, CHAR 9/139B/191.

was to ensure that his contribution was properly understood. 'People say my speeches after Dunkirk were the thing. That was only a part, not the chief part', he complained. 'They forget I made all the main military decisions'.[5]

This work has been driven by the same desire to examine and understand Churchill's actions. His words and images remain an important part of the story, but need to be set in their proper context. My aim has been to try and answer the question what did Churchill do? How did he wage war?

Having been lucky enough to work on Churchill's papers for over twenty years, I wanted to follow the evidence, set the context, strip away the layers of hindsight and let the contemporary documents speak. My method has been to enter the Cabinet Room, to look into the despatch box, and to try and follow some of the debates and discussions as they occurred. I wanted to understand how the decisions were reached. It is an approach intended to highlight some of the emotion, humanity, uncertainty, complexity and nuance that are often missing when Churchill is discussed.

We know how the story ends. It is perhaps a self-evident thing to say, but while waging war, Churchill and his contemporaries did not. They were making policy and strategy on incomplete information, wrestling with a multitude of interrelated problems that were not always easy to prioritise or disentangle, and which were often influenced by fears that did not materialise or by factors that turned out to be inconsequential. Events could assume a momentum that it is not so easy for us to discern or understand. By looking at a selection of decisions in context and in detail, I hope that I have been able to give insights into Churchill's style of leadership, but also to reveal something of the mindset, constraints and challenges within which he was working. My aim has been to put the spotlight on history in the making, and to challenge some of the more simplistic assumptions about Churchill's wartime ministry.

The ten key moments and decisions I have chosen are not intended to be comprehensive. For that, I would need to be another Sir Martin Gilbert, the author of Sir Winston's multi-volume biography, on whose work all Churchill scholars draw. My moments have been chosen because they ask questions that interest me, because they give a good chronological spread and so may provide some insight into how Churchill's approach was shaped and changed by the war, and because they relate to different theatres of conflict and varied types of decision.

---

[5] Lord Moran, *Winston Churchill: The Struggle for survival 1940-1965*, (Constable & Company, 1966), pp.291-292.

What sort of war leader did Churchill want to be and why? How did he cope with the terrible crisis of his first few weeks and respond to the bombardment of the Blitz? Did he have a strategy for taking the offensive? What can be learned from comparing his approaches to Roosevelt and Stalin? How did he respond to the setback of Singapore? And what drove his personal interference in military commands and his sacking of Auchinleck? Why did he endorse the Atlantic Charter and embrace the concept of unconditional surrender? How did he survive illness and pressure? What were his concerns about D-Day, and how did he overcome them? Why were Greece and Poland so important to him in those final months of European conflict, and what led him to fight and lose the 1945 election in the way that he did?

These are windows on key moments, and inevitably partial and selective, but taken together I believe they do provide insights into Churchill's manner, motivation and method of waging war. The figure that emerges is more political, often more conflicted, less omniscient, more consultative though not always more considerate, inevitably more human and in my view much more interesting than the icon.

My approach is perhaps best illustrated by a quote that leads us into the first chapter. It is from an unpublished memoir by John Martin, a civil servant who joined Churchill's inner team as a private secretary in the spring of 1940. When reflecting on those momentous days, he was prepared to admit with the luxury of hindsight that they may have formed 'the finest hour', but that was not how they had seemed at the time: then, they had been 'a time of agony piled on agony'.[6]

---

[6] CAC, Martin Papers, MART 1.

Chapter 1

Chairman or Chief Executive?

Why did Churchill choose to become Minister of Defence as well as Prime Minister?

J ust before 18.00 hours on the evening of Friday, 10 May 1940, Winston Churchill took the short car journey from his offices at Admiralty House along the Mall to Buckingham Palace. It was a surprisingly low-key moment in an otherwise dramatic day. There were no crowds to greet him outside the famous royal gates. The British parliament, press and public were as yet unaware that Neville Chamberlain had resigned as their Prime Minister and that Churchill was about to replace him.

What might have gone through Churchill's mind as he gazed out of the car window at a London braced for war? On passing the soldiers in Horse Guards parade, maybe his thoughts went back to his youth: to his own experiences of battle as a cavalry officer in the Victorian empire. Could it really be almost forty-three years since he had served on the Indian north-west frontier? Did the portly, balding, cigar-smoking man of sixty-five still identify with the thin, ginger-haired, twenty-two-year-old, who, fresh from action, had dashed off an excited note to his mother describing how:

> I rode on my grey pony all along the skirmish line where everyone else was lying down in cover. Foolish perhaps but I play for high stakes and given an audience there is no act too daring or too noble. Without the gallery things are different.[1]

Now, in May 1940, the stakes could not be higher, and it was the whole world that was watching. That very morning Hitler had launched his *blitzkrieg* offensive against France and the Low Countries. The war was

---

[1] CAC, Churchill Papers, CHAR 28/23/57.

1

entering a new and possibly decisive phase. It was time to steel himself to play the gallery once again.

With Big Ben and the Palace of Westminster in view, perhaps he pondered upon his immediate task. The will of the House of Commons was that a national government be formed, bringing together representatives of all the major political parties. As early as October 1902, when serving as the newly elected member for the northern town of Oldham, he had confessed that, 'the idea of a central party, fresher, freer, more efficient yet above all loyal and patriotic, is very pleasing to my heart'. Certainly, he had never been a fierce party man, changing his political allegiance twice; crossing the floor from the Conservatives to the Liberals in 1904, and back again twenty years later. But this had made him enemies in both camps. Where he had been consistent was in his opposition to the Labour movement, which, even in 1902, he had regarded as 'anti-national, irreligious and perhaps communistic'[2]. Yet now Labour was the second biggest party in the Commons and he had to lead a coalition that would depend on their support.

As he swept through Admiralty Arch, maybe he paused to consider his dramatic rise and fall during the First World War. There is no doubt that the Gallipoli campaign continued to cast its long shadow, as he would later admit, writing:

> I was ruined for the time being in 1915 over the Dardanelles, and a supreme enterprise was cast away, through my trying to carry out a major and cardinal operation of war from a subordinate position. Men are ill- advised to try such ventures. The lesson had sunk into my nature.[3]

In his multi-volume history, *The World Crisis*, he had already set out his analysis of the failings of British leadership during the Great War:

> No one possessed plenary power. The experts were frequently wrong. The politicians were frequently right. The wishes of foreign Governments, themselves convulsed internally by difficulties the counterpart of our own, were constantly thrusting themselves athwart our policy. Without the title deeds of positive achievement no one had the power to give clear brutal orders which would command unquestioning respect. Power was widely disseminated among the many important personages who in this period formed the governing instrument. Knowledge was very unequally shared.[4]

---

[2] CAC, Churchill Additional Papers, WCHL 1/24.
[3] Churchill, W., *The Second World War*, Vol. II *Their Finest Hour*, (Cassell & Co Ltd, 1949), p.14.
[4] Churchill, W., *The World Crisis*, Vol.II 1915, (Thornton Butterworth Ltd, 1923), p.498.

These were the mistakes that he believed he had to avoid this time round. His conclusion was clear. Being Prime Minister in name only was not enough. He could not drive through major operations in war unless he had the executive power to do so. If he were to lead from the front, if he were to forge an effective coalition, then he needed to establish his control over both the political and military elements. Such convictions would only have been reinforced as he reflected on his strange path to power.

Churchill had first entered the British Cabinet in 1908, at the age of just thirty-three, and over the course of the next twenty years he had served in many of the major Offices of State. Yet, in the decade leading up to the outbreak of war, he had been excluded from high office. To some of his political contemporaries he was a reactionary figure who had told the suffragettes he would not be henpecked and had dismissed Gandhi as a 'half naked fakir'. His opposition to self-governing status for India, and his ill-judged support for Edward VIII during the Abdication Crisis had contributed to an increasing political isolation. Some had even dismissed his calls for rearmament in the face of Hitler's growing power as a cynical ploy designed to undermine Prime Ministers Baldwin and Chamberlain. His long and controversial career, with its changes of party, had made him enemies on both sides of the House of Commons. Such fears, suspicions, rivalries and jealousies were only exacerbated by Churchill's forceful personality; a combustible mix of eloquence, self-confidence and energy with a tendency to dominate that did not always make him a congenial colleague.

Throughout the 1930s Winston had made no secret of his desire to return to front bench politics. He had remained a member of parliament and a Privy Counsellor, and had been brought onto the newly created Air Defence Research Sub Committee in 1935, but he had been kept out of the Cabinet. In March 1936, when Prime Minister Stanley Baldwin created the new position of Minister for the Co-ordination of Defence to help oversee the beginnings of a new rearmament policy, he was felt by many to be the obvious candidate, having considerable interest and experience in military matters. He had already served as First Lord of the Admiralty for the navy, as Secretary of State for War for the army, and as Secretary of State for Air for the air force, and while this new post did not replace or outrank the three existing armed service ministers, and had no department of its own and no real executive authority, it would have provided Churchill with a way back into government. His personal papers show that he was following the issue closely and it is clear from his memoirs that he would have accepted the position.

In the event, Baldwin gave the job to the politician and lawyer, Sir Thomas Inskip, a former Attorney General: a move that was famously felt by Churchill's friends to be the 'most remarkable appointment since the Emperor Caligula made his horse a consul'[5]. Yet one strong reason for Churchill's exclusion is revealed in the letter that he had already received from his friend and fellow member of parliament, Admiral Sir Roger Keyes. Summarising a conversation with Baldwin in a corridor at the Palace of Westminster, Keyes relates that when he told Baldwin, 'Well, it would be a very good appointment, both in your interests and those of the Country' – He [Baldwin]said "I cannot only think of my interests I have to think of the smooth working of the machine".[6] Chamberlain, then the powerful Chancellor of the Exchequer and Baldwin's most likely successor as Prime Minister had almost identical views, writing to his sister Ida that Churchill was 'in the usual excited condition that comes on him when he smells war, and if he were in the Cabinet we should be spending all our time in holding him down instead of getting on with our business'.[7]

Churchill must have been equally disappointed not to get the post in January 1939, when Neville Chamberlain, by then Prime Minister, gave it to Admiral Lord Chatfield. For, even though Churchill's public reputation was now rising as his warnings about nazism were seen to be increasingly prescient, there remained many within Westminster and Whitehall who were wary of him. Chamberlain, upon whose patronage any return would depend, certainly considered him a potentially disruptive presence in any Cabinet or council. He wrote that although he could not help liking Winston, 'I think him nearly always wrong and impossible as a colleague'; later remarking, 'That is Winston all over. His are summer storms, violent but of short duration and after followed by sunshine. But they make him uncommonly difficult to work with'.[8]

Yet, with the outbreak of hostilities, Chamberlain had no choice but to bring Churchill into government. Large sections of parliament, press and public opinion were now demanding it. He returned as First Lord of the Admiralty, the position he had held at the beginning of the First World War. But this does not mean that there was an immediate

---

[5] Who first coined this phrase now seems uncertain. See Lord Ismay, *The Memoirs of Lord Ismay*, (William Heinemann Ltd, 1960) p.75, cites it as 'the comment overheard in a certain club'.

[6] CAC, Churchill Papers, CHAR 2/251/90-91.

[7] Self, R. (ed) *The Neville Chamberlain Diary Letters*, Vol. IV, (Ashgate, 2005), p.179, (letter to Ida, 14 March 1936).

[8] Self, *The Neville Chamberlain Diary Letters*, Vol. IV, p.311 (letter to Hilda, 27 March 1938), p.438 (letter to Ida, 5 August 1939).

acceptance of him within the corridors of power. Jock Colville was to become one of Churchill's closest advisers and greatest admirers, instrumental in the founding of both Churchill College and its Archives Centre. But Colville was in No. 10 before Churchill. He began the war as one of Neville Chamberlain's private secretaries. His diaries for the period September 1939 to May 1940 reflect sceptical views about Churchill, which were widespread not just in Downing Street but throughout Whitehall. Colville listened to Churchill's first wartime broadcast of 1 October 1939, and commented:

> He certainly gives one confidence and will, I suspect, be Prime Minister before this war is over. Nevertheless, judging from his record of untrustworthiness and instability, he may, in that case, lead us into the most dangerous paths. But he is the only man in the country who commands anything like universal respect, and perhaps with age he has become less inclined to undertake rash adventures.[9]

Churchill certainly chafed at being tied to the Admiralty. Chamberlain had created a War Cabinet of nine to provide overall direction during the conflict, comprising himself, the Chancellor of the Exchequer, the three armed service ministers, the Secretary of State for Foreign Affairs, the Minister for Military Co-ordination, the Lord Privy Seal, and a Minister without Portfolio (former Cabinet Secretary Lord Hankey), and to which other ministers, key civil servants and the Chiefs of Staff could be summoned. This replaced the normal much larger peacetime Cabinet, and was modeled on the body set up at the latter end of the First World War by Prime Minister Lloyd George in 1916.

Military strategy was developed independently of the politicians by the professional heads of the three services sitting together in the Chiefs of Staff Committee: The First Sea Lord for the navy; the Chief of the Imperial General Staff for the army; and the Chief of the Air Staff for the Royal Air Force. From October 1939, a Standing Ministerial Committee on Military Co-ordination was introduced to try and act as an intermediate body, reducing pressure by controlling the flow of military proposals to the War Cabinet. Its remit was, 'To keep under constant review on behalf of the War Cabinet the main factors in the strategic situation and the progress of operations, and to make recommendations from time to time to the War Cabinet as to the general conduct of the war'.[10] This body brought together the three

---

[9] Colville, J., *The Fringes of Power. Downing Street Diaries 1939-1955*, (Hodder & Stoughton, 1985), p.29.

[10] Ismay, *Memoirs*, p.109.

service ministers and the Minister of Supply and was chaired by Lord Chatfield, as the Minister for Military Co-ordination.[11]

From the outbreak of war and his return to government, Churchill proved an active but restless presence on these bodies. He was determined to take the fight to the enemy and was frustrated by his lack of ability to command the whole scene. In his own memoirs he is candid about his decision to bombard Chamberlain and his other colleagues with a stream of letters on matters related to the 'general view', quoting examples from September 1939 on the reuse of post-First World War heavy canon, the creation of a ministry of shipping, and his thoughts on the war situation. This did not always have the right effect, prompting Chamberlain to complain: 'getting very tired with the barrage of letters from Winston, arriving every day & increasingly devoted to matters outside his sphere at the Admiralty. The latest of these went so far and looked so like a document for the Book that I resolved to put an end to it. I sent for him and had a very frank talk'.[12]

The new Standing Ministerial Committee on Military Co-ordination, though nominally chaired by Chatfield, was, from the outset, dominated by Churchill. In part this was because the navy was more active than the other services during the period of phoney war, in part no doubt because Churchill was better prepared for the meetings, but the force of his personality was also a factor. Ian Jacob, the member of the War Cabinet Secretariat who had to administer the committee, reflected that, 'Churchill was so much larger in every way than his colleagues on this committee that it ran like a coach with one wheel twice the size of the other three, and achieved very little with much friction'.[13]

These problems intensified in April 1940 just as the real fighting started in Norway. Chamberlain persuaded Chatfield to resign, and rather than replace him as Minister for Military Co-ordination, he bowed to the inevitable, abolished the post and allowed Churchill as the senior service minister to chair the Military Co-Ordination Committee. It did not go well. The problem was that Churchill had drive and strong views but no executive authority to order action. How could he chair the committee while also representing the Admiralty, one of the three service ministries? In the end he had to ask Chamberlain to preside. The wonderfully named General Sir Edmund Ironside, Chief of the

---

[11] For a good summary of these arrangements and the new structure under Churchill that came to replace them see Ismay, *Memoirs*, chapters VIII & XIII.

[12] Churchill, *The Second World War*, Vol. 1, p.355 & Self (ed), *The Diary Letters of Neville Chamberlain*, Vol. 4, p.457.

[13] Wheeler-Bennett, J. (ed), *Action This Day: Working with Churchill*, (Macmillan & Co Ltd, 1968), p.161. Also, CAC, Jacob Papers, JACB 5/2.

Imperial General Staff, observed in his diary that Churchill's 'physique must be marvellous, but I cannot think that he would make a good Prime Minister. He has not got the stability necessary for guiding the others'.[14] Colville was equally damning: 'his verbosity and restlessness make a great deal of unnecessary work, prevent any real practical planning from being done and generally cause friction'.[15]

The paradox of Churchill's position on the eve of his premiership, a would-be war leader with responsibility but no executive authority, is nicely captured by Leo Kennedy, diplomatic editor of *The Times* in his diary entry for 4 May 1940:

> There is a drive against Chamberlain. I can't quite see who can advantageously take his place. Curiously enough what is really needed is that <u>Winston</u> should be made to take a rest. He is overdoing himself and taking the strain by stoking himself unduly with champagne, liquers etc; Dines out and dines well almost every night. Sleeps after luncheon, then to the House O' Commons, then a good and long dinner, and doesn't resume work at the Admiralty till after 10 pm, and goes on till 1 or 2 am. He has got into the habit of calling conferences and subordinates after 1 am, which naturally upsets some of the Admirals who are men of sound habits. So there is a general atmosphere of strain at the Admiralty which is all wrong. Yet Winston is such a popular hero and so much the war-leader that he cannot be dropped. But he ought somehow to be rested![16]

Six days later he was Prime Minister, and when Colville heard the news he wrote: 'He may, of course, be the man of drive and energy the country believes him to be and he may be able to speed up our creaking military and industrial machinery; but it is a terrible risk, it involves the danger of rash and spectacular exploits, and I cannot help fearing that this country may be manoeuvred into the most dangerous position it has ever been in'.[17]

How then had this outcome, dreaded by many in Whitehall, come to pass?

The tenth of May 1940 was an extraordinary day for everyone, but especially for Winston Churchill. He had woken confident in the knowledge that Chamberlain was preparing to resign and that he was in a strong position to succeed him.

---

[14] Macleod, R. & Kelly, D. (eds), *The Ironside Diaries, 1937-1940*, (Constable & Company Ltd, 1962).

[15] Colville, *Fringes of Power*, p.108.

[16] CAC, Leo Kennedy Papers LKEN 1/23.

[17] Colville, *Fringes of Power*, p.122.

Chamberlain had been brought down by the military shambles of the Narvik campaign, in which the Germans had outmanoeuvred the Allies and established their domination over Norway and Denmark. Churchill was lucky not to be censured himself. As First Lord of the Admiralty and Chair of the Military Co-ordination Committee, he had played a key role in planning the campaign, and later admitted that 'it was a marvel' that he survived and did not face the opprobrium heaped on Chamberlain.[18] Yet, the mood of the House of Commons had turned decisively against the Prime Minister. It was a salutary reminder of how quickly a leader could lose the confidence of his political colleagues, and one which Churchill would not forget.

Things had come to a head on 8 May. Having only narrowly won a vote of confidence Chamberlain had recognised that a national coalition was needed, and had asked the main opposition Labour Party if they would serve under him. An answer from their National Executive Committee, meeting at the Party conference in Bournemouth, was awaited. It was expected to be negative. The situation in the House of Commons is most eloquently described in the letter sent to Churchill on the evening of 9 May by his friend and fellow Conservative member of parliament, Bob Boothby:

> The Labour party won't touch Chamberlain at any price. Nor will Archie. [A reference to Archibald Sinclair, leader of the Liberal Parliamentary Party] Nor will our group [meaning the Conservative rebels who had opposed Chamberlain]. Therefore, it is inconceivable that Chamberlain can carry through a reconstruction of the Government.

The letter concludes with these prophetic words, 'In fact, I find a gathering consensus of opinion in all quarters that you are the necessary and inevitable Prime Minister – as I wrote to you some weeks ago. God knows it is a terrible prospect for you. But I don't see how you can avoid it'.[19] Then, at three in the morning, Germany launched her blitzkrieg offensive against Belgium, the Netherlands and Luxembourg. Suddenly all eyes in London were turned towards the continent. Churchill was already active by six, when he asked the French ambassador to clarify whether Allied troops would now move into

---

[18] See Shakespeare, N., *Six Minutes in May*, (Harvill Secker, 2017) for description of Churchill's role in Norwegian campaign; Churchill, *Second World War*, Vol. I, p.523; David Reynolds, *In Command of History*, (Allen Lane, 2004), p.126.

[19] CAC, Churchill Papers, CHAR 2/392B/146-147.

Belgium, before attending a meeting of the War Cabinet at eight to discuss the new emergency. At ten he received Kingsley Wood, a close political ally of Chamberlain's, who came hotfoot from a meeting with the Prime Minister. Chamberlain had questioned whether the German offensive meant he should stay, it not being a good moment for a change at the top, and Kingsley Wood had urged on him the need to go so that a coalition government could be formed. Churchill then attended further War Cabinet meetings at eleven and four-thirty, while managing to conduct Admiralty business and fit in a meeting with some shell shocked Dutch ministers in between.[20]

According to Churchill, it was immediately before the second War Cabinet of the day at around eleven, that his fateful meeting took place at 10 Downing Street with Chamberlain and the Foreign Secretary Lord Halifax, Churchill's main rival for the premiership within the majority Conservative Party. Chamberlain raised the question as to which of them might succeed him. For once, Churchill remained silent, prompting Lord Halifax to decline on the grounds that he would not be able to lead a wartime administration from the House of Lords. It left Churchill as the only possible Prime Minister and famously feeling, 'as if I were walking with destiny, and that all my past life had been but a preparation for this hour and for this trial'.[21]

Yet as many historians have noted, the contemporary accounts of others challenge the chronology of the Churchill account.[22] Both the diaries of Jock Colville and Alexander Cadogan agree that the crucial meeting between Churchill, Chamberlain and Halifax had in fact already taken place on 9 May, and by the next day the corridors of Whitehall were already echoing to the rumours that Halifax had declined the premiership and Winston had accepted it. Yet the decision remained hypothetical, and on the tenth Chamberlain was still Prime Minister, and, as we have seen, showing signs of wanting to stay.

It seems strange and unlikely that Churchill would have misremembered such a key moment in his political life. Perhaps there were indeed multiple conversations between the main protagonists over the two-day period, with the position not absolutely finalised until the afternoon of 10 May. Perhaps Churchill's memoirs are deliberately simplifying and dramatizing

---

[20] Churchill's day is reconstructed from a number of sources, including Churchill, *The Second World War*, Vol. I, pp.523-527 & Woodward, L., *British Foreign Policy in the Second World War*, Vol I (HM Stationery Office, 1970).

[21] Churchill, *The Second World War* Vol. I, pp.526-27.

[22] See, for example, Gilbert, *Winston S. Churchill*, Vol. VI, (Heinemann, 1983), p.301, footnote, or more recently Reynolds, *In Command of History*, p.127; Shakespeare, *Six Minutes in May*, pp.361-375.

what must have been a very confused, highly complex and rapidly evolving political situation. Another possible explanation is that the story as presented by Churchill places him at the centre of a narrative that was actually controlled by others, for it was only during the third War Cabinet meeting of the 10 May, at about five in the evening, that Chamberlain received a note of a telephone call from Clement Attlee. He had rung from the Labour Party conference in Bournemouth to confirm that it was the view of the Party's National Executive Committee that they would not serve under Chamberlain in a coalition government. Chamberlain's letter to his sister Ida of 11 May makes very clear that it was only at that moment that his situation became truly untenable and his resignation inevitable.[23] Within the hour, he had visited the Palace and informed the King, and Winston had been summoned to his 18.00-hour appointment at the Palace.

Churchill had not chosen to become Prime Minister, though it was a role he was never going to refuse. Nor was he elected to the office. His ascendancy was the result of a unique and specific political and military crisis. Nor did he really have any option but to form a national government. Though a long time anti-socialist, his elevation was dependent on the support of the Labour Party. He was not the natural choice of either his own Conservative party or the civil service establishment, though they grudgingly recognised that his anti-appeasement credentials and his bellicosity meant that he could form a cross-party administration. In fact, his political position was not a strong one. He had little room to manoeuvre. To form his coalition, he would have to find roles for Chamberlain and Halifax, who remained powerful within the Conservative Party; giving prominent seats to both his predecessor and his main rival for the top job. He would also have to accommodate the Labour leaders, Attlee and Greenwood, without whose support he could not sustain his coalition. The faces staring back at him from around that famous Cabinet table would not be his natural bedfellows.

Once inside the Palace, Churchill was ushered into the presence of the King for a private audience. Their exact conversation is not known, though according to Churchill's later account the Sovereign broke the ice by joking, 'I suppose you don't know why I have sent for you?', to which Churchill replied equally disingenuously, 'Sir, I simply couldn't imagine why'. The King then asked Churchill to form a government, and Churchill confirmed his intention to create a new national coalition of all three major political parties.[24]

---

[23] Self (ed), *The Neville Chamberlain Diary Letters*, Vol. IV, pp.528-530.
[24] Churchill, *The Second World War*, Vol. I (Cassell & Co Ltd, 1948) p.525.

Churchill also became, 'with the King's approval', the country's first Minister of Defence. This was his first real decision as war leader, and it was one that set the tone for his war premiership. He was not going to play the chairman's role, sitting above the fray and dispensing the wisdom of Solomon, adjudicating between the competing claims of the ministers below him. He was going to get his hands dirty and take direct personal control of the day to day running of military policy.

In his own memoirs Churchill chooses to downplay his adoption of this new role, arguing that:

> In calling myself, with the King's approval, Minister of Defence I had made no legal or constitutional change. I had been careful not to define my rights and duties. I asked for no special powers either from the Crown or parliament. It was however understood and accepted that I should assume the general direction of the war, subject to the support of the War Cabinet and of the House of Commons.[25]

Yet to Major General Sir Hastings Ismay, the chief of staff to the new Minister of Defence, this was Churchill's 'first, and most far-reaching change'.[26] It mattered because of the power vested in this new office when, and only when, it was combined with that of the Prime Minister: unifying in one person the oversight of the political and military direction of the war. As such it was a radical break with the position prior to May 1940. In becoming Minister of Defence, Churchill had deliberately put himself at the heart of the British war machine.

His creation of the new post helped strengthen his weak political hand. As Prime Minister, the new Minister of Defence chaired the War Cabinet. Moreover, he did so not alongside but in place of the three service ministers, who were stood down from this inner circle, thereby effectively removing them from the sphere of strategy and high policy, and relegating them to the role of departmental ministers. They could be summoned to the War Cabinet but would attend when necessary rather than by right. The role of Minister for Military Co-ordination, which had already been abolished by Chamberlain in early April 1940, was also now absorbed within this new position. At a stroke, Churchill had subsumed in his two roles five of the seats in Chamberlain's War Cabinet. This allowed him to streamline the War Cabinet, reducing its

---

[25] Churchill, *The Second World War*, Vol. II, pp.15-16
[26] Ismay, *Memoirs*, p.15

membership from nine to five. The members were now just Churchill, Chamberlain (now Lord President of the Council) and Halifax (Foreign Secretary) from the Conservative Party, and Attlee (Lord Privy Seal) and Greenwood (Minister without Portfolio) from the Labour Party. It is true that none of the four were natural allies of Churchill, though it probably strengthened him that the Labour and Conservative leaders both distrusted each other perhaps a little more than they distrusted him. By reducing the numbers, he ensured himself the casting vote. Moreover, only Halifax was a departmental minister, running the Foreign Office, which meant that this core group was free to focus on the immediate crisis. Others, including the Chiefs of Staff and the service ministers, could be summoned as required, with the control of attendance firmly in Churchill's hands.

The new Prime Minister clearly felt he had to give one of the service ministries to each of his main coalition partners. The Conservatives got the War Office, the Liberals the Air Ministry and Labour the Admiralty. Yet two of the three ministers, Anthony Eden at the War Office and Archibald Sinclair at the Air Ministry, were also chosen because they were close to Churchill. Eden had been a fellow Conservative critic of Chamberlain, and Sinclair, though the leader of the Liberal Party, had served Churchill in the field during the First World War as an officer in the Royal Scots Fusiliers, and thereafter as his personal military secretary at the War Office and private secretary at the Colonial Office. Churchill placed these allies in key subordinate positions because he knew he could rely on their loyalty. His trust was not misplaced.

But the service ministers were to be further weakened anyway, for the new Prime Minister wanted direct reporting lines from his Chiefs of Staff. The Military Co-ordination Committee was abolished and the Minister of Defence now chaired the Defence Committee, which was divided into the two panels of Operations and Supply. In theory Churchill chaired both, though in practice he could and did delegate that responsibility, allowing him to pick and choose, and where needed to convene, the most important meetings. It was rare for him not to chair the Operations Committee, which as its name suggests, was a small forum for planning, directing and taking executive decisions relating to key military operations. The composition could be changed depending upon the issue, but it normally included the three service ministers and was attended by the Chiefs of Staff.

Nor did the link between the new Minister of Defence and the Chiefs of Staff have to be filtered through any Cabinet committees. Churchill would personally attend twelve Chiefs of Staff meetings in 1940 and

44 in 1941.[27] While the appointment of Ismay as his representative, as an ex-officio member of the Chiefs of Staff Committee with a watching brief, effectively gave Churchill a permanent presence on this highest military body. The immediate result was a much closer contact between Churchill and his most senior commanders, whom as Minister of Defence he could and would summon independently. 'Thus for the first time the Chiefs of Staff Committee assumed its due and proper place in direct daily contact with the executive head of the Government, and in accord with him had full control over the conduct of the war and the armed forces'.[28]

The new arrangements also came with their own expert administrative staff in the shape of the military wing of the War Cabinet Secretariat, formerly the secretariat of the Committee of Imperial Defence, with a long pedigree in running sub committees on all aspects of defence planning, everything from home and overseas defence, to manpower, to raw materials and intelligence. Run by Ismay, with the assistance of a small but specially selected team led by colonels Leslie Hollis and Ian Jacob and Mr Lawrence Burgis, this office now combined its role in servicing the War Cabinet with the additional but related function of Office to the Minister of Defence, thereby giving Churchill the mechanics as well as the means of liaising with all aspects of military planning and operations.

When combined with the private office in Downing Street and the civil wing of the War Cabinet Secretariat, run by Sir Edward Bridges, and reporting to Churchill in his capacity as Prime Minister, the effect was to create a much larger 'handling machine'; one that was infinitely better geared to meeting the vastly increased business coming across the Prime Minister's desk in wartime.[29]

This handling machine also created a space, outside of the more established 10 Downing Street structures, into which Churchill could place his own people and develop the specialist resources he felt he needed. The new Prime Minister came with his own circle of friends and advisers: men who had helped sustain him during the last decade when he had been out of office, and campaigning against the government, firstly in his opposition to greater Indian independence, and then in his calls for rearmament against the threat of a resurgent Germany under Hitler and the Nazi Party.

---

[27] CAC, Churchill Papers, CHAR 20/60/9, note prepared for John Martin, Churchill's Private Secretary, February 1942.

[28] Churchill, *The Second World War*, Vol. II, pp.15-16.

[29] Ismay, *Memoirs*, p.158.

There was Brendan Bracken, the red-haired Irishman, who had launched himself on British high society by pretending to be an Australian, and by lying about his age to attend Sedbergh School when already an adult, but who from sheer force of will and hard work had become an editor, publisher and newspaper magnate. According to his entry in the *Oxford Dictionary of National Biography*, 'His witty cracks were as renowned as his preposterous lies. When caught out, he would simply laugh'. He had first attached himself to Churchill in 1923 and since becoming an MP himself in 1929 had played the role of Churchill's greatest advocate, assistant and emissary, with the rare ability to jolt Winston out of melancholy or intemperate moods.[30]

There was Frederick Lindemann, the professor of Experimental Philosophy at Oxford University and founder of the Clarendon Laboratory. A teetotal, non-smoking, vegetarian, who the carnivorous, cigar chomping, drink-loving Churchill called simply 'The Prof'. Lindemann had made his name in the First World War by learning to fly his own plane in order to prove his theory of combating spin. He first met Churchill in 1921, and by the 1930s he had become his close friend and adviser on all things scientific and technical, appearing 112 times in the Chartwell Visitors Book before 1939. He was able to explain complex issues in a clear and concise way, and helped Churchill write articles on modern science for money, and to question government statistics and reports on technological developments. He was also a man of strong views and prejudices, who made enemies easily and for the long term.[31]

And then there was Major Desmond Morton, a decorated hero of the First World War with a bullet still lodged near his heart, whom Churchill had helped to find a career in intelligence. Morton repaid his patron by sharing official information with him in the 1930s when head of the Industrial Intelligence Centre, answerable to the Committee of Imperial Defence (with what degree of State sanction is not quite clear, though his latest biographer believes Morton probably exaggerated his actions and only showed Churchill what he was entitled to see as a Privy Councillor and member of parliament). Mary Soames, Churchill's youngest daughter, recalled his regular visits to Chartwell, from his nearby house at Edenbridge, and the added 'apprehension and piquancy' of watching him play tennis with her mother, knowing

30 Tomes, J., 'Bracken, Brendan Rendall, Viscount Bracken (1901-1958)', *Oxford Dictionary of National Biography*, (Oxford University Press, 2004), online, accessed 2017. See also Colville, *Fringes of Power*, biographical note at end of volume.

31 Blake, R., 'Lindemann, Frederick Alexander, Viscount Cherwell (1886-1957)', *Oxford Dictionary of National Biography*, (Oxford University Press, 2004), online, accessed 2017.

that the vigorous exercise might dislodge the bullet and cause him to 'drop down dead'.[32]

They made for an eccentric group, but what united these rather maverick figures was their absolute loyalty to Churchill, and his trust in them for specific functions: Bracken for politics, Lindemann for science and Morton for intelligence. Room would have to be found for them in his Downing Street. Bracken became Churchill's parliamentary private secretary, Lindemann and Morton were to be his personal assistants. They provided constancy and loyalty in an environment that was at least initially filled with suspicious officials and political doubters. Even if, ironically, their very presence often increased those suspicions and doubts among the bureaucrats who regarded them as Churchill's myrmidons.

The suspicions went two ways. Churchill was sceptical of the ability of Whitehall to provide the right information and fearful of its ability to stifle innovation. Colville records him railing against 'feeble and weary departmentalism' and later recalled that when asked which he disliked most, the Foreign Office or Treasury, Churchill replied, 'The War Office'.[33]

Information was power, and Churchill wanted to be able to challenge the information being generated by other departments and used by them to justify decisions or defend inaction. An early act as First Lord of the Admiralty in 1939 was to ask Lindemann to set up an independent statistical unit, called S branch, to collate, challenge, verify and present information for his use. From the beginning this did not restrict itself to purely naval questions, but was briefed to range across all aspects of government policy. The man charged with starting the unit was the twenty-six-year-old Donald MacDougall, and the very first task assigned to him was to find out whether it was really necessary to ration sugar. The unit quickly expanded to contain about half a dozen economists, supported by human computers to undertake calculations and 'chartists' to prepare the hand drawn and coloured graphs and charts that Churchill used to digest complex information. When Churchill became Prime Minister, this unit moved with him.[34]

---

[32] Bennett, G., *Churchill's Man of Mystery*, (Routledge, 2007), p 172; Soames, M., *A Daughter's Tale*, (Doubleday, 2011), p.74.

[33] Colville, *Fringes of Power*, p.150 and Colville in Wheeler-Bennett (ed), *Action This Day*, p.78.

[34] MacDougall, D., *Don and Mandarin. Memoirs of an Economist*, (John Murray, 1987), p.21. For an overview of the work of the unit see also MacDougall, D., 'The Prime Minister's Statistical Section' in Chester, D.N. (ed), *Lessons of the British War Economy*, (Cambridge University Press, 1951).

As did his own map room, which was to remain under the charge of Captain Pim, and which was entirely separate from the central map room in the newly constructed Cabinet War Rooms.

Churchill also feared that departmentalism could stifle innovation, and so personally sponsored the development of a new experimental weapons section, under the command of explosives expert Millis Jefferis, tasked with developing sticky bombs, spigot mortars, limpet mines and other ingenious tools of destruction. Once Prime Minister, he was so concerned that this unit not be absorbed or dismantled by the War Office or the Ministry of Supply that he designated it as part of the otherwise non-existent Ministry of Defence, and it became MDI. A country house in Whitchurch, *The Firs*, was commandeered and a veritable factory established.[35]

We have seen that Churchill could be a source of friction. His task was now to try and forge unity. He had to try and meld into one team the politicians of different hues, the uniformed Chiefs of Staff, the be-suited civil servants and his eccentric personal appointees.

Once in power, Churchill's basic character did not change. His bulldog determination to take the fight to the enemy, his forceful nature and his sheer bloody mindedness feature regularly and prominently in the accounts of those working most closely with or for him. Ian Jacob later reflected that, 'To those around him who came into direct contact with him there was a feeling of powerful character, immense drive and force'.[36] He also described Churchill's method of dominating meetings by browbeating, badgering and cajoling, and felt that 'people put up with behaviour they would have tolerated from no one else'.[37] Norman Brook (later Lord Normanbrook), who joined the War Cabinet Secretariat in 1941, noted, 'when he wanted something done, everything else had to be dropped. The work was heavy, and the pace was hot'.[38] Add to this his eccentric routine – working on his papers from bed in the morning; drinking with lunch; taking a nap in the afternoon; convening meetings after dinner till late at night – and it is easy to see how stresses and strains were placed on those around him. The workload was certainly huge. Other than the occasional film

---

[35] For more detail on MD I see Macrae, S., *Winston Churchill's Toyshop*, (2nd edn Amberley, 2010). Stuart Macrae was the second in command to Jefferis and first published his memoir in 1971. His papers are at the Churchill Archives Centre. See also Milton, G., *The Ministry of Ungentlemanly Warfare* (John Murray, 2016).

[36] Wheeler Bennett (ed), *Action This Day*, p.181.

[37] Wheeler-Bennett, *Action This Day*, pp.185-186.

[38] Wheeler-Bennett, *Action This Day*, p.25.

at Chequers, he rarely relaxed and worked through till the early hours on an almost daily basis. On a bad day he might be chairing three meetings of the War Cabinet, convening other committees, summoning smaller conferences with the Chiefs of Staff and other ministers and having informal conversations with other key figures.

Yet the key change was that Churchill was now at the centre. He was no longer one over-sized wheel putting a stress on the system: he was the engine driving the whole vehicle. This meant that the system was now designed around him and was therefore better able to accommodate his work habits; helping him to maximise his productivity and containing his excesses, while providing a solid administrative framework for his decision making.

He established early on that he expected his colleagues and subordinates to communicate with him in writing, and in clear, concise English. This minimised the time that he needed to spend in meetings and private conversations, and allowed him to choose the issues he wished to focus on at any one given time.

Clementine Churchill advised Edward Spears that writing was the best way of getting her husband's attention, 'He often does not listen or does not hear if he is thinking of something else. But he will always consider a paper carefully and take in all its implications. He never forgets what he has seen in writing'.[39] It is advice that she would take herself in June 1940 when she had to write her husband a particularly difficult letter, as we will see in the next chapter.

Churchill's obsession with brevity even formed the subject of a Prime Ministerial directive to the War Cabinet at the height of the Battle of Britain, in which he expressed his loathing of tortuous constructions like 'Consideration should be given to the possibility of carrying into effect', rejecting 'officialese jargon' in favour of setting out the real points concisely. His government really was to be accompanied by a change in tone.[40]

Similarly, he insisted that all his requests for action should be given in writing by his staff as minutes, so that his wishes were clear and could not be misunderstood, and to prevent anyone acting on the assumption or rumour of what he might have wanted. If they were particularly urgent he would affix a small red label stating 'Action this Day'. There were actually two other gradings, 'Report within Three Days' and 'Report as soon as Possible', and it is telling that these latter two categories were very rarely used.[41]

---

[39] Spears, *Assignment to Catastrophe*, p.101.
[40] CAC, Churchill Papers, CHAR 23/4/4, Prime Ministerial Directive WP (40) 211, 9 August 1940.
[41] Pawle, G., *The War and Colonel Warden*, (George G. Harrap & Co Ltd, 1963), p.29.

Not that there was likely to be any mistaking a missive from the Prime Minister, as it would be dictated in his own highly personalised grandiloquent style and distinctive voice. To Anthony Eden, the Secretary of State for War, he wrote on 17 May 1940 asking, 'Are you proposing to arm the men of the balloon barrages? I understand they have no weapons. Surely they should be included among your parashots?'[42] A civil servant or military officer receiving a minute from the Prime Minister containing an order beginning, 'Pray let me know', would know that it came from the new man at the top.

Many of his inner circle later recorded their own favourite examples of Churchillian language. Lawrence Burgis, an assistant secretary to the War Cabinet, recalled him commenting, when discussing the means of protecting parliament in session from Doodlebugs, 'There are too many eggs in the Parliamentary basket, and though some of them are addled it is our duty to preserve them'. And when the allocation of cement, which was in desperately short supply, was on the Cabinet Agenda he opened the discussion with the words, 'Well, it is the same old story; too many little pigs and not enough teats on the old sow'.[43] James Stuart, his Chief Whip from 1941, recalled him describing Greek general Plastiras as 'Plaster-arse' and expressing the hope that his feet were not made of clay.[44]

Churchill was certainly conscious of playing a key role in great events and of conveying a theatrical sense of the importance of the moment to those around him. He was keenly aware of the possible judgements of history, and there were times, as we have already seen with Chamberlain, when some of his colleagues wondered whether he was writing to them or for posterity and post-war publication. Yet, his tone was constant whether in public or private: his voice unique, so that his contributions can often be guessed at in otherwise anonymised minutes. His use of language was a tool he deployed very effectively in many of his key wartime speeches and broadcasts, as well as in his set piece meetings with colleagues and allies, but it could also come across as overly sentimental, emotional and too oratorical in more private settings, and as we will see, sometimes caused friction with political colleagues and the Chiefs of Staff.

Though not one for small talk, Churchill was clearly a charismatic figure, capable of dominating but also winning loyalty from those

---

[42] CAC, Churchill Papers, CHAR 20/13, Prime Minister's Personal Minutes, May 1940.
[43] CAC, Burgis Papers, BRGS 1/3 (letter from Burgis to General Sir Leslie Hollis, 3 May 1955).
[44] Stuart, J, *Within the Fringe*, (The Bodley Head Ltd, 1967), p.103.

around him. The military and civilian wings of the War Cabinet Secretariat, the private secretaries and civil service staff from Downing Street, the Prime Minister's own personal advisers, even his personal secretaries, household staff and family now became what he dubbed his 'Secret Circle'. They accompanied him by day and night, at home and abroad, and, while he may not always have treated them with consideration, Churchill certainly took them into his confidence. Sir Edward Bridges, later Lord Bridges, the Secretary to the War Cabinet described the frankness and freedom with which he would discuss things with his staff:

> In this sort of discussion he would keep nothing back. He would express the most outspoken views about the probable reactions or attitudes of the most important persons, or about the various ways in which the situation might be expected to develop. And these confidences were not prefixed by 'You must not repeat this'. This was so clearly understood to be the basis of the relationship.[45]

There was certainly no doubting Winston's personal courage. According to US envoy Averell Harriman, 'Churchill had no personal fear and believed that his best security was unannounced appearances. Assassination plots, the Prime Minister once explained to me, took a great deal of planning to have a chance of success'.[46] His was a to be a very visible premiership, still riding up and down the skirmish line for the benefit of the gallery.

The impact of working for a brave, dynamic and charismatic, even eccentric, leader at a time of great national crisis, with that feeling of being at the centre of events, cannot be underestimated. Sceptics like Jock Colville were quickly and fully won over, bowing in the face of his 'indomitable' spirit and admitting by 19 May that, 'perhaps my judgements of him have been harsh'.[47] Churchill created his own court or household and plugged it into the existing prime ministerial and War Cabinet machinery. The result was that all the energy that had been wasted by Churchill trying to assert authority, or by others trying to contain him, could now be channelled through the system. Churchill finally had the executive power that he had craved for so long. He had not sought high office in order to play the role of a company chairman, presiding over competing views and interests, much as Chamberlain

---

[45] Wheeler Bennett (ed), *Action This Day*, pp.222-223.
[46] Pawle, *The War & Colonel Warden*, p.2.
[47] Colville, *Fringes of Power*, p.136.

had done. His instincts, character, and experience all pointed towards a hands-on chief executive role, in which he would personally direct the successful prosecution of the war on which his premiership depended.

But at least initially the exercise of that power might be limited by his political weakness. Though the head of a national government, and theoretically free to create a Cabinet of all the talents, his position was constrained by the need to work with the existing Conservative and Labour leaders. He could not afford to alienate Chamberlain, Halifax, Attlee or Greenwood. It was by making himself Minister of Defence that he was able to rearrange the structures and carve out a space that would allow him to take control of military affairs. It enabled him to chair the key strategy meetings and to summon senior officers, to be involved in the appointment and sacking of Chiefs of Staff and commanders in the field, and to appoint special advisers and emissaries. The military were now effectively reporting to the War Cabinet and the civil arm through him, and this greatly strengthened his hand.

As Minister of Defence, Churchill became not just the head of the government, but the clear head of the war effort. It was a decision that set the priorities and the style for his premiership, but it also posed challenges. He was taking on an immense personal burden, he was running the risk of identifying himself directly with failure in the field, and by focusing on military affairs he would have to delegate the running of civil matters to others. Yet given the scale of the military crisis that was about to engulf his new regime, it is surely difficult to argue that his immediate priorities were wrong. The ramifications of this first decision reverberate through subsequent chapters.

Chapter 2

Britain or France?

How did Churchill respond to the collapse of his ally?

At 17.54 hours on Wednesday, 3 July 1940, Vice-Admiral Somerville ordered the British ships of Force H to open fire on the French fleet in the North African harbour of Mers-el-Kébir, just outside Oran. Ten minutes later, when the guns stopped and the smoke cleared, a scene of carnage and destruction was revealed. The modern French battle cruiser *Dunkerque* was crippled, the older battleship *Bretagne* had exploded, and many other French ships were damaged. Nearly thirteen hundred French sailors were dead.[1] Until a few days before, these men had been allies of the British. How had this come to pass?

Between Churchill's assumption of the premiership and the sinking of the French fleet lie just eight weeks, but they must surely rank among the most complex, dramatic and difficult faced by any incoming British Prime Minister. At their heart were a series of inter-related decisions on questions of British and French national survival; decisions that must have brought home to Churchill very quickly the true meaning of 'victory at all costs'.

Let us return 10 May 1940. It was the assumption of the British military that, in the event of a German campaign in Western Europe, they would be fighting alongside France, and that, if so, the much larger French army, supported by the British Expeditionary Force (BEF) and the Dutch and Belgians, would bear the brunt of the land fighting while the British navy would seek to blockade Germany and the Royal Air

---

[1] For details of the operation, see Roskill, S., *The War at Sea*, Vol I (HM Stationery Office, 1954), pp.240-245.

Force would bomb German targets and provide support to engaged Allied forces on the ground.

The initial British divisions of the BEF were already in France, supplemented by the RAF with an Air Component of fighters and an Advanced Air Striking Force of light and medium bombers. The British troops formed a discrete force under the command of General Lord Gort, and were charged with holding a dedicated sector of the line, but were subordinated to overall French command. This would be a campaign in which French troops outnumbered the BEF by a ratio of about 10:1 and were engaged in defending their homeland, and so the British had agreed to a French plan under the direction of General Gamelin.

The plan anticipated that the strong French fortifications on the German border, known as the Maginot line, meant that the German attack would come in the north-west through the Low Countries. It saw the Allied forces responding by moving to a predetermined defensive line in northern Belgium, thereby protecting industrial areas in northern France and barring access to the Channel ports. Further south, other French armies would continue to guard the Maginot line and the rest of the frontier with Belgium and Luxembourg.

When the German attack came, it at first appeared in line with Allied predictions. But both Britain and France were in the process of changing their governments and the Anglo-French forces had to be invited into Belgium. It was the quick execution of this move that had so exercised Churchill on waking to the news of the German offensive. The Dutch were quickly overwhelmed, and the Allies struggled to reach and prepare all their agreed defensive lines. It was only then that the full genius of the German masterplan became apparent. Heavily armoured panzer divisions supported by a ferocious aerial bombardment crashed into the unsuspecting French centre through the Ardennes Forest, an area which had been considered unpassable by a mechanised army. They simply bypassed the Maginot line on the German frontier and quickly opened up a gap in the Allied lines.

Churchill, in his war memoirs, tried to explain this failure in Allied foresight by emphasising that Britain was always the junior partner. Yet he also highlighted potential flaws in the plan that cannot be blamed exclusively on the French: such as the failure of Belgium and Holland to integrate their defensive plans for fear of provoking the Germans; and the failure of the Allies to learn the lessons of Poland about the 'revolution effected by fast-moving heavy armour'. According to Spears, who accompanied Churchill on a visit to the Maginot Line in August 1939, Winston had also questioned the vulnerability of the

Ardennes area to attack. With the benefit of hindsight, Churchill and his colleagues in Chamberlain's War Cabinet must accept some of the blame for these deficiencies in military planning.[2] But, hindsight is a wonderful thing, and in the early days of May 1940 the British leadership remained confident in the strength of the French army to resist, as it had done in the war of 1914-18.

It was certainly in Churchill's nature to rate the martial virtues of the French. He was a lifelong Francophile. His mother, though American, had grown up at the court of Louis Napoleon III. The bust on Churchill's desk was that of his hero Napoleon. During the First World War he had worked alongside French Ministers and fought alongside French soldiers, and had been a witness to the huge sacrifice of the French people. He knew most of the famous French political and military figures of his age and praised the warlike qualities of Marshal Foch and Georges Clemenceau in his book *Great Contemporaries*.[3]

It is impossible to read the contemporary accounts, whether they be the official minutes of the War Cabinet, or the private diaries of Jock Colville in Downing Street, Alexander Cadogan in the Foreign Office, or Oliver Harvey, in the British Embassy in Paris, without being struck by just how quickly and unexpectedly the Allied military situation in France deteriorated. By Tuesday 14 May, the Dutch had been brought to the point of surrender. By Wednesday, the Germans had emerged from the Ardennes, crossed the Meuse and broken through at Sedan. The forces pouring into this gap could now threaten Paris, or turn westwards and encircle the Allied forces falling back from Belgium. They chose the latter, reaching the coast at Abbeville just five days later on the 20 May.[4]

For the first forty-eight hours, the fog of war on the battlefields and the aftermath of the political transition seems to have obscured a realisation of the true seriousness of the situation in London.

The War Cabinet learned at their second morning meeting on Friday 10 May of the broad German battleplan, 'advancing through Luxemburg and the Ardennes to the line of the Meuse, and at the same time advancing through Belgium to the Albert Canal'.[5] Over the

---

[2] Churchill, *The Second World War*, Vol II, Chapter II; Spears, *Assignment to Catastrophe*, Vol I, pp.6-7.

[3] Winston Churchill, *Great Contemporaries*, (Thornton & Butterworth, 1939).

[4] The events of May – June 1940 in this chapter are reconstructed from a number of different accounts, but both Woodward *British Foreign Policy in the Second World War* pp.174-225 & 251-288, and Churchill *The Second World War*, Vol. II, pp.26-pp 190 are useful in giving the broad narrative of the campaign.

[5] TNA, CAB 65/7, WM (40) 118.

weekend, Alexander Cadogan, sitting in the Foreign Office, noted a 'very confused' situation, but it is only on Monday that his diary entry turns darker, recording, 'Things look pretty black. Holland cracking and Belgium not too good…'. Though on the Saturday he vents his frustration that these are, 'Most critical days. And here we are Cabinet-making'.[6] By the Sunday evening, the Chief of the Air Staff, Sir Cyril Newall, is reporting the loss of seventy-six aircraft with a further forty damaged, but a meeting of leading ministers with Churchill in the chair (his new government not yet fully constructed) is being told that the German advance has slowed considerably and that the French and British forces have a 'very good prospect of establishing themselves on the Antwerp-Namur line'.[7]

Yet, by the time of Churchill's first full War Cabinet at 18.30 hours on Monday 13 May, just three and half hours after his first speech to parliament as Prime Minister, the general situation was not encouraging. The whole front was showing strong German mechanised forces advancing in a number of directions, with the RAF engaged in 'continuous action against waves of enemy bombers', the situation in 'fortress Holland' was described as 'very precarious' with the 'Germans landing more and more troops in the Rotterdam area'.[8] On 14 May, Oliver Harvey, British First Minister in the Embassy in Paris, noted the unexpected speed of the German thrust at Sedan, and the first of many French appeals for greater British air support.[9]

The rapid developments in France posed Churchill and his colleagues with two inter-related questions: firstly, what measures could and should Britain take to support her ally and sustain her in the conflict; and secondly, if France were to cease fighting, what should Britain do to prevent French resources being turned against her? The greater the crisis in France, the more she would ask of her ally. But the greater the crisis, the more likely France might collapse. The more that was given to France; the more that would be eaten up in combat and the less there would be available for the defence of Britain. Could France be kept in the fight, and, if not, at what point would Britain have to start thinking in terms of self-preservation rather than alliance?

The initial instincts of the War Cabinet were to try and support the battle in France. Decisions were taken within the first two days to despatch an additional four squadrons of Hurricane fighters, to add

---

6   Dilks, D. (ed), *The Diaries of Sir Alexander Cadogan*, (Cassell, 1971), pp.281-282.
7   TNA, CAB 65/7, WM (40) 119C.
8   TNA, CAB 65/7, WM (40) 120.
9   John Harvey (ed), *The Diplomatic Diaries of Oliver Harvey, 1937-1940*, (Collins, 1970), p.357.

to the six already operating across the Channel; to prioritise bombing raids in support of the Belgian Army; and to send the only Armoured Division with heavy tanks to Lord Gort.[10] Yet, the first crunch point was not long in coming. Churchill began the evening War Cabinet meeting on Tuesday, 14 May, by reading out a message from Prime Minister Reynaud of France, reporting the German breakthrough at Sedan and asking for ten more squadrons of fighters to help hold the line. If accepted, this would constitute a doubling of the British fighter presence in France, and would leave just twenty-nine squadrons in Britain. Moreover, it was already clear that the RAF fighters were taking heavy casualties in France.

Cadogan, who was present at this meeting in Downing Street, reports the French request and describes the meeting as 'very gloomy and unpleasant', labelling it the 'worst that I have ever attended in that beastly room'.[11] Still, it was finished in just over an hour and ended with some consensus. The Deputy Chief of the Air Staff reported that he had already redeployed three of the existing fighter squadrons in Northern France to operate on the Sedan front, making six in total. Churchill felt that 'we should hesitate before we denuded still further the heart of the Empire' and that the priority should be to use our existing air resources to support the French counter-attack. The Chief of Air Staff expressed the view that, 'Additional fighter squadrons for France could be drawn only from this country; and he was convinced that these squadrons would never return to this country once they were established on the other side of the Channel, as the majority of them would be lost'. The decision was not to rush any decision, but to see how events developed.[12]

In the event, they developed very quickly. Churchill was awoken the next morning by a desperate telephone call from Reynaud announcing, 'We are beaten, we have lost the battle'.[13] Having spoken with French field commander General Georges and received a telegram from General Gamelin, he then reported to the morning War Cabinet, informing them that the French Prime Minister had said that the road to Paris was open. The question of additional fighters for France was back on the War Cabinet agenda. The discussion was clearly sensitive and was recorded as a confidential annex, which was kept out of the main minutes. Air Chief Marshal Sir Hugh Dowding, the officer in

---

[10]   TNA, CAB 65/7, WM (40) 117, WM (40) 119, WM (40) 119A.
[11]   Dilks (ed), *Cadogan Diaries*, p.283.
[12]   TNA, CAB 65/7, WM (40) 122.
[13]   Churchill, *Second World War*, Vol. II, p.38.

charge of Fighter Command, was summoned to attend. The British line remained firm. Churchill was not inclined to support the request as no official demand had been received from the French military authorities, and, in reply to the Prime Minister's point-blank question, the Chief of Air Staff refused to recommend a further despatch. The rate of attrition was already high, with Newall reporting that thirty-six out of sixty-seven aircraft were unaccounted for from the attacks made the previous day at the Meuse crossing. Instead, the War Cabinet finally decided to approve bombing raids on German industry in the Ruhr. They did so in the knowledge that these were likely to provoke a retaliatory attack against Britain, but in the hope that these might draw some pressure off France. A telegram to this effect was despatched to Reynaud.[14]

Yet the issue resurfaced at the next Cabinet on the following morning. And whereas the Chief of the Air Staff had hitherto used RAF losses as an argument against despatch, he was now moved by the mounting burden falling on his airmen in France to argue for reinforcement, and so recommended that the equivalent of four additional squadrons be sent. Churchill thought it a 'very grave risk' but felt that 'it seemed essential to do something to bolster up the French'. Indeed, it took interventions from others to persuade him against withdrawing a further two squadrons from the defence of the navy in Scotland at Scapa Flow. It is clear from these minutes that Churchill had not yet appreciated the enormity of events on the ground in France. He still felt that the French defeat was more psychological than physical, and that 'Armoured vehicles could not conquer the whole of France', but faced with the possibility of the BEF withdrawing from its current line, he resolved to cross the Channel in order to see the situation for himself and to stiffen Allied resolve.[15]

The narrative of Churchill's trip to Paris is well known. In the words of his own colourful account he met with Reynaud, Daladier and Gamelin only to find 'utter dejection was written on every face'. He listened with mounting concern as the speed and extent of the breakthrough was described, was horrified to learn that there was no military reserve, and gazed out of the window at the burning French archives of the Quai d'Orsay.[16] Oliver Harvey's diary reveals that, a few streets away, the British archives were burning too, while the Embassy ladies were being evacuated. Churchill told Lady Campbell,

14 TNA, CAB 65/13, WM 123 (40).
15 TNA, CAB 65/13, WM 124 (40).
16 Churchill, *Second World War*, Vol. II, p.42.

the departing British Ambassador's wife, 'This place will shortly become a charnel house'.[17] He was now only too aware of the extent of the German breakthrough, and immediately telegraphed to the War Cabinet in London asking for a further six squadrons of fighters in addition to the four they had already promised that morning.

At 23.00 hours, with Neville Chamberlain minding the shop in the chair, the War Cabinet acceded to this request with no dissension and seemingly little discussion. The Chief of the Air Staff explained that, because there was not room at the bases in the north of France for a further six squadrons, these would have to operate out of Kent, refuelling and reservicing in France on a rotation basis. He did point out that they were the only complete Hurricane squadrons in Britain, and that the fighter defence of the country was now down to just twenty-nine squadrons. Yet, despite all of the previous British reservations and discussions, the French were now getting the ten squadrons that they had asked for just forty-eight hours before[18].

Did Churchill have any choice? On 16 May the French were already demoralised and Paris was preparing for an evacuation. But the battle was still raging, and there were large French and British forces in the field with at least the hypothetical potential to counter-attack. If Churchill had not provided air support in response to the urgent French request, then he would have been announcing to Reynaud that he thought the alliance over and the battle lost. He had only been Prime Minister for six days. To start cutting his losses at this point would surely have had a devastating effect on morale, not just in France, but also in Britain, where the public was not yet aware of the Allied reverses. It would have been at odds with his stated policy of blood, toil, tears and sweat.

True, he had taken a lead in asking for the additional six squadrons, but only after seeing the situation for himself, and only with War Cabinet authorisation. Since May 10, the War Cabinet, with the agreement of the Chiefs of Staff, had increased the Air Component operating in France from six squadrons, to ten, to fourteen and now to twenty. Churchill knew it was 'a very grave risk' that left Britain vulnerable, with close to the bare minimum of fighters recommended for its defence. No doubt he also had an eye to the judgement of posterity, but he was probably right in his telegraphed request to the War Cabinet that, 'The position would not be good "historically" if the French request were denied, and their ruin resulted'.[19] The next day, he told his colleagues

---

[17] Harvey, *Diplomatic Diaries*, p.359.

[18] TNA, CAB 65/7 WM 125 (40).

[19] Woodward, *British Foreign Policy*, Vol. I, p.193.

that he felt they 'had been faced with the gravest decision that a British Cabinet had ever had to take'.[20]

Churchill's intervention in Paris may have helped bolster French morale but only for the short term. Reynaud restructured his government on 18 May, appointing First World War hero Marshal Pétain as his deputy, and recalling General Weygand from North Africa to replace Gamelin and attempt a rally of the French armies. When Churchill visited Paris again on 22 May, he was impressed by Weygand's energy and his plans for a counter-attack, and on his return to London, he appointed Edward Spears as the liaison officer with Reynaud to improve communications. Yet these political moves did not result in an improvement of fortunes on the battlefield. The Germans continued to advance, and, despite spirited defences by the Allied garrisons, took the Channel ports of Boulogne on 25 May and Calais on the morning of the 27 May. Then came another hammer blow. The King of the Belgians ordered his troops to surrender, exposing the French northern army and the BEF to attack on their flank. Cut off on three sides, unable to fight their way across the German lines to join up with other Allied forces, and running low on supplies and ammunition, they had no option but to make a fighting retreat to the port at Dunkirk. About three hundred and thirty-eight thousand were successfully and famously evacuated by the Royal Navy and a flotilla of small ships, between 26 May and 4 June.

Against this bleak backdrop, it was inevitable that French requests for further British support should intensify. Reynaud visited London on Sunday 26 May and painted a grim picture of the French inability to carry on by land, sea or air, before proposing that the Allies ask Mussolini for terms that would ensure Italy's non-belligerency. This would allow the release of ten French divisions from the Italian border, but at a price that was likely to include British concessions in Gibraltar, Malta and Suez.[21] Churchill reported on the conversation to the War Cabinet at 14.00 hours, causing Cadogan to note, 'Reynaud doesn't say that France will capitulate, but all his conversation goes to show that he sees no alternative... '.[22] It is no coincidence that Lord Halifax chose this moment to raise the question of whether Britain should use the French initiative to investigate possible peace terms through Italy; a discussion which continued in subsequent War Cabinets. These

---

[20] TNA, CAB 65/7 WM (40) 126.

[21] TNA, CAB 65/13, WM (40) 140.

[22] Dilks (ed), *Cadogan Diaries*, p.290.

debates have been the subjects of a much speculation in print, as well as on stage and screen. They occurred at a most vulnerable moment when they could easily have derailed Churchill's whole policy of waging war.[23]

Here then was a very real and very early test of Churchill's leadership. He was now fighting on several interrelated fronts. The military situation was desperate. If enough troops could not be rescued from the beaches of Dunkirk, Britain might lack the numbers to mount any effective defence from invasion. But the need to defend the beachhead from German air attack was also putting an additional strain on British Fighter Command, which was having to send planes across the Channel from home bases. Dowding sent a message to the Chief of the Air Staff on 28 May to say that his 'fighter defences were almost at cracking point' and that if the 'exceptional effort had to be repeated over Dunkirk the following day, the situation would be serious'.[24] Meanwhile, on the diplomatic front, Churchill had to respond to the capitulation of Belgium and Reynaud's defeatism, while also taking seriously his Foreign Secretary's desire to investigate peace terms.

Churchill's response to the crisis shows him exploiting to the full his power to convene the meetings and control the agendas. In effect, over the course of the next two days, he held two parallel series of War Cabinet meetings. The discussions about an approach to Mussolini were restricted to a very small group; the five members of the War Cabinet, supplemented from 27 May by Alexander Cadogan and Archibald Sinclair, the latter in his capacity as leader of the Liberal Party (and key coalition partner) rather than Secretary of State for Air. The small group held three separate meetings to thrash out the issue; in Admiralty House mid-afternoon on 26 May, at 16.30 in Downing Street on 27 May, and at 16.00 in the Prime Minister's Room at the House of Commons on the 28 May. These meetings were then alternated with fuller War Cabinets concentrating on the wider military situation, attended by the Chiefs of Staff, the service ministers and others at 11.30 and 22.00 in Downing Street on 27 May, and at 11.30 on 28 May. It meant that the inner War Cabinet was in almost constant session.

---

[23] John Lukacs, *Five Days in London, May 1940*, (Yale Nota Bene, 2001). The play was called *Three Days in May*, and the episode featured prominently in the film *Darkest Hour* (2017).

[24] TNA, CAB 65/7, WM (40) 144.

By separating the meetings Churchill allowed the politicians to focus on the key political issue as a smaller group, but he also contained the damage that might have been caused had discussions about possible peace terms taken place within the larger meetings. There would have been a greater risk of leakage, but also the strong possibility that the issue would have dominated and would have started to impact on the military questions and the resolution of those tasked with overseeing operations. Furthermore, by bringing Sinclair into the smaller meetings he strengthened his own position, as he would have known that the Liberal leader would take a robust view against any move towards negotiation, thereby giving him a majority as long as the Labour leaders remained staunch, which they did. The records of those tense and sometimes acrimonious meetings show a more nuanced debate than is sometimes portrayed. Halifax wanted to explore the possibility of mediation in order to avoid bloodshed, but was only prepared to go so far in ceding British independence. Churchill feared that any exploration of terms was a slippery slope, and that Britain was likely to get a better deal after she had demonstrated her resolve and capacity to fight, but, faced with the dire military situation, he had to be careful to take his colleagues with him.

His final ploy on the afternoon of the 28 May was to break the smaller discussion half way through to call his first meeting of all the ministers outside of the War Cabinet. Seizing the moment, he addressed the wider group with a stirring extempore speech in which he outlined the serious nature of the crisis, and pledged to go down choking in his own blood rather than countenance surrender. It was a bravura performance which won an ovation from a hardened and usually cynical political audience. But, more crucially, it gained their support at this key moment for his policy of continuing to wage war. Leo Amery, the Secretary of State for India, was a near contemporary of Churchill's and a not uncritical friend. He was at the meeting, which took place in the Prime Minister's Room in the House of Commons, and wrote that it, 'left all of us tremendously heartened by Winston's resolution and grip of things. He is a real war leader and one whom it is worth while serving under'.[25] It prompted Amery to write to Churchill the next day:

Leaving your room yesterday there came to my mind a remark once made about Chatham when he took over in a pretty dark hour, followed

---

[25] CAC, Amery Papers, AMEL 7/34.

soon after by the great year of victories, that 'No one went out of his presence without feeling a braver man'. You certainly did that to all of us yesterday and I for one am deeply grateful to you. I see no reason whatever for doubting our final victory, whether with France or single-handed, and I am sure it would be fatal to show weakness by even hinting that there are concessions that we can make either to Italy or to the Germans. More power to your elbow.

Amery went on to compare Churchill to Lincoln in the American Civil War, quoting some satirical verse lines from Lowell's Biglow papers, ending, 'An' so his "Forrards" multiplied an army's fightin' weight by twenty'.[26] Churchill, with his love of poetry and language, is likely to have known the reference. Churchill the historian would have appreciated the comparison and the resonance, and Churchill the war leader would have understood its significance in changing the tone of the debate.

When the War Cabinet meeting resumed at 19.00, immediately after Churchill's speech, it was clear that he had effectively won the argument against any exploration of negotiations. In this, he was undoubtedly helped by the fact that President Roosevelt had made his own unsuccessful offer of mediation, by sources which were suggesting that Hitler would not allow Mussolini to play the role of mediator, and by the beginning of the successful evacuation from the Dunkirk beaches. He had also secured the agreement of his Chiefs of Staff that Britain could resist an invasion, as long as the air force remained in being and morale could be sustained.[27] The timing of his intervention had been critical, and Churchill had played his hand well, keeping his Cabinet together and preparing his government for the collapse of their ally.

Those at the centre of the British war effort now had to face the real likelihood that France might be defeated or surrender. Colville's diary for 27 May notes that, 'The French seem to be demoralised and there is now a serious fear that they may collapse', and by 1 June Cadogan felt that the French were now 'evidently worse than useless! Dreadful! I should like to be quit of them'.[28] In the aftermath of the destruction of the northern armies, on 30 May, Churchill summarised the new situation to his colleagues:

---

[26] CAC, Amery Papers, AMEL 2/4/4.
[27] TNA, CAB 80/11/69, COS (40) 397, WP (40) 169.
[28] Colville, *The Fringes of Power*, p140 & Dilks (ed), *Cadogan Diaries*, p.293.

The Prime Minister drew the attention of the War Cabinet to the requests that were being received from the French for further divisions to help on the Somme Front, for RAF assistance, for co-operation in appeals to President Roosevelt and for concessions to Italy, and said that he could not resist the conclusion that, when we refused these requests, as we must, the French would use these refusals as an excuse for giving up the struggle.[29]

It was clearly in the British interest to help keep the French fighting for as long as possible. The battle was destroying German troops and equipment, and was keeping Hitler's focus on the other side of the Channel. It was the view of the British Chiefs of Staff that Germany would seek to finish France before turning on Britain, and thus the continuation of hostilities in France bought time for Britain to re-equip her evacuated army, pull professional troops back from overseas, receive reinforcements from the Dominions and strengthen her defences. Yet, at the same time, it was no longer in the British interest to pump troops and aircraft into France, where they would take heavy casualties, when they might subsequently be needed to fight in Britain. The best hope now was to do enough to sustain hostilities in France for a few months, in the hope that Germans might become overstretched, or that the Americans would become more involved, and to build up British forces at home before contemplating a return in strength to the continent.

This dilemma was the tightrope that Churchill was now walking, and it was magnified by the contradictions inherent within his own character. Churchill the politician, with four decades of experience, and fuelled by his insatiable appetite for maps and statistics, could see that the emphasis had shifted. Britain needed to prioritise her own defence. Churchill the man of destiny, the historian, the Francophile, did not want to remembered as the new British leader who abandoned France in her hour of need. Nor was it in his nature not to fight.

It was a case of head versus heart that played out over the next few days. On 31 May, Churchill flew to Paris to meet Reynaud and Weygand. He shed tears over the French plight, pledged to 'fight to the water's edge' and the last man of the rear-guard at Dunkirk, and cajoled the French to hold on for a few more months until British forces could be brought back. He used all his oratorical skills and the force of his personality to dominate the meeting and instil resolve, but he did not go beyond the line agreed in the War Cabinet, and refused to

---

[29]   TNA, CAB 16/13, WM (40) 148.

promise more fighters. Moreover, he had the level heads of Clement Attlee, Generals Dill and Ismay with him. Churchill may have been the charismatic front man, but Spears describes the British team he brought with him as: 'business-like and precise. They gave the impression of men who had to deal rapidly with important affairs in a short time. No-one seemed worried or showed fatigue'.[30]

It was clear that final battle in France was about to begin. The view of the French government was that this would be decisive, not just for France but for Britain as well, and their politicians and military leaders united in bombarding London with requests for troops and planes. The requests went beyond anything that had been asked for before. General Vuillemin, the commander of the French air forces, was now requesting that 320 British aircraft to be based in France. The War Cabinet addressed the issue in the knowledge that, 'to decline to respond might mean collapse of French resistance, if Paris fell they might conclude a separate peace'.

Churchill was bullish and keen to offer as much support as was practicable. On 2 June, there was discussion on the advantages to French morale of the despatch of further fighter squadrons to France. The Prime Minister was clearly in favour, and Churchill's colleagues sought to contain him by referring the matter to the Chiefs of Staff, buying time to prepare their defences against the move. On 3 June, when Churchill noted that there were now fewer British fighters in France than at the beginning of the campaign, he was strongly opposed by the Chief of the Air Staff, and most significantly by Air Chief Marshal Dowding, attending for this item, who argued that, 'our fighter operations must be regulated by the rate of output in such a manner as to ensure that we were not squandering the capital of our fighter aircraft'. Churchill seemed to accept this, but only with the proviso that the matter could be reconsidered in ten days, and not without observing that to the French 'it looked as though we had some 500 fighters of incomparable quality which we would be withholding at a moment when they would be making a supreme effort on land'.[31] But if his colleagues thought that was the end of the matter, they must have been sorely disappointed the following morning. The Prime Minister, having delayed communicating any decision to Reynaud, was still unhappy that Britain now had fewer squadrons operating in France than in early May, noting that production had increased the number of squadrons in the United Kingdom from twenty-nine to

---

[30] Spears, *Assignment to Catastrophe*, Vol.I, p.294.
[31] TNA, CAB 16/13, WM (40) 152 and WM (40) 153.

forty-five. It took the combined efforts of Sinclair, Eden and Halifax, marshalling an impressive array of arguments to convince him to hold the pre-agreed line.[32]

Ten days later the issue was largely academic. For, having defeated the Allied armies in the north, the Germans could now pivot southwards. They reached Rouen on 8 June, crossed the river Seine on the 10 June, and entered Paris on the 14 June. The French government fell back on Tours in the Loire Valley, and then retreated to Bordeaux. There was nowhere left to go, other than the French overseas colonies in North Africa, and Prime Minister Reynaud's administration resigned on the 16th. The new French government under Marshal Philippe Pétain opened negotiations for an armistice with Nazi Germany. France had fallen. British fighters had continued to operate from bases in France and Britain right up to the end, and one man at least was relieved when that end came. Air Chief Marshal Dowding sent Churchill a handwritten note thanking him for the gift of a book, and stating, 'Well! Now it is England against Germany, and I don't envy them their job'.[33]

The question before Churchill in this last phase was deciding what could be saved from this wreck? The policy adopted can best be described as the carrot and then the stick.

There must have been times in those final days when he found the constant pressure of demands from France unbearable. To Oliver Harvey, at the Embassy in Paris, it looked 'as if every Frenchman who knew an Englishman had received a *mot d'ordre* to go and see him and urge necessity of greater air support'.[34] According to Colville, Churchill was annoyed by a telegram from Reynaud on 2 June which he found 'grasping', and it is clear that he was incensed by Vuillemen's accusations that the RAF had been slow to arrive over the battlefield in May.[35] He rang Spears twice on 5 June to complain about the French, 'At the moment they were trying him almost beyond endurance, but the mood did not last'.[36]

Yet, both at the Supreme War Council meetings with the French and in the British War Cabinet, Churchill emphasised the need to avoid recriminations. Instead he worked hard to keep channels of

---

[32] TNA, CAB 16/13, WM (40) 154. The arguments included the higher losses when fighting in France, the disorganisation of the existing squadrons in the UK, the lack of pilots and the greater German threat now they had occupied the Channel ports.

[33] CAC, CHAR 2/393/112.

[34] Harvey (ed), *Diplomatic Diaries of Oliver Harvey 1937-1940*, p.381.

[35] Colville, *The Fringes of Power*, p.146 & p.150.

[36] Spears, *Assignment to Catastrophe*, Vol. II, p.58.

communication open, installing Spears as a trusted emissary within Reynaud's camp, and making repeated – and increasingly hazardous journeys across the Channel. In the final hours of the Third Republic, he flew to meet Reynaud in the Loire Valley at Briare on 11 June, returned to London on the following day, before going back to Tours on the 13th. He was sitting on a train at Waterloo station, preparing to set off for yet another meeting off the Brittany coast on the evening of 16th, when the news came through that Reynaud had resigned.

The minutes of the final meetings of the Supreme War Council at Briare and Tours read like the scripts of a Shakespearean tragedy, capturing something of the authentic voices of the participants. As you read the pages, you can hear Weygand's defeatism, Reynaud's vacillation between hope and despair, and Churchill's determination to keep the French fighting. He suggested counter-attacking across the Lower Seine, fighting street by street for Paris, establishing a bridgehead on the Atlantic seaboard, conducting a guerrilla war, or fighting on from the North African Empire. He urged the French to hold on for a few weeks to allow Britain to rebuild her strength and the United States to become more involved. The Prime Minister sympathised, cajoled and used all his powers of persuasion: 'She [Britain] would fight in the air, she would fight with her unbeaten navy, and she would fight with the blockade weapon' and 'The British had not yet felt the German lash but were aware of its force. They nevertheless had but one thought: to win the war and destroy Hitlerism'.[37] The final passages of that last meeting in Tours could not be more poignant:

> Mr Churchill said that this was certainly the darkest hour for the Allied cause. Nevertheless, his confidence that Hitlerism would be smashed and that Nazidom could not and would not over-rule Europe remained absolutely unshaken.
>
> M. Reynaud said that his confidence remained equally firm; else he could not endure to go on living.[38]

Churchill's appeals, though they may have had a momentary effect on Reynaud, could not delay the reality of French defeat. Without the prospect of American belligerency, which President Roosevelt could not deliver, and with Britain unwilling to increase its air support and unable to supply more troops, the battle was lost. In his head, Churchill certainly knew this. At their morning meeting on 12 June, while the

---

[37] CAC, Churchill Papers, CHAR 23/2.
[38] CAC, Churchill Papers, CHAR 23/2.

Prime Minister was still returning from Briare, the British War Cabinet discussed at length their 'plans to meet a certain eventuality'. These included the measures needed to secure French military equipment, shipping, cables, gold, securities, secret documents and machine tools, as well as plans to destroy oil supplies and set up subversive activities.[39] At his final meeting with Reynaud at Tours Churchill emphasised the importance of the French handing over captured German airmen, and was careful not to release the French from their treaty obligation not to conclude a separate peace.[40] It was vital that the British now strengthened their own position, while maintaining as much leverage as possible over the French in advance of their seeking terms.

The ultimate manifestation of the 'carrot' policy was the dramatic offer made by the British War Cabinet on 16 June 1940 of a Franco-British union: a full merger of the two nations, providing for joint organs of defence, foreign, financial and economic policies, under which the people of the two countries would enjoy common citizenship. This was not Churchill's idea, but rather the brainchild of Jean Monnet and René Pleven, prominent French officials based in London, working with Desmond Morton, Sir Robert Vansittart and others. It secured the support of General de Gaulle, who was in London on a mission for Reynaud, and was first brought to the War Cabinet on 15 June by Neville Chamberlain.[41] The fact that it was so speedily endorsed is in part a testament to the scale of the crisis. Colville wryly observed that, 'Meanwhile the King does not know what is being done to his Empire. The Lord President is going to see him at 7.00 and will break the news. Who knows, we may yet see the "fleur de lys" restored to the Royal Standard'.[42]

Yet the move did not come out of nowhere and was a natural extension of Churchill's existing policy. On 13 June, the War Cabinet had already agreed that there should be 'an announcement in dramatic terms of the solidarity of France and Great Britain...proclaiming the indissoluble union of our two peoples and our two Empires'.[43] This was not just a romantic gesture, it was a continuation of British policy to keep France fighting, and – faced with collapse in France – it was a mechanism by which the British could legitimately acquire all French personnel, equipment and supplies. Churchill was certainly not overly concerned with the details of the proposed union or the form of the

---

[39] TNA, CAB 16/13, WM (40) 162.
[40] CAC, Churchill Papers, CHAR 23/2.
[41] Woodward, *British Foreign Policy in the Second World War*, Vol. I, pp.276-280.
[42] Colville, *The Fringes of Power*, p.160.
[43] TNA, CAB 65/13, WM (40) 165.

new joint government, suggesting that it could be dealt with by the simple expedient of more frequent meetings of the Supreme War Council.[44] Defeated by Germany and clinging to the last vestiges of their independence, the French government chose to reject the plan.

The offer of union has to be seen alongside the attempts that were being made to get the French government to come to Britain or go to North Africa, but above all it has to be viewed in the light of British fears about the French fleet; fears which were being discussed in the War Cabinet on the same day as the proposed union. The French had the fourth largest navy in the world, and some of the newest and most powerful battleships. If the French fleet were combined with the German and Italian fleets, Britain would lose all control of the Mediterranean, her important sea routes to the Empire would be threatened, and her ability to enforce a blockade of Europe and resist invasion diminished. All but the fastest merchant shipping was already being rerouted away from the Mediterranean around the Cape, but now even the Atlantic sea-lanes might be threatened from French bases in West Africa.[45]

The initial hope of the British was that the French fleet would fight on under a French administration in North Africa, or voluntarily move to British ports, or failing that would scuttle itself rather than fall into enemy hands. Churchill's initial 'stick' had been to try and make it an absolute condition of British consent to any French investigations of peace terms that the French fleet should sail immediately for British ports. This was to be conveyed to Reynaud on 16 June, but was deliberately delayed to allow the 'carrot' of the offer of union to be dangled. After the fall of Reynaud's government, the position was repeatedly stated to his successor Marshal Pétain, and to Admiral Darlan, the commander of the French navy, but the new administration was clearly determined to enter into an armistice, and the British were shut out of all consultations with their former ally.

On 22 June, as the French and Germans met to conclude their armistice at Compiègne, the British War Cabinet considered the various locations of the French fleet. There were powerful ships at Alexandria, Casablanca, Dakar and Oran, and smaller units in British home waters at Portsmouth, Plymouth and Southampton. The First Sea Lord, Admiral Sir Dudley Pound, felt that Admiral Darlan 'had taken all possible steps to safeguard our interests' by putting in place orders and arrangements to ensure that the fleet was to be 'held against the enemy; and that the fleet was not to accept any orders from a foreign

---

[44] TNA, CAB 65/13, WM (40) 167.
[45] Roskill, *War at Sea*, Vol. I, p.271.

government'. Churchill was not convinced. He was adamant that 'in a matter so vital to the safety of the British Empire we could not afford to rely on the word of Admiral Darlan'; he was particularly concerned about the new modern battleships *Richelieu* and *Jean Bart*, which he felt had the power to 'alter the whole course of the war'; and stated that, 'In no circumstances whatsoever must these ships be allowed to escape'. When Lord Halifax tried to argue that 'we should exhaust every means of persuasion before using force'. Churchill replied that we could not, 'run the mortal risk of allowing these ships to fall into the hands of the enemy. Rather than that, we should have to fight and sink them'.[46]

Thereafter his view did not waver. Writing later, Churchill cast Admiral Darlan as the villain of the piece castigating him for throwing his lot in with the new French government, and for rejecting the opportunity to lead the fight against Germany from French North Africa or to scuttle his ships. Instead of becoming a focus of French resistance, 'he went forward through two years of worrying and ignominious office to a violent death, a dishonoured grave, and a name long to be execrated by the French Navy and the nation he had hitherto served so well'.[47] This is surely partly deflection on Churchill's part. Viewed from France, Darlan was acting to try and preserve the last shreds of national independence, and had given orders that his ships should resist German occupation. But viewed from Britain that independence was too precarious, too dependent on German good will, and complicated by the risk that the new Vichy regime might turn hostile.

The British impounded those French ships in Britain, hemmed in the force at Alexandria, and monitored movements at Oran, Casablanca and Dakar. Inevitably, they began to face demands from the French for the free movement of their ships. The War Cabinet discussed the issue three times on 24 June, and at its evening meeting considered an appreciation by the Admiralty of actions that might be necessary against the French fleet. This identified the *Force de Rade* at Mers-el-Kebir, just outside Oran, with the battlecruisers *Dunkerque* and *Strasbourg*, two other capital ships and a large force of destroyers and submarines, as the most important units to be eliminated. Once again, the First Sea Lord questioned whether such an attack was worth the risk of damage to British ships, given the assurances by Darlan and the French Admirals that the ships would not be surrendered to the Germans, and armistice terms which allowed for them to be

---

[46] TNA, CAB 65/13, WM (40) 176.
[47] Churchill, *The Second World War*, Vol. II, p.202.

demilitarised. In the ensuing debate, Churchill was scathing about the French promises: 'The covert German occupation of French territory was complete, and the French government were entirely at their mercy, there was nothing to prevent Germany imposing peace terms more onerous than those to which the French had agreed for the purpose of the Armistice'.[48] On 1 July, he said that, 'discussions as to the armistice could not affect the real facts of the situation'.[49]

With the risk that the *Dunkerque* and *Strasbourg* might sail to a French or Italian port, the decision to act was taken on 27 June. The date for action was set as 3 July, the earliest date by which a large British naval force under Vice Admiral Somerville could reach Oran, and would take the form of a simultaneous operation against all the French naval forces in their various localities. The French ships in British waters would be seized, those in foreign waters would be given the options of sailing with the British, sailing to British or overseas ports in the French West Indies, putting themselves beyond use, or being sunk. The operation was code-named *Catapult*, and the French government were not forewarned so as to preserve the crucial element of surprise.

Churchill watched these events unfold from London, sitting up late into the night with the Chiefs of Staff and the First Sea Lord to review progress as the reports came in.[50] The escape of some French ships from Oran, including the battle cruiser *Strasbourg*, meant that the operation was not a complete military success. But when Churchill addressed the House of Commons to explain the action on the following day, he was cheered to the rafters, even by those Conservatives who had hitherto remained loyal to Chamberlain. Colville described seeing him 'visibly affected' and hearing him say, 'This is heartbreaking for me'. And by Friday, both Cadogan and Colville were able to remark on the psychological effect of the action. Colville quotes his mother as saying, 'there is a strange admiration for force everywhere today, even among those who suffer from it', while Cadogan observes, 'Winston had a triumph in the House yesterday on French fleet. What funny people we are! Of course it was right and vital, but I should have thought there might have been a more regretful tinge in it. It was very necessary, but it was not pleasant! Like having a tooth out'.[51]

The action was not popular with the navy, who thought it unnecessary and dishonourable. Reservations were expressed beforehand in the War

---

[48]   TNA, CAB 65/13, WM (40) 180.
[49]   TNA, CAB 65/14, WM (40) 190.
[50]   TNA, CAB, 69/1, DO (40) 19.
[51]   Colville, *Fringes of Power*, p,185 & Dilks (ed), *Cadogan Diaries*, p.311.

Cabinet by the First Sea Lord and afterwards by Admirals Cunningham, North and Somerville, the three British naval commanders on the spot in the Mediterranean.[52] They felt with more time, the French fleet at Oran could have been persuaded to disarm itself under British supervision, as did happen at Alexandria. The action also ended all possibility of future cooperation with independent French naval forces in North Africa, and risked alienating many who might have otherwise have flocked to the Free French banner of General De Gaulle in London.

The key point perhaps is that Churchill did not know how much time he had. His decision to force the pace of events at Oran must be seen in the broader context of what was crossing his desk at that point. Italy had entered the war against Britain on 10 June. It was widely feared that Spain might be about to do the same, meaning that the British bases at Gibraltar and Malta were at risk.[53] The Mediterranean Sea routes had been declared unsafe for all but the fastest shipping, the British were facing an increased burden in the western Mediterranean because of the French collapse, and the French force at Oran had already been identified as a threat and a priority by the Admiralty. This was about reasserting naval dominance and deterring potential aggressors.

In addition, a German invasion of Great Britain was felt to be possible, even if Churchill doubted it was imminent. Cadogan's diary for 1 July notes that, 'This is the zero hour for Hitler's invasion of England – the actual date favoured by the tipsters being about 8 July'.[54] On the very day of the operation at Oran, the War Cabinet was also considering dispositions for the British Home Fleet against invasion and measures for the possible evacuation of the civil population from east and south-east coast towns. The Chief of the Imperial General Staff and the Chief of the Air Staff were united in warning that, 'there were many signs which pointed to an attempt to invade this country in the near future and which could not be ignored'.[55]

There was also a definite American dimension. Churchill had made repeated and unsuccessful appeals to President Roosevelt for aid or some statement of support, and had watched as the French did the same. As early as 15 May, he had warned, 'But I trust you realise, Mr President, that the voice and force of the United States may count for nothing if they are with-held too long'. Thereafter, he kept Roosevelt

[52] Stephen Roskill, *Churchill and the Admirals*, (Collins, 1977), p.158.
[53] See for example TNA, CAB 69/1, DO (40) 18.
[54] Dilks (ed), *Cadogan Diaries*, p.308.
[55] TNA, CAB 65/8, WM (40) 192.

informed of the deteriorating situation in France, sending telegrams on 18 and 20 May, and on the 11 (twice), 12, 14, and 15 (twice) of June. In the last of these he tried to reinforce the desperate French attempts to secure American belligerency before they collapsed, and admitted that Britain might reach a point in the struggle, 'where the present ministers no longer have control of affairs and when very easy terms could be obtained for the British Islands by their becoming a vassal state of the Hitler empire'. In such circumstances, he warned that the combined German, British, French, Italian and Japanese fleets would then be able to threaten America.[56]

When the fall of France failed to secure American intervention, Churchill drew the conclusion that further appeals were futile for the time being, and that the Americans needed to see action, and to be convinced that the British were not going to capitulate. He also knew that the White House was disappointed with the surrender of the French fleet, describing it as 'the most degrading surrender in history' and that President Roosevelt would not only allow seizure but that any British action would most likely 'be applauded in the United States'.[57] Writing to Lord Lothian, the British Ambassador in Washington, on 28 June, Churchill put the situation with regard to the Americans very bluntly, 'I don't think words count for much now. ... Only force of events can govern them. Up till April they were so sure that the Allies would win that they did not think help necessary. Now they are so sure we shall lose that they do not think it possible'.[58]

In his speech to the House of Commons on 4 July, Churchill defended the sinking of the French fleet by leaving the judgment of his action, 'with confidence', to parliament, the nation, the United States, 'to the world' and to history'.[59] The action was the logical culmination of his stated policy to wage war 'whatever the cost may be' and to achieve 'victory at all costs'. Behind the rhetoric, it had quickly become a Britain first policy which had aimed to keep France fighting for as long as possible while preserving an independent British capacity to fight, and which sought by carrot or stick to prevent French military resources from falling into enemy hands.

How does Churchill emerge from this first crisis? There is certainly no doubting his commitment and level of activity. For most of the

---

[56] CAC, Churchill Papers, CHAR 20/14.
[57] TNA, CAB 65/14, WM (40) 187 & WM (40) 192.
[58] CAC, Churchill Papers, CHAR 20/14.
[59] CAC, Churchill Papers, CHAR 9/140B/176.

two-month period he was in almost constant session with his Chiefs of Staff and political colleagues. The War Cabinet was meeting at least daily, but often twice a day – morning and afternoon – and occasionally in the evening as well. Outside of these main sessions there were meetings of related committees and smaller gatherings of key individuals. The Defence Committee (Operations), usually with the Prime Minister and Minister of Defence in the chair, met nineteen times between 10 May and the 3 July[60]. By Friday 17 May, just one week after the launch of the German offensive, Cadogan was writing in his diary: 'Never did I think one could endure such a nightmare. … very tired. But how these Chiefs of Staff (and the P.M.) endure – never getting any rest – I can't think'.[61]

Imagine a small group of increasingly weary men (for the only women were secretaries and administrators) meeting almost constantly, day after day, night after night, in the same, smoke-filled rooms, receiving ever worsening news and trying to come to terms with what they had believed unthinkable. The atmosphere must have been tense and claustrophobic, and it is not surprising that tempers occasionally flared. There were no easy answers. Can Halifax, as Foreign Secretary, really be criticised for raising the possibility of diplomatic mediation? Could Churchill, as Prime Minister and Minister of Defence, really be certain that Britain had the air and naval supremacy to be able to fight on?

To this almost perpetual round of meetings in London must be added Churchill's five trips to France, in increasingly hazardous conditions, and his parliamentary or public speeches and broadcasts on 13, 19, 23, 28 of May, the 4, 17, 18, 20 and 25 June, and 4 July.

There were clearly times when this pressure got to him, and examples have been cited above of his occasional flashes of anger with the French. The only known letter to survive from Clementine Churchill to her husband in 1940 is her famous and much published missive of 27 June in which she warns him that, 'One of the men in your entourage (a devoted friend) has been to me & told me that there is a danger of your being generally disliked by your colleagues & subordinates because of your rough sarcastic and overbearing manner', noting that 'I must confess that I have noticed a deterioration in your manner; & you are not so kind as you used to be'. Clementine clearly agonised over this letter, which by her own admission she had first written the previous Sunday at Chequers and then torn up. This means it was

---

[60] TNA, CAB 69/1. Conclusions of the Defence Committee Operations, May – December, 1940. It met twice on 10 May 1940, once with Churchill in the chair, and twice on 25 May, both with Churchill in the Chair.

[61] Dilks (ed), *Cadogan Diaries*, p.285.

originally written on 23 June, just after the French armistice, when Churchill was wrestling with all of the implications of that terrible collapse.[62]

At times, he clearly annoyed his colleagues in the War Cabinet. On 26 May, Cadogan felt Churchill to be 'too rambling and romantic and sentimental and temperamental'; while the following day his diary records a conversation with Lord Halifax at which the Foreign Secretary expressed the view that he could no longer work with Winston; and on 29 May refers to Churchill's clash with Chamberlain and Halifax over Churchill's 'theatrically bull-doggish' insistence that the British rear-guard fight to the death at Dunkirk.[63] Yet these conversations were occurring at a moment of the very highest tension, against the backdrop of the evacuation from the beaches and the discussion of the possible approach to Mussolini, when all involved will have needed to let off steam. It would be strange indeed if such sentiments did not surface periodically within the War Cabinet given the personal histories and rivalries of those involved and the awful pressures they were now under. Similarly, there were real concerns from the Air Staff about Churchill's willingness to despatch fighter squadrons to France in early June; and from the Admiralty about his hard line on the French fleet a month later in early July.

The important thing is that these frustrations were not allowed to fester and develop into the sort of bitter enmities that further hastened the demise of the French government, and where policy and military strategy were regarded as completely separate spheres. The official minutes sanitise the language of the debates in the War Cabinet and other meetings and make them seem more coherent and harmonious than they undoubtedly were, but they also show a system that was working; where the issues were being addressed systematically, with the Chiefs of staff and the War Cabinet meeting and working as one, and with other ministers and military officials being brought in as and when was necessary to offer their specialist advice. Churchill can hardly be accused of a lack of consultation.

No doubt the level and intensity of the crisis focused all concerned on trying to work harmoniously. But Churchill also had a role to play in binding everyone together. He was not rough and sarcastic all the

---

[62] CAC, Baroness Spencer-Churchill Papers, CSCT 1/24, published in Mary Soames, *Speaking For Themselves*, (Doubleday, 1998), p.454.

[63] Dilks (ed), *Cadogan Diaries*, pp.290-292.

time, as this wonderful vignette of the Prime Minister at Chequers at the end of a very long day on 15 June makes clear:

> About 1.00 am Winston came in from the garden and we all stood in the central hall while the Great Man lay on the sofa, puffed his cigar, discoursed on the building up of our fighter strength, and told one or two dirty stories. Finally saying 'Goodnight, my children', he went to bed at 1:30.[64]

Throughout the Battle of France, Churchill was consistently the most bellicose member of the War Cabinet. He pushed for as much air support for the French as could be spared; just as he took a strong line on the action against their fleet. Yet he remained at pains to take his colleagues with him, literally in the case of his meetings in France, with Attlee, Beaverbrook, Eden and Halifax all accompanying him at different times. Halifax's proposal to enquire after terms from Mussolini was debated and rejected over three days in May; Churchill's desire to send additional fighter squadrons to France was discussed and defeated over three days in June; and the action against the fleet was endorsed by the War Cabinet and the First Lord of the Admiralty, and took place with the agreement, if not the active support, of the First Sea Lord. The structure that Churchill had established allowed for continuous engagement with the Chiefs of Staff throughout the crisis, but it also enabled him to control the key political debates and to maintain consensus around the top table. This was not government by dictatorship.

Churchill's grandiloquent style may have sometimes bored or annoyed his War Cabinet colleagues, but it helped secure the backing of the wider group of government ministers at a key moment on 28 May, and eased relations at the hideously difficult Supreme War Council meetings with the French leadership. In public, the defiant language of his speeches and broadcasts helped limit the wider fallout from the military crisis. Dunkirk and Oran were the results of a catastrophic failure in the field, yet in both cases the swift action of the War Cabinet coupled with Churchill's words snatched advantage from the jaws of defeat.

Few leaders in modern history can have been faced with such a baptism of fire. Churchill could not have won the Battle of France, but he could have been led into negotiations with the enemy or succumbed to rash military promises to his ally that would have lost the Battle

---

[64] Colville, *Fringes of Power*, p.158.

of Britain. That he avoided these pitfalls is a testament not just to his resolve, but also to his skills of political management and timing. But what of victory? In July 1940, it must have seemed a distant prospect, and it was not clear that words or actions would be enough without America. Especially as the bombs started to fall on Britain.

Chapter 3

Defence or Offence?

Why did Churchill embark on his Middle Eastern Strategy?

It was at the end of the summer of 1940 that the bombs started to fall on the cities. After weeks of attacks on airfields, the German tactics changed. Industrial centres such as Portsmouth, Liverpool, Bristol and Birmingham were hit first. Then the suburbs of London were targeted. But at around 17.00 hours on Saturday, 7 September 1940, the real onslaught against Britain's capital city began. A total of 348 enemy bombers, protected by 617 Messerschmitt fighters, filled the skies above the East End, dropping 300 tonnes of high explosives and incendiaries onto the docks below. Stepney, Whitechapel, Poplar, Shoreditch, West Ham and Bermondsey were all set ablaze. The initial attack was followed up by further waves throughout the night. This was only the beginning. The bombers would return for the next fifty-six consecutive nights, and for seventy-five nights thereafter excepting only 2 November.[1] No modern city had ever suffered such a concentrated and sustained assault from the air.

The war had now arrived on Churchill's doorstep. The King and Queen had a narrow escape when Buckingham Palace was bombed on 13 September.[2] Downing Street was repeatedly damaged. A large part of the neighbouring Treasury was destroyed. Churchill was forced to work and sleep underground in the Cabinet War Room, while a second, deeper underground command centre was prepared for his use at Dollis Hill in north west London.[3] Even his old school at

---

[1] Overy, R., *The Bombing War*, (Penguin Books, 2014), pp.82-86; Crang, J. & Addison P. (eds), *Listening to Britain*, (The Bodley Head, 2010), p.401.
[2] CAC, Churchill Papers, CHAR 1/355/62.
[3] Colville, *Fringes of Power*, p.241, pp.242-243, p.267-268.

47

Harrow on the Hill was hit, though the only casualty reported by the Headmaster was an overenthusiastic boy who put out several bombs with his helmet and 'then burnt himself quite badly by replacing it on his head!'[4] Horse Guards Parade, the War Office, the National Gallery, the Carlton Club, the BBC and St Paul's Cathedral all soon joined this growing roll call of iconic central London institutions to suffer bomb damage.[5] By Wednesday 16 October, Colville was describing Leicester Square as a desert.[6]

But Churchill's preoccupation was not with Westminster and Whitehall. It was with the citizens of London and particularly those in the most heavily bombed industrial and dockland areas. Would the city continue to function? Would morale hold? The story of the Blitz has become part of the British national mythology: a tale of Londoners pulling together in adversity, motivated by the spirit of quiet defiance epitomised by the slogan 'keep calm and carry on'. Of course, there were many great acts of personal heroism, sacrifice and generosity, yet these were accompanied by occasional civil disturbances, and the picture was inevitably more nuanced than the stoic endurance and noble resistance that the Ministry of Information and Churchill needed to convey at the time and sought to perpetuate afterwards. Historians have since described the social response as 'complex and fractured', and the national unity as 'provisional, conditional and potentially fragile'.[7] Strip away the layers of hindsight, remember that the wartime generation had been brought up to fear the utter devastation that might be wrought by the new weapons of air power, and you can see why Churchill and his colleagues would be worried. They were on the defensive: uncertain of the intensity and duration of the bombardment, and apprehensive about the reaction of the British people.

Published Home Intelligence reports for September 1940 give a vivid insight into the varied responses to the attacks, both in London and around the country. These were collated from reports at the time by local sources, and must therefore be regarded as impressionistic rather than scientific, but they do provide a street level view of events. Initial reactions in the capital included shock and fear. Within three days there were 'visible signs of nerve cracking' from 'constant ordeals', with some old women and mothers accused of 'undermining morale of young women and men by their extreme nervousness and lack of resilience'.

---

[4] CAC, Churchill Papers, CHAR 20/5/56-58.
[5] Colville, *Fringes of Power*, p.258, p.260 & p.264; CAC, Churchill Papers, CHAR 20/7/39.
[6] Colville, *Fringes of Power*, p.267.
[7] Overy, *The Bombing War*, p.126; Calder, A., *The Myth of the Blitz*, (Jonathan Cape, 1991), p.90.

By day four, many were simply voting with their feet, 'Families in the Deptford area were making for the hopfields of Kent, taking with them such of their belongings as they can carry', while those further west were, 'making for the main line stations'. Nerves were 'worn down to a fine point', the conditions of living almost impossible, with worrying signs of rising class tensions and anti-semitism.[8] Thereafter the reports give hints of the ongoing psychological effects of consistent sleep deprivation, constant bombardment and the paralysis introduced by the destruction of the infrastructure.

But these accounts also testify to the presence of another very powerful human emotion: hatred. In the late summer of 1940 London was not well defended. Most of the British fighter planes could not operate effectively against the German bombers at night, and there were only ninety-two heavy guns protecting the city.[9] For the first two nights the guns remained silent. When they fired on the night of 12 September, they did little damage to the Germans, but they did a huge amount to boost the city's morale, as 'in public shelters people cheered and conversation shows that the noise brought a shock of positive pleasure'.[10] The same day, the report for London noted:

> Most prevalent emotion anger with the Germans and irritation over constant raids. Real hatred and savagery flash out at times from those who have come in contact with actual tragedies. 'We must wipe them off the face of the earth', is working man's comment heard today.[11]

Nor was this response limited to London. Reports from Belfast, Birmingham, Bristol, Cambridge, Newcastle, Nottingham and Reading all supported the bombing of Germany, particularly Berlin, and some specifically called for 'reprisals' against the civilian population.[12]

It is a response that Churchill experienced for himself. Both his memoirs, and those of Lord Ismay, describe a visit to a bomb-damaged area, Churchill places it in Peckham, Ismay in the dock lands. The Prime Minister's entourage arrived at the remains of an air raid shelter that had taken a direct hit, and in which about forty people had been killed. It must have been a moment of some tension. The arrival of Churchill's car had quickly attracted a crowd. He cannot have been sure how they would react. Would their grief and anger be directed

---

[8] Crang & Addison, *Listening to Britain*, pp.407-411.

[9] Overy, *The Bombing War*, p.78.

[10] Crang & Addison, *Listening to Britain*, p.414.

[11] Crang & Addison, *Listening to Britain*, pp.419-420.

[12] Crang & Addison, *Listening to Britain*, pp.413-457.

against him and the establishment, for leading them into such peril and for failing to provide better protection? Instead, according to Ismay, '"Good old Winnie", they cried. "We thought you'd come and see us. We can take it. Give it 'em back"'.[13] In Churchill's account he notes how as he departed 'a harsher mood swept over this haggard crowd. "Give it 'em back" they cried, and "Let *them* have it too". I undertook forthwith to see that their wishes were carried out; and this promise was certainly kept. ... Alas for poor humanity!'[14]

Churchill remained in central Westminster and shared the experience of the Londoners. On 15 September Archibald Sinclair, who had come under fire with Churchill in the trenches during the First World War, took issue with him for remaining in 10 Downing Street during the nightly bombardments.[15] This, no doubt coupled with the intensity of the bombing, seems to have had some effect, for we know from Colville's diary that Churchill was sleeping in his underground bedroom at the Cabinet War Room on the nights of the 16th and the 18th. Which is just as well, given that Colville also recorded bomb damage to Downing Street during this period.[16] Two days later, Churchill admitted to Mrs Chamberlain that he was moving his possessions out and that he proposed 'to lead a troglodyte existence with several "trogs"'.[17]

On 14 October, he was dining in the garden-room of No.10 Downing street with three of his ministers, Archibald Sinclair, Oliver Lyttelton and Moore-Brabazon, when two high explosive bombs fell on the adjacent Treasury. The kitchen and pantry were destroyed, though fortunately, just after the Prime Minister, 'acting on a providential impulse', had sent the cook and servants into the shelter.[18] Churchill wrote to Neville Chamberlain, now dying of cancer in the countryside, and shared with his predecessor the latest damage to the building that had served as an official home to them both. He described how these 'very near misses', which had killed five and wounded at least two others, had shattered the windows and doors on the exposed side of Downing Street, and rendered 'the greater part of the house uninhabitable'. As if to point out that the attack had failed in destroying the heart of British government, he mentioned that the Cabinet Room was intact, but of the future he

---

[13] Ismay, *Memoirs*, pp.183-184.
[14] Churchill, *The Second World War*, Vol. II, pp.307-308.
[15] CAC, Churchill Papers, CHAR 20/8/13.
[16] Colville, *Fringes of Power*, pp.240-242.
[17] CAC, Churchill Papers, CHAR 2/393/35.
[18] Churchill, *The Second World War*, Vol. II, pp.305-306.

could only assert his hopefulness and his belief that 'we shall wear them down and break them up. But it will take a long time'.[19]

Moore-Brabazon, the Minister for Transport, wrote to him the next day, thanking him for 'a lovely dinner, bomb and all!!', but also enclosed a copy of the report describing the destruction of a block of flats in Stoke Newington. Many of the occupants had been in the basement shelters, and it was feared that two hundred people had been buried, with 'little chance of their being rescued alive'. The letter goes on to mention that Moore-Brabazon was off to Balham to inspect the site of 'the most tragic of all our tube disasters'.[20] Over sixty people had been drowned when a bus had crashed into a bomb crater, rupturing water and sewage pipes and flooding the station below. And these were just two incidents within a two-day period. At such times, Churchill must have felt the responsibility of his office very keenly. The death and destruction was all around him, and it continued to mount. He had been given the premiership on the understanding that he was a war leader, and he had taken office on the pledge to wage war, by all the means at his disposal, until final victory. And yet the intensity of the enemy attack meant that Britain was now firmly on the defensive.

In his history, *The Second World War,* Churchill makes the argument that the Blitz was ultimately a turning point in Hitler's attempt to defeat Great Britain. The switch from attacking RAF stations in the south and east of England to night attacks on London, while they killed and wounded many civilians, in effect provided 'a breathing space of which we had the utmost need'.[21] If the RAF had been defeated as a force and lost control of the skies, then invasion would have been possible. While the Luftwaffe concentrated on London, the British could regroup, increase fighter numbers, and harry and reduce German bomber forces. This was easy to argue with hindsight, but at the time the Blitz must have raised new questions.

For, in the autumn of 1940, it cannot have been immediately clear what the effect of the bombing offensive was going to be. Was the intensive bombardment of the capital a signal that the German invasion was about to be launched? Hitler was known to be assembling barges in Channel ports, and the code word 'Cromwell' signalling 'invasion imminent' had been mistakenly issued by Home Forces in the Southern and Eastern Commands in response to the scale of the German airborne

---

[19] CAC, Churchill Papers, CHAR 20/2A/66-67.
[20] CAC, Churchill Papers, CHAR 20/4A/88-89.
[21] Churchill, *The Second World War,* Vol. II, p.292.

attack on 7 September.[22] The War Cabinet was now promoting the voluntary evacuation of the civil population from threatened south coast towns.[23] Might the combined German U-boat campaign and air assault exert a stranglehold on the British economy? Steel production was already down by 50,000 tons because of air raid warnings before the September bombings.[24] On 11 September the First Sea Lord reported the loss of 29,000 tons of shipping in the London docks. This was better than first thought, but the bombers were still coming, and the U-boats were still sinking merchant shipping in the Atlantic.[25]

What if civilian morale collapsed and there were fresh political calls for a negotiated settlement? Hitler had made a cursory appeal to Britain in a speech of 19 July, and a further overture through Switzerland had been quickly rejected as the bombs had started to fall on London in September. In the second week of October Churchill was vitriolic in the War Cabinet about articles that had appeared in the *Sunday Pictorial* and *Daily Mirror* newspapers. He felt they stood for something 'most dangerous and sinister, namely an attempt to bring about a situation in which the country would be ready for a surrender peace'. The Attorney General and the Home Secretary were both consulted, and though the matter ended in an informal warning to the papers concerned, it occupied time at several War Cabinet meetings, and reveals that the Prime Minister was clearly rattled.[26] By mid-October, incidents like Balham and Stoke Newington were felt to be having a marked effect on civilian morale, with the public having realised 'that practically no kind of shelter was invulnerable'. It was felt desirable to show fewer images of bomb damage in London, and more of Berlin.[27]

There was also an international dimension. Would President Roosevelt and the Americans be stirred into action by the scenes from the British capital, or would they retreat into isolationism, feeling that all was now lost and fearing that any American supplies sent across the Atlantic would simply be sunk or bombed? British prestige had been seriously damaged. There were fears of nationalist agitation in India from the Congress Party. What if Spain were to enter the war and seize Gibraltar, or Vichy France were to ally with Germany? The

---

[22] Churchill, *The Second World War*, Vol. II, p.276.

[23] TNA, CAB 65/9, WM (40) 245.

[24] TNA, CAB 65/9, WM (40) 249.

[25] TNA, CAB, 65/9, WM (40) 247.

[26] For September peace offer see Dilks (ed), *Cadogan Diaries*, p.325. Entry for 10 September 1940: for War Cabinet discussions on press articles, see TNA, CAB 65/9, WM (40) 267 & WM (40)268 (40).

[27] TNA, CAB 65/9, WM (40) 271 & WM (40) 272.

Italian and Japanese vultures were now circling the colonial Empire, in the Middle and Far East. All these issues occupied time and space on the agendas of the War Cabinet meetings, and all were influenced by events in London. As Churchill later acknowledged, 'We did not know how long it would last. We had no reason to suppose that it would not go on getting worse'.[28]

When he came to publish his diary for this period, Colville confirmed that in the summer and autumn of 1940 the Prime Minister suffered from an ill-tempered phase, albeit one that was passing and never constant.[29] This has already been touched on in the last chapter when discussing Clementine's letter, and surely reflected the huge stresses and workload of coping with the collapse of France and the attack on Britain. But by the time of the Blitz there was a new element with Colville's diary recording Churchill's increasing anti-Germanism. On Thursday 19 September, just after he had first been forced out of Downing Street, he was so infuriated by the indiscriminate use of German parachute mines, with their potential to devastate an area of up to 400 yards, that he advocated hitting back against their cities in a similar vein dropping 'two for every one of theirs' (something that British Bomber Command lacked the resources to undertake even if it had been deemed strategically appropriate, as became apparent when Churchill took the issue to a meeting of the Defence Committee). The following day, after seeing the bomb damage at Wandsworth, Colville noted that his boss was 'becoming less and less benevolent towards the Germans'.[30]

Churchill had stated that 'wars are not won by evacuations', but the British had been evacuated from France and with that retreat their whole war strategy had unravelled. Germany had routed the Allied army that was meant to win the war in mainland Europe. The Royal Navy could no longer enforce a naval blockade against an enemy that controlled the continental coastline from Norway to the Bay of Biscay. American political and public opinion was not yet willing or able to offer the required material aid. The Italian intervention meant that the British were challenged in the Mediterranean. The United Kingdom was enduring constant air attack. Churchill tended to be robust about the unlikely prospect of an invasion attempt, but he could not rule it out, which meant keeping substantial forces pinned down for home

---

[28] Churchill, *The Second World War*, Vol. II, p.326.
[29] Colville, *Fringes of Power*, p.281.
[30] Colville, *Fringes of Power*, pp.244-245.; see also TNA, CAB 65/9, WM (40) 254 & CAB 69/1, DO (40) 31.

defence. Yet he was under a mounting pressure, which accorded with his own instincts and nature, to find a strategy that went beyond defence and presented some hope or vision for how the war might be won.

On the very day that he wrote to Neville Chamberlain about Downing Street's near miss, 20 October 1940, a British raid was taking place on Berlin. Based at RAF Waddington, Group Captain Charles Anderson, a friend who had supplied Churchill with information about British air strength in the 1930s, sent the Prime Minister an extract from the summary of operations. It stated that four 5000lb bombs had been dropped on Hitler's Chancery building, and claimed (unfortunately erroneously) that the target had been consumed by fire and destroyed.[31] The fact that this document was kept in his papers is perhaps illustrative of Churchill clutching at a scrap of good news. Here was one way that the Germans might be worn down and one way for him to 'give it 'em back'.

In public, Churchill remained resolute and defiant. Broadcasting to the nation on 11 September, and speaking in the knowledge that the huge bombardment might be a prelude to invasion, he invoked the spirits of Drake and Nelson, British heroes who had obstructed previous enemy attempts to cross the Channel. He described the 'cruel, wanton, indiscriminate bombings of London' as 'part of Hitler's invasion plan', accused the enemy of 'killing large numbers of civilians and women and children' in an attempt to 'terrorize and cow the people of this mighty Imperial city', and expressed his confidence in 'the tough fibre of the Londoners'. He spoke in very general terms of Hitler having 'lighted a fire which will burn with a steady and consuming flame until the last vestiges of Nazi tyranny have been burnt out of Europe'.[32]

In parliament, on 8 October he addressed the question of reprisals directly: 'On every side there is the cry: "We can take it", but with it there is also "give it 'em back"'. He defended the British policy of bombing military targets, saying that he did not want to debate the 'moral issue' or enter into 'a sterile controversy' on what constituted reprisals, but promised to 'batter continually with forces which steadily increase in power each of those points in Germany which we believe will do the Germans most injury and will most speedily lessen their power to strike at us'. In doing so, he admitted the comparative weakness of the

---

[31] CAC, Churchill Papers, CHAR 20/3/37-39. For information on Anderson's role in the 1930s see Gilbert, M., *In Search of Churchill*, (Harper Collins, 1994), pp.115-117.

[32] CAC, Churchill Papers, CHAR 9/144/64-66.

British bomber forces and hinted at the pressure he was coming under to unshackle the RAF and authorise a more unrestricted bombing campaign. Having then proceeded to brief the house on the failure of the combined British and Free French operation against Vichy forces at Dakar, he ended with the assertion that, 'we must improve our methods but redouble our efforts. We must be baffled to fight better, not to fight less'.[33] The frustrations of being on the defensive were evident.

Behind the scenes, he focused on finding a way to take the initiative. After the intense pressure of his first few weeks, his government was now able to settle into a steadier rhythm. The War Cabinet tended to meet just once a day, around noon or early in the evening, with the Prime Minister doing more business directly with the military leaders in the Chiefs of Staff or Defence Committees. A Prime Ministerial directive of 27 June, almost certainly produced with the help of Ismay, (and just possibly in response to Clementine Churchill's letter of that day), sought to further streamline War Cabinet meetings: instituting a written Daily Intelligence Summary to reduce the oral reporting requirements on the Chiefs of Staff, introducing a rota system for attendance at weekends, and seeking to regulate the attendance of additional ministers.[34] On 9 October, it was agreed that any government department which had not given effect to orders issued by the War Cabinet was required to report back and explain itself. This was a tightening of the reins.[35]

But it was around the top table that Churchill needed to strengthen his position. The dramatic nature of his accession to the premiership, and the suddenness and speed of the French collapse, had meant that he had initially lacked the time and the political capital to make changes to the people around him. He had no choice but to include Chamberlain and Halifax in his War Cabinet, as to do otherwise would have alienated a large part of the Conservative Party and led to a dislocation in decision-making at a moment of supreme national crisis. Similarly, he had inherited the Chiefs of Staff, and could hardly restructure the High Command during a period when the military and political leaders were in almost constant session. The same applied further down the chain, as Churchill later wrote, 'The existing organisms remained intact. No official personalities were changed'.[36]

Yet, as has been seen, this was not quite true. Churchill had compensated for his initial political weakness by making himself

---

[33] CAC, Churchill Papers, CHAR 9/142A/8,9,27.
[34] CAC, Churchill Papers, CHAR 23/4/3, Prime Minister's Directive, WP (G) (40) 164.
[35] TNA, CAB 65/9, WM (40) 268.
[36] Churchill, *The Second World War*, Vol. II, p.15.

Minister of Defence, taking over the structure of the War Cabinet Secretariat, and by bringing his own team of special advisers and assistants into Downing Street. By the end of the summer of 1940, he had not only weathered the immediate crisis, but had won the argument for his war policy in the War Cabinet, strengthened his position in the House of Commons with the sinking of the French fleet, and consolidated his reputation in the country through his series of broadcasts and reported speeches. But these gains might be temporary, and there had been times in those first two months when he had faced strong opposition from political colleagues and the military commanders. If he was going to drive forward with an aggressive war policy, then he needed a like-minded team at the top. This is what he now set about building.

The first to go was the head of the army, the Chief of the Imperial General Staff, General Sir Edmund Ironside. He had known Churchill since the Boer War, and had served under his political direction in Russia and Iraq in the period immediately after the First World War. Ironside had become Chief of Staff at the beginning of the new conflict, in September 1939, just as Churchill was joining the War Cabinet, and had initially enjoyed the full backing of the new First Lord of the Admiralty. Yet, there was soon friction between them on the Military Co-ordination Committee over the conduct of operations in Norway, and, before Churchill had become Prime Minister, General Sir John Dill had already been recalled from France, made Vice Chief of the Imperial General Staff, and established as a potential successor. Ironside who, in the words of one historian, was an 'open-air soldier', 'disliked the confines of desk work', and 'held a low, if not contemptuous view of politicians', admitted that the he was not temperamentally suited to the role, wishing that he were 'fighting instead of making war in an office'.[37] Some of his private diary entries during the Battle for France also reveal a pessimism that, even if not openly stated, must have been sensed and would have been at odds with the offensive spirit being demanded by the Prime Minister. Accepting his fall from favour, he stepped aside, agreeing to become Commander in Chief Home Forces. He did not last long in his new post, being removed and retired in July, when his plans to resist invasion were criticised by Generals Brooke and Montgomery, and ultimately by Churchill, for being too static.

Next it was the turn of Air Chief Marshal, Sir Cyril Newall, the head of the Royal Air Force. He had fought hard to prevent British

---

[37] Bond, B., 'Ironside' in Keegan J. (ed), *Churchill's Generals*, (Weidenfeld & Nicholson, 1991), pp.17-18; Macleaod & Kelly (eds), *The Ironside Diaries*, p.303.

fighter strength being dissipated over France, but was criticised by Lord Beaverbrook for not getting to grips with aircraft production, by Lord Trenchard, the founding father of the RAF, for not implementing a greater bombing offensive, and by Churchill for wanting to remove Air Chief Marshal Dowding prior to the Battle of Britain. There was an orchestrated campaign against him by elements within his own service, who saw him as representing an out of touch old guard, which was backed by Lord Beaverbrook and which reached the desks of prominent political figures, including that of the Prime Minister. It manifested itself in an ongoing and festering row about whether Newall had concealed the true nature of comparative British and German air strengths.[38] In October, he was replaced by Air Chief Marshal Sir Charles Portal and sent half way round the world, to be Governor General of New Zealand.

The Prime Minister may not have been the sole mover in either of these changes. Both commanders were damned by the judgements of their military peers in the immediate aftermath of the first phase of the war, but equally neither leader could have been removed without Churchill's support and ultimate sanction. In terms of their successors, Portal was a favourite of Lord Trenchard, with whom Churchill had first worked in 1919, and as Head of Bomber Command was known to back the sort of offensive bombing strategy that the Prime Minister now favoured; while at the end of May 1940 Churchill had no real option but to promote Dill, the existing Vice Chief of Imperial Staff, as continuity was clearly critical and the alternative army commanders were engaged in the battle for France. Yet, Churchill never seems to have warmed to Dill, and was writing to Eden at the War Office as early as 10 July in very blunt terms to complain that, 'I do not think we are having the help from General Dill which we hoped for at the time of his appointment, and he strikes me as being very tired, disheartened and over-impressed with the might of Germany'.[39]

As Minister of Defence Churchill expected to be fully involved in all appointments and removals to high level military commands: as Prime Minister he reserved to himself ultimate right of approval. Once the Battle of France was over, these rights were exercised. In a pattern that would repeat itself throughout the war, Churchill wanted commanders who would be bold, bellicose and take the offensive. He wanted Chiefs of Staff who would share his vision, even if they would often disagree over the means of achieving it.

---

[38] Ritchie, S., 'A Political Intrigue Against the Chief of the Air Staff; The Downfall of Air Chief Marshal Sir Cyril Newall' in *War & Society*, Vol. 16, Number 1, pp.83-104.
[39] CAC, Churchill Papers, CHAR 20/1/49.

The changes to the Chiefs of Staff left Admiral Sir Dudley Pound, the First Sea Lord and head of the Royal Navy, as the only surviving member of the original triumvirate. Not that he can have felt very secure in his seat. Colville noted the fall of Newall in his diary for Wednesday 2 October, and wrote that 'the Chiefs of Staff, who are sound, but old and slow, are being purged'. He wrongly thought that Pound would cease to be First Sea Lord.[40]

Newall's removal was timed to coincide with a wider political restructuring. In August, Churchill had brought Lord Beaverbrook, the Minister for Aircraft Production into the War Cabinet. No-one could dispute the importance of aeroplane numbers in the summer of 1940, but Beaverbrook was also a long-time, if often critical, friend of Churchill's with a direct line to the Prime Minister. At the beginning of October, with Neville Chamberlain's failing health having led to his resignation, Churchill grasped the opportunity to further strengthen his grip on the centre. The overall number of ministers in the War Cabinet was increased to eight. Chamberlain's title of Lord President of the Council and his chairmanship of the key Cabinet committee for the Home Front was taken over by Sir John Anderson, a senior civil servant and accomplished administrator. In came the Chancellor of the Exchequer, Sir Kingsley Wood, a former Chamberlainite whose crucial defection in May had helped ease Churchill's path to power. While for balance, Ernest Bevin, the Minister of Labour, joined his fellow Labour Party members Attlee and Greenwood in the Cabinet Room. He brought with him his influence over the trade union movement. This was a team that could focus on the key problems of home defence, production and supply, and was capable of mobilising the labour force and economy. Churchill clearly hoped that they would ease his burdens in these areas, allowing him to concentrate on military operations and grand strategy.[41]

The 'official personalities' had certainly changed. This shuffle meant that, while Halifax remained in the War Cabinet, as Foreign Secretary he was now isolated. Even more so when Churchill took Chamberlain's role as Leader of the Conservative Party, rubbing salt in the wounds by asking Halifax to propose him. Then, in December, after the sudden death of Lord Lothian, the British Ambassador to the United States, Churchill asked Halifax to take up the vacant role at the Embassy in Washington DC. It was a move that allowed him to install his own choice, Anthony Eden, as Foreign Secretary, thereby establishing a

---

[40] Colville, *Fringes of Power*, p.256.
[41] Churchill, *The Second World War*, Vol. II, p.326.

much closer and generally more harmonious relationship between Downing Street and the Foreign Office. For the moment at least, Churchill's control over his government seemed secure. These moves, however, were not without risks. The new War Cabinet contained two very strong and politically opposed personalities in the form of the union boss Bevin and the newspaper magnate Beaverbrook. As a body, it was larger and therefore perhaps less wieldy than that which had navigated Britain through the fall of France, and though Churchill had strengthened his personal position with the demise of Chamberlain and the removal of Halifax, he had lost his two most experienced ministers, and with them any shield that these vestiges of the last government provided by acting as lightning rods for criticism of the direction of the war effort. It was now very clear who would take responsibility for success and for failure.

While Churchill was making changes to his team, he was also focusing on what their future direction might be. As the bombs were falling in September and October, and while wrestling with all the problems caused by the Blitz, he found time to write and circulate three directives touching on forward strategy. His paper on 'The Munitions Situation', dated 3 September 1940, is far more than a survey of military requirements. It set out in eight points his road map for how Britain should regain the initiative. It began with the bold assertion that:

> The Navy can lose us the war, but only the air force can win it. Therefore our supreme effort must be to gain overwhelming mastery in the Air. The Fighters are our salvation, but the Bombers alone provide the means of victory. We must therefore develop the power to carry an ever-increasing volume of explosives to Germany, so as to pulverise the entire industry and scientific structure on which the war effort and economic life of the enemy depends. … In no other way at present visible can we hope to overcome the immense military power of Germany…

He therefore gave priority to the claims of the RAF over those of the army or navy. The paper admitted that the main short-term focus would have to be consolidation. The army was to be built up to its planned fifty-five divisions as quickly as possible, but the process was unlikely to be completed before the end of 1941. In the meantime, though invasion was 'unlikely to materialise,' strong forces would need to be maintained in the UK against its perpetual threat. This would limit the scope for offensive operations before the spring of 1941, thereby giving the country eight months to concentrate on 'an enormous improvement in our output of war-like equipment, and in which steady and rapid accumulations may be hoped for', with particular attention being given to devising new weapons and developing scientific leadership. Yet it was clear that he was not prepared to give up the offensive completely, urging the Admiralty to consider 'aggressive schemes of war' and the bombardment of enemy held coasts, particularly in the Mediterranean, and identifying the potential for bringing Imperial troops into action in the Middle East, and for aggressive amphibious warfare in North Africa.[42]

The production programmes that would be needed to underpin such a forward strategy formed the subject of a subsequent directive on 'Priorities', issued on 5 October 1940. Aircraft production remained the top priority, but emphasis was also placed on acquiring the motorised transport needed to build up the army's armoured divisions, and on increasing production of rifles and ammunition. The paper was clearly intended as a call to arms against failure to meet production targets, rebuking 'laggard elements', suggesting that horses might be used in England to free up resources for overseas, and stating that, 'Any attempt to make heavy weather out of this problem is a failure to aid us in our need'.[43] His third paper, circulated on 15 October, just after the bombing of Downing Street, was on 'The Mediterranean', and urged the wholesale reinforcement of the theatre with ships, troops and aircraft.[44]

The conclusion reached by Churchill was that there were two primary areas in which the country might not have to sit back and take it, and could 'give it 'em back': the first was the bombing of Germany; the second, action in the Mediterranean theatre.

Britain had in fact been bombing Germany from the very beginning of Churchill's premiership. His predecessor had been more cautious. As late as 10 May, Chamberlain had delayed a decision on the bombing of German industry in the Ruhr and had warned against doing 'anything which could render us liable to be accused of having initiated unrestricted air bombing'.[45] There was a particular fear of alienating the United States, as Roosevelt had called on all sides not to bomb civilians. Yet Churchill had presided over the foundation of the Royal Naval Air Service prior to the First World War, had served as the first Secretary of State for Air in 1919, and had been a proponent of building

---

[42] CAC, Churchill Papers, CHAR 23/4/8, Prime Minister's Directive WP (40) 352.
[43] CAC, Churchill Papers, CHAR 23/4/9, Prime Minister's Directive, WP (40) 416.
[44] CAC, Churchill Papers, CHAR 23/4/10, Prime Minister's Directive, WP (40) 421.
[45] TNA, CAB 65/7, WM (40) 118.

up Britain's bomber forces during the 1930s. He believed in meeting fire with fire and was more robust in his approach to the Americans, whom he believed needed to see proof of British fighting spirit.

Not surprisingly then, one of his first actions as Prime Minister had been to sanction the raid on the German industrial centre of München Gladbach on the night of 11-12 May, which had resulted in four deaths.[46] As early as the evening of 12 May he had stated that German wartime actions had already given the Allies 'ample justification for retaliation' which meant that 'we were no longer bound by our previously held scruples as to initiating "unrestricted" air warfare'. The debate in the War Cabinet at that point had not been primarily about whether it was right to use the bombers on industrial targets, with the consequent likelihood of civilian casualties, but whether it was more effective to use them against the Ruhr or in support of ground troops in the land battle. Throughout the discussions, Churchill had been a consistent advocate of launching a bombing offensive against German industry. In this he had been backed by all three Chiefs of Staff, who saw such action as a means of wresting the initiative from the enemy.[47] On the morning of the 15 May the Prime Minister had chaired the War Cabinet which had authorised Bomber Command to strike against marshalling yards and oil refineries in the Ruhr and elsewhere in Germany.[48] These were legitimate military targets, albeit ones that would clearly involve civilian casualties. This was the first round in a debate that would continue on how best to use the bombing arm, and whether it should be deployed in support of other operations or unleashed as a campaign in its own right.

It is clear from the summaries of the discussions in May that Churchill had always expected British bombing to bring German retaliation. His view had been that it was better to take the initiative and try and inflict as much damage as possible while British air defences were still strong, and while such action might relieve pressure on the French. In any case, he felt sure it would only be a matter of time before the Germans attacked the United Kingdom. After the fall of France, and faced with the Luftwaffe in British skies, he continued to support the regular bombing of military industrial targets in Germany as a means of weakening the enemy. In late August, after the bombing of British industrial centres and attacks on the outskirts of London, he ordered two small retaliatory raids on Berlin. Hitler immediately used these

---

[46] Overy, *The Bombing War*, p 244.
[47] TNA, CAB 65/13, WM (40) 119C; WM (40) 120; WM (40) 122.
[48] TNA, CAB 65/13, WM (40) 123.

as a pretext for the Blitz, though the attack had already been planned as part of a wider strategy to subdue Britain ahead of an invasion attempt.[49]

Churchill, then, had already been deploying a 'Give it 'em back' strategy prior to September 1940. Now, the sheer scale of the Blitz, and the related public demands for retaliation, contributed to an escalation. On 10 September, he supported the War Cabinet view that our raiders over Germany ought to be instructed not to return home with their bombs if they failed to locate their targets, though this was not implemented because a similar instruction had already been issued and Sinclair feared it might discourage British bombing crews from making all efforts to find their targets.[50] On 11 September there was further discussion about whether to retaliate by bombing any one of twenty German towns, but the conclusion was to delay any decision and to continue to focus on military targets.[51] This remained the view of the Chief of the Air Staff when Churchill pushed the adoption of parachute mines at the Defence Committee on 24 September, with Newall continuing to favour the attack on military objectives with bombs, albeit noting that many would be near centres of population so that their bombing would also affect morale and living conditions.[52] It is only in October, after more than a month of bombardment, and faced with all the pressures described above, that the War Cabinet approved Churchill's proposal for 'a somewhat broader interpretation of our present policy'. The emphasis remained on military targets, but 'we should also for the time being take as our primary objectives military targets in built up areas'.[53]

The bombing of London, and the death and damage seen at first hand, had undoubtedly increased Churchill's resolution. But there were other factors. Bomber Command under Portal's leadership was keen to show what it could do, the Italians had just attacked Greece, and the War Cabinet had received a telegram from Belgrade suggesting that 'the cocksureness of the German civil population was disappearing, and that the German people seemed to have less power of resistance to air bombardment' than the people of Britain. This latter was wishful thinking, if apparently backed by 'a recent secret report'.[54]

---

49 Overy, *The Bombing War*, pp.83–84.
50 TNA, CAB 65/9, WM (40) 246.
51 TNA, CAB 65/9, WM (40) 247.
52 TNA, CAB 69/1, DO (40) 31.
53 TNA, CAB 65/9, WM (40) 280.
54 TNA, CAB, 65/9, WM (40) 279.

In reality, the policy of bombing Germany was born as much from frustration as revenge. To paraphrase his letter to Chamberlain, Churchill needed to find a way of wearing the enemy down and breaking them up. It was RAF dogma that Bomber Command could provide such a weapon. Prior to Germany's success in France it had been envisaged that her defeat would be achieved through a combination of military attrition on the Western Front and sea blockade by the Royal Navy. Churchill's paper of 3 September recognised that, 'The weapon of sea blockade had become blunted' and 'less effectual' on account of Germany's ability to exploit her new land conquests'.[55] Newall's replacement by Portal had signalled the shift to an alternative; a more aggressive bombing policy. But it would still take time to build up, was yet to prove itself, and was unlikely to deliver final victory on its own.

Then there was the Mediterranean. Britain's status as a global empire had led her to build up a strong position to protect the key trade route through the Mediterranean, via the Suez Canal to India, Hong Kong, Singapore, Australia and New Zealand. Naval bases had been established at Gibraltar, Malta and Alexandria. Egypt, though nominally independent, was a client state, while the British and Egyptians jointly administered the Sudan. Palestine and Trans Jordan were held as a mandate under the League of Nations. Somaliland was a protectorate, and Aden, Cyprus and Kenya were Crown colonies. The British also retained a strong interest in Iraq and Iran, with their critical reserves of oil. In 1940 this huge area, comprising several million square miles, formed the Middle Eastern command of General Sir Archibald Wavell, and was defended by total forces of just 90,000, a handful of air squadrons, and two fleets, based at either end of the Mediterranean in Gibraltar and Alexandria.[56] The British fear was that their position would be challenged by Fascist Italy, who had taken advantage of British and French weakness to enter the conflict on 10 June, and that Mussolini was intent on carving out a new Roman Empire in the region. The French surrender had left Britain without an ally in the theatre, and the precarious neutrality of the French colonies in North Africa and Syria was now a major headache, with the risk that the Vichy regime might turn hostile.

Churchill was emphatically not a 'Little Englander'. He was a child of the Empire, and a child that had been schooled in the Mediterranean theatre. As a young Victorian cavalry officer, he had fought in the

---

[55] CAC, Churchill Papers, CHAR 23/4/8.
[56] Beckett, I., 'Wavell' in Keegan, *Churchill's Generals*, pp.74-75.

Sudan against the Mahdist uprising. His political apprenticeship had been served at the Colonial Office as an Under Secretary of State in the Edwardian era. As First Lord of the Admiralty from 1911 he had toured the fleet bases of the Mediterranean. After the First World War, he had advocated using air power to control Iraq. In 1921 he had chaired the Cairo conference, supporting the implementation of the Balfour Declaration to give the Jews a home within Palestine and fixing the borders of modern day Iraq and Jordan. The Middle East, unlike the Far East, was a region that he had visited, that he could visualise, and which he now saw as central to the war effort of his administration.

Central because it was now threatened by a huge build-up of Italian forces. Wavell's best estimate in August 1940 was that there were 280,000 enemy troops in Libya and they were starting to mass on the border with Egypt.[57] It was a fear that was compounded by the threat that the Germans might move into the Balkans. The loss of the Eastern Mediterranean, following on from the reverses in Norway, France and at Dakar, would be another crushing blow to British prestige. It would also sever the already threatened and restricted links with the eastern hemisphere through the Suez Canal, compounding supply problems to and from the United Kingdom. But also central because the theatre provided an opportunity: for here were substantial British and Imperial forces that were not tied up in home defence, that were not pinned to the British Isles, and which might be able to take the offensive. Hence the stress Churchill had placed on the Mediterranean in his various directives. Now he just had to convince the Chiefs of Staff and commanders to act.

The situation was not immediately promising. When Wavell visited London in early August he was very cautious. Some degree of withdrawal might be necessary, there was a danger that German armoured forces might appear, the position would remain unsatisfactory unless the state of British forces could be improved, there was a general shortage of equipment, large numbers of troops were needed for internal security duties within Egypt, and resources would not allow an offensive from within Kenya.[58] It is tempting to picture Churchill listening to this litany, his grip tightening on his chair arm, his cigar clenched firmly in his scowling jaw.

Things did not go any better in his private meetings with the taciturn Wavell. Churchill now wrote to Eden, as Secretary of State for War, noting

---

[57] Playfair, I., *The Mediterranean and the Middle East*, Vol I (HM Stationery Office, 1954), p.188.

[58] Playfair, *The Mediterranean and the Middle East*, Vol I, pp.188-189.

Wavell's lack of 'mental vigour and resolve to overcome obstacles'.[59] Research by David Reynolds has revealed that he even considered replacing Wavell with the New Zealander, General Bernard Freyberg, whom he knew and admired, and whom he felt to be a fighter.[60]

Realising that he could not really remove Wavell without a better reason, particularly while he commanded the confidence of Dill, Churchill confined himself to micro management. He sent an extremely full directive to his Commander-in-Chief in the Middle East, specifying in great detail exactly how Wavell should deploy his troops in defence of Egypt and even including appendices detailing the methods he should use in contaminating water supplies, using delay-action mines, and destroying the one asphalt-surfaced road on the African desert coast.[61] It shows the level of interest Churchill was taking in the campaign, but also highlights his tendency to 'prod' his commanders, especially when he was worried that they were not doing enough. In the words of General Playfair, the official historian of the war in the Mediterranean and the Middle East, the military could have been left in no doubt 'that there was indeed a central direction of the war, and a vigorous one'.[62] Yet, the initial British reverses that followed, with the evacuation of British Somaliland in August, and an Italian advance into Egypt in September, can hardly have increased Churchill's optimism or confidence.[63]

Yet, in spite of any reservations, Churchill made himself the key advocate for building up forces in the Middle East. He refused to countenance the withdrawal of the British fleet from the eastern Mediterranean. In August, he enthusiastically backed a plan to send half of Britain's tanks to Egypt. He even urged that they be sent through the Mediterranean, rather than via the safer Cape route, in order to hasten their arrival in the theatre of battle. In Churchill's words, 'sharp argument was maintained'. He felt the Admiralty was 'taking an unduly pessimistic view of the risks involved', but ultimately deferred to the wishes of the First Sea Lord, Admiral Pound, who feared that 'the chances of the convoy getting through unscathed were remote', and General Wavell, who felt it was more important that the tanks arrived safely.[64] In September, Churchill overruled Lord Beaverbrook

---

[59] CAC, Churchill Papers, CHAR 20/2/42-43.
[60] Reynolds, *In Command of History*, pp 190-191, citing CAC, Churchill Papers, CHUR 4/167/127-128.
[61] TNA, CAB 69/1, DO (40) 28.
[62] Playfair, *The Mediterranean and the Middle East*, Vol. I, p.200.
[63] Playfair, *The Mediterranean and the Middle East*, Vol. I, pp.246-248.
[64] Churchill, *The Second World War*, Vol II, p 397. TNA, CAB 69/1, DO (40) 25.

in support of despatching more aircraft and in October he pushed through the reinforcement of Malta.[65] Playfair has calculated that in the last third of 1940 Wavell was reinforced with 126,000 personnel (not all of whom were combatants), as well as with forty-one Wellington bombers, eighty-five Blenheim IV's, and eighty-seven Hurricanes.[66] This was a clear statement of intent, not least because it included the 2nd Armoured Division, three tank regiments and three field artillery regiments from the United Kingdom, all of which would be sorely needed were Hitler to launch an invasion of the British mainland.

Having taken these steps, Churchill began to share his thinking more widely. At 11.00 hours on Thursday, 31 October 1940, he convened a conference of the leading military commanders of British Home Forces. The small Cabinet War Room beneath the Treasury in Whitehall, central London, must have been packed. It contained the First Lord of the Admiralty, the Secretary of State for Air, the three Chiefs of Staff, the three Vice Chiefs of Staff, General Ismay, five further Admirals, two more Vice Admirals, one Rear Admiral, one full General, two more Lieutenant Generals, two further Air Chief Marshals, one Air Marshal and one Air Commodore. If a German bomb had penetrated the concrete ceiling, it would have wiped out most of the British High Command. This would explain both the choice of this secure venue and the morning timing, as the heavy bombing raids usually came at dusk.

Churchill summarised the situation as he saw it. He believed the invasion threat had greatly diminished but that it would be maintained by the Germans so as to pin down substantial forces in Britain. There must always be sufficient forces retained in this country to deal with invasion, but, subject to that proviso, it was intended to send reinforcements overseas to maximum extent within the limits of shipping. Britain had already sent 72,000 men to the Middle East; and 53,000 more would arrive from the UK and from other parts of the empire by the end of the year. More than half our best tanks had been sent to the Mediterranean, and in spite of the great air battles over this country, we were in the process of firstly re-equipping and then increasing our air forces overseas.

He acknowledged that Britain could not expect to undertake decisive operations in 1941, forecast that Germany might provoke Russia to fight over the fate of the Baku oil fields, and stated that we might need to support Turkey as Germany advanced towards Suez. He concluded

---

[65] TNA, CAB 65/9, WM (40) 260; TNA, CAB 69/1, DO (40) 34.
[66] Playfair, *The Mediterranean and the Middle East*, Vol. I, pp.246-248.

by addressing the key question, 'How are we win to the war?' His answer was that 'for the moment' all Britain could do was continue the blockade of Germany, 'accompanied by the remorseless bombing of Germany and Italy'. By 1941, we to it might be able to undertake medium operations of an amphibious nature; and by 1942, we should be able to deliver very heavy oversea attacks'.[67]

On 5 November in the House of Commons, Churchill spoke of the need to develop 'a strong, fine army, well-equipped, well-armed, well-trained, well-organized', as without such a force 'and the sea power which gives so wide a choice of action, the war might be needlessly prolonged, might even drift towards a disastrous stalemate'. He mentioned reinforcing the armies in the Middle East to the limits of shipping capacity. It was a tacit admission that bombing on its own was not enough, and an indication of what might be planned in the Mediterranean. He was very clear that:

> Only in this way shall we reach a position where instead of being forced to suffer all the measureless vexations of a widespread defensive attitude, – being hit now here, now there, and often inevitably too late, – we shall regain the initiative and make the enemy wonder where and how we are going to strike at them.[68]

This, then, was the plan. To take the offensive where possible, by bombing Germany and fighting Italy in the Mediterranean. This is how Britain would start to wear her enemies down. In the short term, there were some unexpectedly quick gains. On 11 November, Admiral Cunningham's torpedo planes inflicted great damage on the Italian fleet at harbour in Taranto. While in December, General Wavell launched Operation *Compass*, an initially limited assault on the enemy positions in the Libyan desert, that ended up forcing an Italian retreat of some five hundred miles.

Yet in war the goal posts are always moving. Even as Churchill was outlining his plans to his commanders and to parliament, Mussolini was opening a new front at the other end of the Mediterranean by invading Greece. Italian troops crossed the border from Albania on 28 October. Britain and France were bound by a 1939 agreement to support Athens in the event of an attack, and Churchill made it clear that Britain would offer what limited support she could. In his speech at the Mansion House on 9 November 1940 he declared that, 'To the

---

[67] TNA, CAB 69/1, DO (40) 39.
[68] CAC, Churchill Papers, CHAR 9/142A/57-61.

valiant Greek people and their armies now defending their native soil from the latest Italian outrage, we send from the heart of London our faithful promise that amid all our burdens and anxieties we will do our best to aid them in their struggle...'[69]

There was much debate within the Chiefs of Staff, Defence and War Cabinet Committees about what form such aid might take, and whether it might allow for the creation of a new Balkan bloc with Yugoslavia and Turkey joining Greece to create a front against any southward German advance. This was complicated by the unexpected success of the Greeks in pushing the Italians back into Albania, and by the Greek fear that direct British military intervention might lead to immediate German retaliation. Churchill chose to prioritise Wavell's offensive in the Western Desert, and it was only in the face of a German military concentration on the Greco-Bulgarian border, and after Eden and Dill had visited the Middle East and recommended military intervention in Greece, that he and the War Cabinet ratified the decision to halt the advance in Libya and send troops to stand alongside the Greeks.[70]

The minutes of the key Cabinet meetings for the 5, 6 and 7 March show the Prime Minister wrestling with the issues. On 5 March he introduced the discussion by admitting that 'it was still open to us, if on consideration this seemed the wisest course, to tell the Greeks that we would liberate them from any undertaking' and that they would be free to make terms with Germany. He was worried that if we landed in Greece and were driven out, the effect on Spain and North Africa might be worse than if we simply 'remained Masters of the Delta'. In a telegram to Eden he was prepared to admit that, 'We have done our best to promote Balkan combination against Germany (stop) We must be careful not to urge Greece against her better judgment into a hopeless resistance alone when we have only a handful of troops which can reach scene in time (stop)'. Perhaps remembering Gallipoli, he was also concerned about sending what were primarily Australian and New Zealand troops on such a hazardous enterprise.[71] On the 6th, 'He did not wish us to expose ourselves to the charge that we had caused another small nation to be sacrificed' but, having just seen the text of the military agreement that General Dill had signed with the Greek General Papagos on 4 March, he was clear that we could not go back on it, 'unless the Greeks themselves released us'.[72] By noon on the

---

[69] CAC, Churchill Papers, CHAR 9/145/48.
[70] For detailed analysis of these debates see Lawlor, S., *Churchill and the Politics of War, 1940-1941*, (Cambridge University Press, 1994), pp.165-256.
[71] TNA, CAB 65/22, WM (41) 24.
[72] TNA, CAB 65/22, WM (41) 25.

following day, his attitude had hardened. Eden had cabled him that the Greeks were going to fight anyway, the report from the commanders on the spot was more optimistic about being able to hold the Germans, and he still felt it possible that Yugoslavia might enter the fray on the Allied side. You can almost see him allowing himself to be persuaded, until finally giving his suitably Churchillian endorsement that, 'we should go forward with a good heart'. And that in spite of the fact that the following item on the agenda was Turkey's likely decision to go back on her undertaking to support Greece.[73]

In the light of the subsequent British defeat in Greece, the decision to intervene has been seen as a mistake. Major-General Eric Dorman O'Gowan (formerly Dorman-Smith), a senior officer in Cairo, whom we shall meet again in a later chapter, felt that an enormous opportunity had been lost to drive the Italians completely out of North Africa in exchange for 'the pious hope that a few British divisions in Greece would induce Turks and Jugoslavia to join up in some nebulous military undefined adventure'.[74] This does not seem quite fair, and it rests on the assumption that Libya could have been cleared before the arrival of German reinforcements in North Africa. By March 1941, Churchill knew the chances of creating a Balkan combination against Germany were slight, and he also knew that intervention in Greece came with a high-risk of failure. It was done partly to honour an alliance, but also as a means of taking the fight to the main enemy. Churchill had known for months that it was only a matter of time till the Germans entered the Mediterranean theatre, and had predicted their move through the Balkans in his conference speech to his military commanders in October 1940. By supporting Greece, whatever the outcome, he had now demonstrated again that Britain would fight to hold her position in the Middle East. He did it with the active encouragement of Eden, his new Foreign Secretary, and with the backing of the Chiefs of Staff, who had already given him an assurance that defeat in Greece would not imperil Britain or mean defeat in the war.[75] This was a battlefield that kept the fighting away from the homeland and away from the British powerbases in Cairo and Alexandria. If successful it would strengthen Britain's position in the Middle East and the Balkans and her prestige worldwide. Yet, if unsuccessful, as Churchill acknowledged in his telegram to Eden of 5 March, the 'Loss of Greece and Balkans by no means a major

---

[73] TNA, CAB 65/22, WM (41) 26.
[74] CAC, Barnett Papers, BRNT 2, (letter from O'Gowan to Correlli Barnett, 14 June 1958).
[75] TNA, CAB 65/22, WM (41) 25.

catastrophe for us provided Turkey remains honest neutral', as this would bar any easy enemy advance into Syria, Iran or Iraq and thence towards the Suez Canal.[76]

The British offensive action inevitably brought a strong enemy response thereby beginning a widening of the war in the Mediterranean, and what General Ismay later labelled the 'Middle East See-Saw'.[77] Hitler sent Rommel and the armoured divisions of the *Afrika Korps* to reinforce the Italians in the Western Desert, and then in April 1941 launched an invasion of Greece through Bulgaria. The British soon found themselves overextended and fighting on two fronts. By the end of April Rommel was besieging Tobruk, which was being stubbornly defended by a force composed primarily of Australians, and had pushed the rest of the British and Imperial troops back to the Egyptian border. Greece had been overrun, Athens had fallen, and the remaining British forces were concentrated on Crete, from whence they would be evacuated after a German parachute assault at the end of May. Egypt was once again threatened.

Churchill set out his response to these setbacks in a characteristically bullish directive to his Chiefs of Staff. Dated 28 April 1941, it stated that, 'The loss of Egypt and the Middle East would be a disaster of the first magnitude to Great Britain, second only to successful invasion and final conquest'. It was 'to be impressed upon all ranks, especially the highest, that the life and honour of Great Britain' depended 'upon the successful defence of Egypt'. All plans for the possible evacuation of the country were to be 'called in', and 'no whisper' of their existence was to be allowed. 'No surrenders by officers and men' would 'be considered tolerable unless at least 50 per cent casualties' were 'sustained by the unit or force in question', and Generals and staff officers were to use their pistols in self-defence.[78]

The week before, while staying at Ditchley Park (a country house retreat lent to the Prime Minister during the war by its owners, Ronald and Nancy Tree), Churchill had received telegrams from Wavell detailing both his shortage of tanks, and the latest intelligence about the arrival of new German armour. One of these may have been Wavell's telegram of 18 April, in which the General had remarked, 'In this desert warfare it is armoured strength that counts especially armour with speed and range and this [sic] where I am so weak'.[79] Deeply troubled, the Prime Minister

---

[76] TNA, CAB 65/22, WM (41) 24.

[77] Ismay, *Memoirs*, p.190.

[78] CAC, Churchill Papers, CHAR 23/9/24; also cited in Butler, J., *Grand Strategy*, Vol II, September 1939-June 1941, (HM Stationery Office, 1957), Appendix IV, p.577.

[79] CAC, Churchill Papers, CHAR 20/37/121.

immediately ordered that the Chiefs of Staff be convened to consider a resurrected version of the plan to send fast tank-carrying ships through the Mediterranean, minuting to Ismay that 'all may turn on a few hundred armoured vehicles. They must be carried there, if possible at all costs… Speed is vital. Every day's delay must be avoided'.[80]

At the Defence Committee meeting the next day, Monday 21 April, he drove this suggestion through, adding an additional ship to include an extra sixty-seven Mark VI Cruiser tanks, the type of faster armour that Wavell most needed. In his later published account of this episode, Churchill was cutting about the opposition of General Dill, who felt that the vehicles ought to be prioritised for home defence.[81] The resulting operation was codenamed *Tiger*. One ship was lost to a mine, which Churchill likened to a tiger losing one claw, but the remaining convoy reached Egypt on 12 May and successfully delivered forty-three Hurricane fighters and 238 tanks.[82] Churchill was clear about his personal involvement in the episode 'for which I took a more direct measure of responsibility than usual', illustrating both the importance he attached to the Middle East, and the risks he was prepared to run to regain the offensive.[83] His determination to see the theatre properly reinforced is clear in a minute that he sent to the First Lord of the Admiralty, First Sea Lord and Minister of Aircraft Production on 30 April, urging a similar operation for air reinforcements and expressing his fear that the 'fighting value' of our army in the Middle East might be 'frustrated and even destroyed by a temporary hostile superiority in tanks and aircraft'. He justified making the necessary accommodations and running the inevitable risks on the grounds that failure to win in Egypt might well determine the decisions of Turkey, Spain and Vichy, and even 'strike the United States the wrong way'.[84]

It was an argument that he used again in a telegram to President Roosevelt a few days later, on 4 May 1941. Responding to the President's desire to prioritise the Atlantic, he explained that he could not regard the loss of the Middle East as 'a mere preliminary to the successful maintenance of a prolonged oceanic war' and that 'if all Europe, the greater part of Asia and Africa' were 'a part of the Axis system, a war maintained by the British Isles, United States, Canada and Australasia against this mighty agglomeration would be a hard, long and bleak proposition'. In other words, this was not just about saving the British

---

[80] Churchill, *The Second World War*, Vol. III, pp.217-220; TNA CAB 69/8 DO (41) 18.
[81] Churchill, *The Second World War*, Vol. III, p.220; TNA, CAB 69/8, DO (41) 18.
[82] Butler, *Grand Strategy*, Vol II, p 453; Colville, 'Fringes of Power', p.385.
[83] Churchill, *The Second World War*, Vol. III, p.217.
[84] CAC, Churchill Papers, CHAR 20/36/4.

Empire, it was about keeping control of a key junction between continents, blocking the Axis advance, and deterring others from joining the war on their side. Faced with 'growing pessimism in Turkey, the Near East and Spain', he urged the United States to declare herself a belligerent power, and warned the President, 'not to underrate the gravity of the consequences which may follow from a Middle Eastern collapse, in this war every post is a winning post and how many more are we going to lose?'[85]

But perhaps more important was the need to win the argument within his own camp. The Chiefs of Staff responded to his directive of 28 April by issuing their own minute. While they backed the decision to fight in the Middle East, they felt that Churchill was overstating the case by arguing that the life of Great Britain depended on the defence of Egypt, and held that the priority must remain the protection of Britain, pointing out that, for the Germans, 'a successful invasion is the only quick way of ending the war', and warning that Hitler might still seek 'a knock-out before American help destroys his last hope of success'.[86]

One of their number, Sir John Dill, the Chief of the Imperial General Staff, was prepared to go even further. Churchill's directive had been motivated in part by a debate about whether the Far East should be more substantially reinforced. Britain was not yet at war in the Pacific but Dill was an advocate for building up forces to defend against any possible attack against the main naval base at Singapore. Australia and New Zealand had supplied troops for the Middle East on the understanding that the British would watch their back, and that Japanese aggression in the Pacific would be deterred or countered. As Dill perhaps unwisely pointed out, Churchill himself while still First Lord of the Admiralty on 17 November 1939, had sought to reassure the Australian government that if it ever came to a choice between 'defending Australia against a serious attack, or sacrificing British interests in the Mediterranean, our duty to Australia would take precedence'.[87] Yet it had proved impossible to send substantial reinforcements east to the main British Pacific base while defending Britain and fighting in France and then the Middle East, and the Commander-in-Chief in the theatre had now been told to prepare Singapore for a siege of 180 days before a relief force might arrive.

The Prime Minister was not to be swayed from his main focus. In his directive, he was clear that 'Japan is unlikely to enter the war' and

[85] CAC, Churchill Papers, CHAR 20/38/61-65.
[86] Butler, *Grand Strategy*, Vol. II, Appendix IV, p.580.
[87] Butler, *Grand Strategy*, Vol. II, Appendix IV, pp.580-81.

that priority was to be given to the Middle East. If conditions changed, it would be the responsibility of the politicians to give the military enough time to prepare.[88] The Chiefs of Staff as a group accepted this, but pointed out that they would require at least three months to reinforce the Far East given the distances involved.[89] But Dill was prepared to push further, pointing out that Singapore had traditionally ranked above Egypt in British strategic priorities. This earned him a furious slap down from the Prime Minister, who accused him of being prepared to face the 'loss of Egypt and the Nile Valley, together with the surrender or ruin of the Army of half a million we have concentrated there, rather than lose Singapore'. He made it clear that he did not share this view, and that even if Japan did come into the war, the United States would in all probability join on the British side, while Japan would be unlikely to besiege Singapore.[90] The inference was that Dill was dealing with hypotheticals in the Far East, while Churchill was facing realities in the Middle East. Dill justified his position on the grounds that it was difficult 'for a soldier to advise against a bold offensive plan' but, his only concern was that 'we should not repeat our previous mistake of under-rating the enemy', while, 'Quite a small addition at Singapore will make all the difference between running a serious risk and achieving full security'.[91]

It was a debate that must have been influenced by the conclusions of the first substantial American, British, Canadian Staff talks, which had just taken place in Washington DC. The Americans had made it clear that their Pacific Fleet would remain at Pearl Harbor in Hawaii and would not reinforce Singapore. However, they had offered to move more ships into the defence of the Western Atlantic, thereby freeing the Royal Navy to send a force to the Far East.[92] This would have strengthened Churchill in his conviction that a combined American and British naval presence would be enough to deter Japanese aggression.

The will of the Prime Minister prevailed. The Mediterranean was prioritised. When Wavell failed to deliver a successful offensive he was removed to India and replaced as Commander in Chief, Middle East, by General Auchinleck. After Dill's objections, his days as Chief of the Imperial General Staff were also numbered. He was replaced

---

[88] CAC, Churchill Papers, CHAR 23/9/24. Also cited in Butler, *Grand Strategy*, Vol. II, Appendix IV, p.577.

[89] Butler, *Grand Strategy*, Vol. II, Appendix IV, p.580.

[90] CAC, Churchill Papers, CHAR 20/36/5.

[91] Butler, *Grand Strategy*, Vol. II, Appendix IV, pp.580-81.

[92] Reynolds, D., *The Creation of the Anglo-American Alliance 1937-41*, (The University of North Carolina Press, 1982), pp.184-185.

by General Alan Brooke on Christmas Day 1941; a firm supporter of the Mediterranean strategy.[93] Huge military resources had now been allocated. British prestige, and Churchill's political capital, had been invested. Yet at the same time, British resources were finite and the nation's financial reserves were dwindling.

Churchill's response to the Blitz was to seek to take the fight to the enemy. Having seized the opportunity provided by victory in the Battle of Britain, he strengthened his position by bringing in Anderson, Beaverbrook, Bevin, Eden, Portal and ultimately Brooke. This left him freer to lead on military policy. Responding to a public mood which accorded with his own instincts, he embraced the bombing of Germany. Yet he also recognised the limitations of such a bombing campaign. It would take time to build up, and an enemy-dominated Europe meant that it remained more hazardous for the RAF to bomb Germany than for the Luftwaffe to bomb Britain. Rather than sit back and strengthen British defences, he chose to reinforce the Mediterranean theatre. By doing so, he was responding to a real threat to British Imperial power and influence, where there were obligations to Egypt, Palestine and Malta, and promises to Greece. He did so because he was the leader of an Imperial power, and because to abandon the Empire was anathema to his world view, but also because to do so would have further diminished Britain in the eyes of the world and increased pressure on him for negotiation with the Axis powers. He was not alone in these beliefs, and enjoyed the backing of his colleagues. There were debates about priorities, over whether to strengthen Singapore or intervene in Greece, but there was no dissension from the general principle that Britain should defend her Empire. The problem was that they lacked the resources to defend it all. Churchill ignored the advice of his senior military adviser and chose not to split resources and reinforce Singapore. He assigned absolute responsibility to the Mediterranean, seeing it as the next battleground with the Axis powers.

Churchill led from the front in his willingness to take real risks to implement an aggressive policy. He was prepared to denude Britain of armour, and to transport that armour by the quicker but more hazardous Mediterranean route. Yet even these were calculated risks, and ultimately only undertaken with the support of the Chiefs of Staff. Where he differed from those around him was in the intensity of his desire to engage the enemy, obvious in his prodding of Dill and Wavell, and in his clear decision to prioritise the immediate risk to Egypt above

---

[93] Danchev, A. & Todman D. (eds), *War Diaries 1939-1945. Field Marshal Lord Alanbrooke*, (Weidenfeld & Nicolson), p.206.

the hypothetical danger to Singapore. For him it was never just about defence. A policy of ultimate victory depended on being able to take the fight to the enemy on the ground. In 1940-41, the Mediterranean was the only theatre where this was possible.

The implications of Churchill's decisions were profound. His commitment to the offensive meant fewer resources for the defensive. How would Britain continue to defend the Atlantic? How would she fund armies in Britain and the Middle East? Japan had signed the tripartite pact in Berlin with Germany and Italy at the end of September 1940. What would happen if she attacked British possessions in the Far East? To Churchill, the answers lay in the west and with the support that he expected from the United States, but war is never predictable, and his attention was suddenly torn, drawn to the east by the German attack on the Soviet Union. His next decision would be how to respond to this widening war. How far should he go, politically, physically, ideologically and in terms of material aid, to secure the allies he so desperately needed?

Chapter 4

The Devil or The Deep Blue Sea?

How did Churchill approach the Soviet Union and the United States?

It is Sunday 22 June 1941, and Chequers, the country residence of the British Prime Minister, is buzzing with activity. At short notice, Churchill is preparing a speech for an evening broadcast to the nation on the BBC. One of his personal secretaries, Elizabeth Layton, who started work for the Prime Minister in May 1941, has left us a wonderful description of Churchill in full flow, which perhaps allows us to visualise the scene:

> On these occasions he would walk up and down the room, his forehead crinkled in thought, the cords of his dressing-gown trailing behind him (he often wore his favourite red, green and gold dressing-gown when dictating). Sometimes he would fling himself for a moment into a chair: sometimes he would pause to light his cigar, which with so much concentration was neglected and frequently went out. For minutes he might walk up and down trying out sentences to himself. Sometimes his voice would become thick with emotion, and occasionally a tear would run down his cheek.[1]

His preparation is interspersed with hastily convened discussions and telephone calls with his colleagues; among them Anthony Eden, the Foreign Secretary and the American Ambassador Gil Winant, both of whom are staying at Chequers, as well as with Lord Beaverbrook and Moore-Brabazon. The special guest for lunch is Sir Stafford Cripps, the British Ambassador to the Soviet Union, recently returned from

---

[1]   Nel, E., *Mr Churchill's Secretary*, (Hodder & Stoughton, 1958), p.36.

Moscow.[2] The reason for all of this activity is the breaking news that Germany has just invaded the Soviet Union.

Churchill had been getting intelligence since March about the concentration of huge German forces on the Reich's eastern borders with Soviet territory. He would later write that the raw intelligence brought to him in his special boxes by Major Morton with its accounts of the movement of German armour from the Balkans 'illuminated the whole Eastern scene like a lightning-flash'.[3] Thereafter, the build-up was followed very closely by the British Joint Intelligence staff, the Chiefs of Staff and the War Cabinet, with much speculation as to what it might mean. Was this the precursor to a full-blown attack, or was Hitler simply trying to apply pressure in order to obtain economic, political and perhaps even territorial concessions from Russia? Foreign Secretary Eden's meetings in early June with the Russian Ambassador, Ivan Maisky, turned on the question of whether this meant war or just 'a war of nerves'.[4] Stafford Cripps gave a confidential briefing to the War Cabinet on the view from Moscow. He felt that the 'general belief in informed circles...was that Hitler would pitch his demands so high that it would be impossible for the Soviet government to accept them', and that the German dictator was banking on the fact that Russia's military position would be stronger in a year's time, that the anti-communism in 'certain quarters' in the United States would earn him 'considerable sympathy' in America, while a quick Russian campaign now 'might be over in time to stage an invasion of the UK'. Cripps was not optimistic about the Russian ability to resist, and thought the three most likely scenarios were that the Russians might surrender and become vassals of Germany, would fight a short campaign and be defeated, or would seek to buy a peace.[5]

Churchill had to decide how to respond to this information. Here was a man who was a die-hard anti-communist, and who had opposed bolshevism from its inception in the Russian revolution of 1917, famously likening the German decision to allow Lenin to return to Russia in a sealed train to the importation of a plague bacillus. At the time of the Spanish Civil War he had said that if he was forced to choose between fascism and communism, it was not to be supposed that he would choose the latter, even if he did express the hope that he would not 'be called upon to survive in the world under a Government of either

---

2   Colville, *Fringes of Power*, pp.404-405; Gilbert, *Winston S Churchill*, Vol. VI, pp.1119-1120.
3   Churchill, *Second World War*, Vol. III, p.319.
4   TNA, CAB 65/18, DM (41) 56; Gorodetsky, G. (ed), *The Maisky Diaries. Red Ambassador to the Court of St James's 1932-1943*, (Yale University Press, 2015), pp.360-361.
5   TNA, CAB 65/22, WM (41) 60.

of these dispensations'.[6] Moreover, since the signing of the Molotov-Ribbentrop Pact in 1939, the Soviet Union had followed a policy of non-aggression towards Nazi Germany, and had, in Churchill's later words, 'shown a total indifference to the fate of the Western Powers'.[7]

He could simply have allowed events to take their course, knowing that any German operation against Russia would be likely to delay further action against the United Kingdom and would, at the very least, lead to the short-term destruction of some German troops and aircraft without loss to British and Imperial forces. Instead, he saw an opportunity to reach out to Stalin. The longer the Russians could be kept fighting, the greater the pressure on Germany, and the greater the likelihood she might be worn down by having to fight on so many fronts. Psychologically, Britain and the Empire would no longer be waging war alone.

It was a view that was in total accord with his policy of waging war until final victory. He told Roosevelt on 15 June that, 'Should this new war break out we shall of course give all encouragement and any help we can spare to the Russians, following the principle that Hitler is the foe we have to beat'.[8] He put it more memorably, on the eve of the German invasion of Russia, while walking with Colville on the Chequers croquet lawn. His private secretary had teased him that in offering support to the Soviets he might be betraying his principles, to which Churchill replied:

> I have only one purpose, the destruction of Hitler, and my life is much simplified thereby. If Hitler invaded Hell I would make at least a favourable reference to the Devil in the House of Commons.[9]

Writing after the war, Churchill made much of his attempt to send a short and cryptic early warning to Stalin in early April 1941. He blamed Stafford Cripps for not delivering this message promptly to the Russian leader and speculated that, had he done so, it might have prevented the Soviet air force being caught unawares and largely destroyed on the ground.[10] Though as Eden pointed out in October

---

[6] Churchill, W., *The Aftermath*, (Thornton Butterworth, 1929), p.76; Speech in the House of Commons, 14 April 1937. Reprinted in Churchill, W., 'Arms and the Covenant', (Harrap, 1938), p.409.

[7] Churchill, *The Second World War*, Vol. III, p.315.

[8] CAC, Churchill Papers, CHAR 20/39/127; Churchill, *The Second World War*, Vol III, p.330.

[9] Churchill, *The Second World War*, Vol. III, p.331.

[10] Churchill, *The Second World War*, Vol. III, p.323; for full texts of all telegrams see CAC, Churchill Papers, CHAR 23/9/19.

1941, 'at this time the Russians were most reluctant to receive messages of any kind; and, even if Stalin did receive your message, he now probably prefers to forget the fact'.[11] The incident is revealing both of the difficult relationship between Churchill and Cripps, of which more in the next chapter, and of the lack of communication between Churchill and Stalin. By his own admission, this was only the second communication that Churchill had sent to the Soviet dictator since the summer of 1940, and the only attempt at direct contact in the crisis leading up to the German invasion. The contrast with his courting of the Americans and President Roosevelt could not be greater.

The reality was that, even in the first weeks of June 1941, Anglo-Russian relations remained strained and characterised by mutual suspicion. The British feared that the Russians were seeking to undermine them in the Middle East and objected to the recognition that the Soviet government had given to the short-lived regime of the pro-German Rashid Ali in Iraq (which British forces had just overthrown). Meanwhile, Ambassador Maisky felt that Churchill was stirring up reports of Russo-German tensions in the British press.[12] For his part, even after the invasion, Churchill could not resist goading Cripps over lunch at Chequers by declaring that 'not even the slenderest thread connected Communists to the very basest type of humanity'.[13]

Nevertheless, in public, Churchill stuck to his line. At 21.00 hours that evening, he made his broadcast. According to Colville, he was wrestling with the text almost right up to delivery. His heavily annotated notes survive among his papers, and show him formulating his response. He chose to emphasise the 'perfidy' and the brutality of the Nazi regime, describing Hitler as a 'monster of wickedness, insatiable in his lust for blood and plunder'. He contrasted this with the Russian people 'defending their native soil', and guarding their fields and homes. His focus was on the people not the communist regime. Indeed, he described nazism as 'indistinguishable from the worst features of communism', and admitted that, 'No one has been a more consistent opponent of Communism than I have for the last twenty-five years. I will unsay no word that I have spoken about it. But all this fades away before the spectacle which now is unfolding'. He promised to give whatever help Britain could to Russia and the Russian people, and he pledged to bomb Germany in ever increasing measure.[14]

---

[11] CAC, Churchill Papers, CHAR 23/9/19.
[12] TNA, CAB 65/18, WM (41)56; Gorodestky (ed), *Maisky Diaries*, pp.359-360.
[13] Colville, *Fringes of Power*, p.404.
[14] CAC, Churchill Papers, CHAR 9/151.

Maisky thought it, 'A forceful speech! A fine performance' and just what was needed.[15] Churchill's cousin Clare Sheridan, known for her links to Soviet Russia in the 1920s, wrote to Winston congratulating him on cleverly negotiating a delicate situation, 'I was so afraid you wouldn't stand by Russia'.[16] Her remark that she looked forward to hearing the communist 'Internationale' among the national anthems of the Allies played on the radio on a Sunday evening, was perhaps more controversial and insightful than she intended. The Internationale was not played the following week, with Duff Cooper reporting to Maisky that this was on the express orders of Churchill, who did not want the British communists making political capital from it.[17] At the War Cabinet of 23 June, Churchill was equally clear that the Labour members of his government 'should continue to draw a line of demarcation' in any speeches they might make 'between the tenets of the Labour Party and those of Communism'.[18] The message was that Britain was supporting Russia not the Soviet communist regime.

In fact, there was little that Britain could offer in immediate support, or do to alleviate the immediate German *blitzkrieg*. Churchill reported to Stalin on his intensification of the bombing of German cities, and he did send 200 Tomahawk fighter planes, 3 million pairs of ankle boots and 10,000 tons of rubber, but this was not what Stalin really wanted.[19]

On 20 July, Maisky motored to Chequers to hand-deliver Stalin's first message to Churchill. The Prime Minister received him wearing his 'strange grey-blue overalls', which must have contrasted with the very aristocratic setting. Churchill was evidently pleased at having finally received a personal message from the Russian leader, but less so with the contents.[20] Stalin's demand for the immediate establishment of a Second Front 'against Hitler in the West (Northern France) and in the North (Arctic)' was a refrain that would recur almost until continuously until 1944.[21]

In the event, the initial agreement concluded between Britain and Russia on 12 July 1941 and signed by Stafford Cripps for the United Kingdom in Moscow, was a very simple one. The two countries agreed

---

[15] Gorodetsky (ed), *Maisky Diaries*, p.366.
[16] CAC, Churchill Papers, CHAR 9/182A/142.
[17] Gorodetsky (ed), *Maisky Diaries*, pp.371-372.
[18] TNA, CAB 65/18, WM (41) 62.
[19] CAC, Churchill Papers, CHAR 20/132.
[20] Gorodetsky (ed), *The Maisky Diaries*, pp.373-374.
[21] CAC, Churchill Papers, CHAR 20/132.

to provide each other with mutual help, without specifying quantity, quality or detail, and confirmed that neither country would conclude a separate peace. It emphasised that this was a purely practical, military arrangement. There was no pretence at great friendship, no declaration of common war aims. A fuller political treaty was promised but there was no immediate rush to conclude it. As we shall see, the negotiations would not prove to be easy.

Churchill had not sought an alliance with Russia, but he had seen and responded to an opportunity; and he had led from the front. In his broadcast of 22 June, he seized the moment and declared that it was his government's policy to back Russia. He did so without formal approval from his Cabinet colleagues (though the key individuals had been consulted), without the agreement of the Allied Dominion Prime Ministers, and knowing that he would be moving further and faster than wanted by some sections of the British public, mostly in his own Conservative Party. Though to some on the left, he had not gone far enough. He had not yet met Stalin, he had not travelled to Russia, but he had travelled a long way politically. He now had an ally, although ironically it was not the one that he had been seeking. For that, he still had a long way to go.

Let me set another scene. We are in a remote bay, surrounded by green rocky hills. There is a 'soft breeze, sun behind thin clouds, and a beautiful shimmering grey look on the water'.[22] But today the seabirds do not have it to themselves. For here are moored four great, grey, armoured ships of war, screened and protected by a host of smaller destroyers. There are three large ships flying the Stars and Stripes of the United States: the veteran battleship *USS Arkansas* and the two 10,000-ton cruisers, the *USS Tuscaloosa* and the *USS Augusta*. Yet even these giants are dwarfed by the presence of *HMS Prince of Wales,* one of the newest and largest British battleships. Floating at anchor like a 'mighty hill of steel', she displaces almost 44,000 tons, is just short of seven hundred and fifty feet in length, and boasts three turrets of powerful 14-inch guns.[23]

Let us go in closer and stand on her quarter deck beneath the four guns of the after turret. We find ourselves surrounded by hundreds of men in uniform: officers, ordinary sailors and marines; some British and some American, and all somewhat mixed up together. They are gathered in a big arc, in places standing more than ten deep. Their voices

---

[22] CAC, Jacob Papers, JACB 1/9.
[23] Morton, H., *Atlantic Meeting,* (Methuen & Co Ltd, 1943), p.37.

are joined in song. It is a Sunday, and this is a divine service. A special desk with the British and American flags draped on it has been set up for the use of the chaplains. The assembled company sings *O God, Our Help In Ages Past, Onward Christian Soldiers* and *Eternal Father Strong to Save*. These hymns have not been selected at random. They are the personal choice of the British Prime Minister. For here at the heart of this gathering, smiling benignly, sits Winston Churchill. He is bedecked in the uniform of the Royal Yacht Squadron. At his right hand in a blue lounge suit sits the American Commander-in-Chief, President Franklin Delano Roosevelt, while behind the two leaders are standing many of the British and American Chiefs of Staff.[24] To Churchill, it is 'a great hour to live'.[25] It is also one that he has very carefully choreographed.

The date is Sunday, 10 August 1941. The location is Little Placentia Bay at Argentia off the coast of Newfoundland. It is a hugely symbolic occasion. The United States is not yet a belligerent in the struggle against Germany, but here in Atlantic waters is the first wartime meeting of Roosevelt and Churchill, surrounded by all the panoply of war. To cross the Atlantic Ocean at a time when it is being bitterly contested, with the German U-boats attempting to assert their stranglehold over Britain, is a brave and defiant gesture by the British Prime Minister. The collusion of the American President sends a clear warning to Hitler of increasing American concerns and involvement in this theatre.

But beyond the stirring imagery, what did this meeting achieve? The most famous result of the encounter will be a joint declaration of eight points drawn up and refined by Churchill and Roosevelt over the course of the four days of their meeting. To paraphrase the provisions as they will appear in the final text:

Britain and the United States will confirm that they are not interested in territorial aggrandisement and pledge themselves to:

- oppose territorial changes that do not accord with the free wishes of the peoples concerned;
- to respect the right of all peoples to choose their own form of government and wish to see self-government restored to those from whom it has been deprived;
- to endeavour, with respect to their existing obligations, to encourage trade and access to raw materials for all on equal terms;

---

[24] For images of this occasion see CAC, Broadwater Collection, BRDW I Photo 4; For a detailed account of the service see Morton, *Atlantic Meeting*, pp.99-103 & CAC, Jacob Papers, JACB 1/9, pp.35-39.

[25] Churchill, *The Second World War*, Vol. III, p.384.

- to secure improved labour standards, economic advancement and social security;
- to establish peace, after the 'final destruction of the Nazi tyranny' with freedom from fear and want;
- to facilitate freedom of the high seas;
- and to further the abandonment of force, by disarming aggressor nations, 'pending the establishment of a wider and more permanent system of general security'.[26]

These will not be presented as war aims, because America is not at war. They will be painted as the 'common principles in national policies' on which are based 'hopes for a better future for the world'. The document is a declaration rather than a treaty. It is not signed by Churchill and Roosevelt. It is not intended to be ratified by parliament or congress. It is written as a public statement to be broadcast to the world, as it will be at 15.00 hours British standard time on Thursday, 14 August 1941. The *Daily Herald* newspaper will call it 'The Atlantic Charter', Churchill will refer to it by this title in his broadcast of 24 August, and the name will stick.

But Churchill was a leader who admitted, when presenting the Charter in the House of Commons, that he had hitherto deprecated the formulation of war or peace aims when the end of the war was not in sight.[27] He had not gone to Newfoundland with such a statement in draft or in mind. His priority at the Atlantic Meeting had been to bring Roosevelt and the Americans closer to a declaration of war against Germany; his secondary and related objective to secure as much practical support and material aid from them as possible. How then had this led to the Joint Declaration and to what extent did it serve his aims? Was he playing a long-term game, or was this this all about short-term gain?

From the beginning of his premiership, Churchill was optimistic about the ultimate involvement of the United States in the war. He was half American by birth, the son of the Brooklyn-born Jennie Jerome. Moreover, he had toured the States several times, was widely published there, and had built up a good personal network of influential American friends and contacts. He had seen America come to the aid of Europe in 1917, and, when war broke out again, was busy working on his *History*

---

[26] For final text of Charter see CAC, Churchill Papers, CHAR 20/48/13-14.
[27] Robert Rhodes James (ed), *Winston Churchill: His Complete Speeches*, (Chelsea House, 1974), Vol. VI, p.6481.

of the English-Speaking Peoples, which emphasised the shared trans-Atlantic bonds of history, culture and language. He did not believe it was in America's interest to allow Germany to dominate Europe, and he must have been encouraged in that belief when President Roosevelt reached out and opened a private channel of communication to him in September 1939, when he was still First Lord of the Admiralty.[28] To be set against this were the President's known dislike of the British Empire and the opposition of American public opinion to involvement in a European war.

Yet it was only with the fall of France, and the sudden loss of the ability to contain and grind down Germany in Europe, that the question of relations with America had become paramount. Churchill's government's policy of waging war until final victory was now dependent on American supplies, credit and ultimate intervention. Without America, Britain might be able to hold off invasion, but she faced bankruptcy, severe shortages of essential military supplies, and strangulation in the Atlantic. She could not contemplate taking the offensive in North-West Europe. The basic position had been set out in stark terms in a paper prepared for the Chiefs of Staff as early as 25 May 1940, drawn up in response to the possible collapse of France, which posited that Britain would only be able to fight on if the 'United States of America is willing to give us full economic and financial support, *without which we do not think we could continue the war with any chance of success'.*[29] The italics are in the original document.

It must then have been particularly frustrating for Churchill when his initial appeals to President Roosevelt seemed to fall on deaf ears. In his public speeches during this period he remained resolute, but his words were aimed as much at the American audience as the British. At the height of the Battle of Britain, he likened improving Anglo-American relations to the mighty Mississippi, rolling on 'full flood, inexorable, irresistible, benignant, to broader lands and better days'. In response to the Blitz bombing of London, he called on the Old World and the New to 'join hands to rebuild the temples of man's freedom and man's honour, upon foundations which will not soon or easily be overthrown'.[30] This was a concerted charm offensive, conducted publicly in speeches, and privately by letter, telegram and private

---

[28] For history of Churchill's relationship with United States, see Gilbert, M., *Churchill and America*, (The Free Press, 2005); for Churchill's writings and speeches on America see Churchill, W.S. (ed), *The Great Republic*, (Cassell & Co, 2002).

[29] TNA, CAB 80/11.

[30] CAC, Churchill Papers, CHAR 9/141A/68; CHAR 9/144/66.

emissary. As he told Colville, 'No lover ever studied every whim of his mistress as I did those of President Roosevelt'.[31]

But it all seemed so frustratingly slow. In August 1940, Roosevelt had exchanged fifty old destroyers, some planes and torpedo-boats for ninety-nine year leases on a number of British bases throughout the Western hemisphere. This would help the British navy by allowing them to use the American ships to protect convoys in the Atlantic while concentrating their newer vessels against invasion. Yet it would take time to implement, with much wrangling over the extent of the rights being claimed by the Americans in places like Bermuda. Moreover, it was so clearly weighted in America's interest that Roosevelt did not even need to take it to congress. When the President tried to impose conditions about the fate of the Royal Navy in the event of a British armistice, wanting the fleet destroyed or sailed to North America, Churchill promised that the fleet would not be surrendered on his watch, but would and could go no further.[32] By December, the Prime Minister was warning the President that Britain was approaching the crunch point when she would no longer be able to afford to pay cash for much-needed American supplies. He expressed the fear that Britain would be 'divested of all saleable assets' and 'after victory was won with our blood', and 'civilisation saved and time gained for the United States to be armed against all eventualities, we should stand stripped to the bone'. When Roosevelt suggested that American warships remove British gold on deposit in South Africa, Churchill had wanted to reply that this was the action of a 'Sheriff collecting the last assets of a hapless debtor', but for fear of alienating the President he swallowed his words and signalled his assent.[33]

True, things had seemed to improve in the first six months of 1941. Following his 29 December Fireside Chat in which he had urged that the United States must become the great arsenal of democracy, Roosevelt had sent his trusted aide Harry Hopkins to see Churchill in January, and had followed up with a handwritten letter of personal support. In it, he quoted from the Longfellow verse 'The Sailing of the Ship' ending, 'Humanity with all its fears, with all the hope of future years, is hanging breathless on thy fate'.[34] The choice of text was clearly designed to appeal to Churchill's romantic nature, and Winston duly had it framed and hung on his study wall at Chartwell. But it was also a message of support that was intended for public release, and which Churchill broadcast back across

[31] Colville, *The Fringes of Power*, p.624.
[32] Kimball, W., *Churchill and Roosevelt. The Complete Correspondence*, Vol. I, (Princeton, 1984), pp.567-60.
[33] Kimball, *Churchill and Roosevelt*, pp 104-109; CAC, Churchill Papers, CHAR 23/4/11.
[34] CAC, Churchill Additional Papers, WCHL 13/1.

the Atlantic on 9 February, asking, 'What is the answer that I shall give, in your name, to this great man… Here is the answer which I will give to President Roosevelt… Give us the tools, and we will finish the job'.[35] This was diplomacy by rhetoric on the part of both leaders, aimed at bolstering British morale and moving American public opinion. Provision for the tools duly came in the form of the Lend Lease Act, which was signed into law on 11 March, and which authorised the President to transfer arms and other defence materials for which congress had appropriated money to any country whose defence the President deemed vital to the interests of the United States, thereby deftly bypassing both the American neutrality laws and Britain's inability to pay.

America was becoming the 'Arsenal of Democracy' and Britain had gained a valuable lifeline. Then in April, Roosevelt signalled his intention to respond to the increased British shipping losses in the Atlantic by extending the American security and patrol zone to all waters west of longitude 25 degrees, effectively assuming responsibility for protecting convoys as far as Iceland and the Azores. This not only relieved the pressure on the British navy, it also greatly increased the likelihood of conflict between American naval vessels and German U-boats, and therefore the possibility that an incident might bring the United States into the war. The move was naturally welcomed by Churchill who told the President that he had 'no doubts that 25th Meridian is a long step towards salvation'.[36] A long step towards maybe, but even within their security zone, the Americans were still not yet escorting convoys, only patrolling and warning of the location of Axis forces.[37]

Churchill had now been conducting his long-distance courtship for a year. At the beginning of 1941, he had faced awkward questions in the House of Commons about his management of the war effort, and in the first six months of the year his military strategy had brought him little in the way of respite or comfort. The German bombing of British cities had continued, and General Wavell's initial success in defeating the Italians in North Africa had given way to defeat by the Germans in Greece, the fall of Crete with heavy associated naval losses, and to Rommel's rolling back of gains in North Africa. The President and the Prime Minister were still to meet in wartime (they had met once before at the end of the First World War, at an occasion

---

[35] CAC, Churchill Papers, CHAR 9/150A.
[36] Kimball, *Churchill and Roosevelt*, p.166 & p.169.
[37] Reynolds, *The Creation of the Anglo-American Alliance*, p.198.

which Churchill subsequently failed to remember[38]), and the United States still seemed a long way from a declaration of war.

When it finally came, the Atlantic Meeting was actually suggested by President Roosevelt. He did so in response to several complicating factors on the international scene. The American planners were concerned at British defeats in the Balkans and North Africa, and felt that the Eastern Mediterranean was proving an increasing distraction from the Atlantic theatre, where they believed the war could be won, and which they considered more vital to their interests. The German invasion of Russia in June, may have eased the invasion threat to the United Kingdom, but it had raised the whole question of widening the Lend-Lease scheme to include munitions shipments to the Soviet Union, some of which would have to be at the expense of supplies to the British. Tensions were rising in the Pacific in the aftermath of the Japanese occupation of French Indo China, and there were worrying rumours circulating in Washington that the British government was trying to influence any future settlement by making territorial offers to some of the occupied nations, such as promising Trieste to Yugoslavia.

But for Churchill, this was the invitation that he had been waiting for, and which he now jumped at, presuming that the Presidential summons meant that an American declaration of war was now near at hand. He believed that history was made by great men at such moments, and he was supremely confident in his own abilities as a face to face negotiator. He travelled with a small but high-powered delegation, bringing with him the heads of the army and navy and the Vice-Chief of the Air Staff. Lindemann was there to provide scientific expertise; Cadogan to help advise on international affairs; Jacob and Hollis from the War Cabinet secretariat to guarantee administrative efficiency. Harry Hopkins, just back from visiting Stalin, secured a place for his return voyage across the Atlantic. Captain Pim and his portable map room came too, allowing Churchill to keep pace with unfolding developments in all the theatres of war. What the British party lacked was any other heavyweight British political figure (though Lord Beaverbrook was flown in late to discuss the implications of aid to Russia). Churchill clearly wanted quality time alone with the President.

It is noteworthy that the party contained two well-known authors as representatives of the Ministry of Information; the celebrated travel writer H.V. Morton, and the best-selling novelist Howard Spring. They had been hand-picked by Brendan Bracken, newly installed as Minister of Information, and were there to ensure good coverage and maximum

---

[38] Gilbert, *Churchill and America*, p.77.

publicity.[39] Such was the secrecy surrounding the trip that Spring did not even have time to retrieve his dentures from his dentist, and had to travel without teeth. Colonel Jacob's diary also records the presence of official photographers and newsreel men from the War Office and the Admiralty.[40]

Much has been made of the Prime Minister's activities while travelling to Newfoundland. On the train up to Thurso he asked Lindemann to calculate how much champagne he had drunk in his lifetime, only to express his disappointment when it failed to fill half the dining car. At sea, he threw himself into the maritime spirit, reading the historical novel *Captain Hornblower,* and shedding tears as he watched for the fifth time, *That Hamilton Woman* with Laurence Olivier playing Nelson. He surprised the crew by singing along to *Mad Dogs and Englishmen* and the popular tune, *Franklin D. Roosevelt Jones.*[41]

Churchill clearly relished being let out of school for an adventure, but this was no holiday. There was a very real risk that the ship might be caught by U-boats, especially once the American media had guessed and broadcast that a conference with the President was in the offing. The latest sightings appeared as ominous looking black 'coffin' shaped pins on Captain Pim's maps. No British Prime Minister had ever travelled so far from home in wartime. It shows how much he was staking on the meeting.[42]

Unlike later wartime conferences (and unlike the meetings of their respective Chiefs of Staff), the conversations of the Prime Minister and President were not minuted. Jacob complained to his diary on the penultimate day that, 'No-one has any idea of what the Prime Minister has been saying to the President'.[43] These were informal conversations, including six meals together, five of them in Roosevelt's quarters on board the *Augusta.*[44] This makes it impossible to be certain about who said what when. According to Churchill's later account, it was Roosevelt who suggested the idea of a joint declaration at their first meeting on the 9 August, and Churchill who then produced a first draft for consideration on the following day. He proudly pointed out that, 'Considering the tales of my reactionary, Old World outlook, and the pain this is said to have caused the President, I am glad it should be on record that the substance and spirit of what came to be called the

---

[39] H.V. Morton, *Atlantic Charter to Meeting,* pp.19-22.
[40] CAC, Jacob Papers, JACB 1/9.
[41] Pawle, *The War & Colonel Warden,* p.127.
[42] Morton, *Atlantic Meeting,* pp.15-16 & p.67.
[43] CAC, Jacob Papers, JACB 1/9.
[44] TNA, CAB, 65/19, WM (41) 84.

"Atlantic Charter" was in its first draft a British production cast in my own words'.[45]

Except that was not quite true. The text was produced to Churchill's specification and approved and annotated by him, but the actual drafting was done over breakfast by Cadogan.[46]

It was a British production, but one with words which were well chosen to appeal to Roosevelt. The President added two paragraphs to Churchill's first draft; one regarding freedom of the seas, and the other concerning the abandonment of the use of force and the disarmament of aggressor nations. It was not all plain sailing. Churchill successfully resisted American attempts to add the phrase 'without discrimination' to the clause on global trade. He recognised this as an attempt to undermine the system of Imperial Preference, by which the British gave favoured trading terms to Empire and Commonwealth nations, and ultimately protected this position with the insertion of 'with respect to their existing obligations'. Meanwhile Roosevelt, no doubt remembering the failure of American engagement with the League of Nations after the First World War, only grudgingly accepted Churchill's addition to his final clause introducing the concept of a permanent post-war system of general security, the form of which he deliberately kept vague.[47]

To historian Warren Kimball, while the Charter might have been drafted by the British, it was created to Roosevelt's specification and was 'a classic statement of American liberalism'.[48] There were certainly potential hostages to fortune for the British Empire in clauses supporting self-determination. This may explain why, upon telegraphing the draft text of the declaration to Clement Attlee, now Lord Privy Seal, and Deputy Prime Minister in all but name, Churchill gave his firm view that, 'It would be most imprudent, on our part, to raise unnecessary difficulties. We must regard this as an interim and partial statement of war aims…'. He asked Attlee to summon the War Cabinet to meet that night and to give him their views 'without the slightest delay' as he feared that the President would be 'very much upset if no joint statement can be issued, and grave and vital interests might be affected'.[49]

---

45 Churchill, *The Second World War*, Vol. III, p.386.
46 Reynolds, *In Command of History*, pp 260-261; Dilks (ed), *Cadogan Diaries*, p.398.
47 See Churchill, *The Second World War*, Vol III, pp 385-388; Kimball, W., *Forged in War*, (Harper Collins, 1997), pp.9-102.
48 Kimball, *Forged in War*, p.99.
49 CAC, Churchill Papers, CHAR 20/48/5-6.

The War Cabinet obediently met at the ungodly hour of 01.45 in the morning in the Cabinet War Room with Attlee in the chair, and with the addition of Peter Fraser, the Prime Minister of New Zealand, who was visiting London. The fact that they did so surely testifies to the importance attached to the Atlantic Meeting by all in the British government. While 'the Declaration in certain respects fell short of what the War Cabinet would themselves like to have seen issued' they remained certain that 'the right course was to accept it in its present form' subject to minor modification. They suggested a change to the wording of one clause. Upon meeting again in Downing Street at 10.00 hours the following morning they decided to suggest a further clause on social security, which was to become clause five of the final agreement: a decision that may have been influenced by the fact that Fraser was a Labour Prime Minister and the three prominent Labour members, Attlee, Bevin and Greenwood, were all present.[50]

Churchill's actions and the tone of his telegrams to Attlee suggest that his clear priority lay in producing something tangible that the President could sanction before the end of the meeting.[51] Jacob describes Churchill's nervousness on receiving the telegraphed response from Attlee confirming the War Cabinet's ratification: 'On hearing that the telegram was the reply from London, he said to Jo [Hollis], "Am I going to like it?", rather like a small boy about to take medicine"'.[52]

The public results of the Atlantic Meeting were specific and limited. Arrangements for American escort of convoys west of the 25th meridian were approved, but their implementation remained pending on a Presidential order, promised but not yet issued. Roosevelt did agree to a joint mission to Russia to discuss the extension of Lend-Lease to the Soviet Union, though in the short term this would reduce what was available to Britain. In the Pacific, the American President confirmed he would take a harder line with Japan over her incursions in Indo-China, but would not go so far as to issue a joint ultimatum. Elsewhere, Roosevelt indicated that the United States would protect the Azores if the Germans moved against Portugal, and confirmed that the Americans would not interfere with British operations in the Canary Islands or Persia.[53]

---

[50] TNA, CAB 65/19, WM (41) 80 & WM (41) 81.
[51] CAC, Churchill Papers, CHAR 20/48/15-16.
[52] CAC, Jacob Papers, JACB 1/9.
[53] Reynolds, *The Creation of the Anglo-American alliance*, pp.213-216.

The meeting was clearly useful in establishing personal relations at the highest level, and gave each delegation an insight into the thinking and strategic approach of the other. The British came away with a clearer picture of the competing demands on American production and the need for their requests to be better co-ordinated and prioritised. They also became aware of differences in approach between the United States army and navy. The Americans shared the text of the mandate for their new Joint Board, created to guide the President on priorities for the distribution of military equipment to its own or friendly military forces. The British would have been pleased to note that it confirmed the Eastern Atlantic, the European and the Mediterranean areas as 'the decisive theatre'. The British Chiefs of Staff then used the opportunity to present their own paper on future strategy. This confirmed the British policy of blockade, bombing and encouraging subversion, but the Americans queried the priorities given to its two main offensive planks of action in the Middle East and ever-increasing bombardment of Germany. General Marshall questioned to what extent the British should develop operations in the Mediterranean, given potential demands in the Far East and on the new Russian front, saying, 'It was a question of weighing up where the amount of equipment available could produce the best results, while General Arnold broke the news that the American supply of heavy bombers would be a smaller allocation than the British had been led to expect.[54] Jacob found their commanders 'altogether too defensive-minded and doctrinaire', while lower down, 'Not a single American officer has shown the slightest keenness to be in the war on our side'.[55]

The British Chiefs of Staff wrote up their verdict on the meeting while homeward bound aboard the *Prince of Wales*:

> To sum up, we neither expected nor achieved startling results. The American chiefs of Staff are quite clearly thinking in terms of the defence of the Western Hemisphere and have so far not formulated any joint strategy for the defeat of Germany in the event of their entry into the war…. We have, we think, convinced the Americans that our policy in the Middle East is sound. They, in turn, have made us understand their difficulties. A most distressing revelation is the reduction in heavy bomber allocation to us. This we consider a serious matter.[56]

---

[54] TNA, CAB 99/18.
[55] CAC, Jacob Papers, JACB 1/9.
[56] TNA, CAB 99/18.

Though useful and by no means a failure, this was not, as hoped, the triumphal arrival of the United States on the battlefield. Churchill remained intent on getting every little bit of political advantage out of the meeting. The film and still pictures of the joint divine service were certainly powerful, and one of Jacob's colleagues described them as, 'just the sort of thing which the press photographer would dream of after a good dose of hashish'.[57] So too were the reported images of Churchill inspecting British and American troops in Iceland, during a stop-off on his way home; Roosevelt having agreed just weeks before to allow a US garrison as part of American defence of the Atlantic.

Yet the most tangible result of the conference was the Atlantic Charter, which is why the Prime Minister needed to make it seem so significant. You can see him stage-managing the release of the information, even advising Attlee on how the Joint Declaration should be released to the press and introduced when broadcast.[58] If he could not have a formal alliance, then at least he could have a publicity coup and use the Charter and the meeting to make the case that it was imminent. Yet even here fate and the Americans seemed to conspire against him. Roosevelt brought no pressmen with him, which meant that 'in the interests of harmony' Morton and Spring were confined to the *Prince of Wales* and forbidden from immediate reporting.[59] Spring was now figuratively, as well as physically, toothless. Then the British films were delayed in Newfoundland due to bad weather and were consequently unavailable to support the release of the Charter text at 15.00 hours on 14 August. This could not be postponed as it had to coincide with the American morning news, or risk the Germans getting the story first, causing Churchill to cable Bracken that, 'Responsibility must be divided between rotation of earth and climate of Newfoundland'.[60]

Churchill was still at sea on 14 August when the text of the Charter was released, so it was read out by Attlee. The crew of the *Prince of Wales*, eager to find out what they had been facilitating, tuned in and were immediately disappointed. Mass Observation found much of the British population similarly 'underwhelmed'.[61] By his very act of traversing the Atlantic, Churchill had raised and now dashed expectations that the United States was about to enter the war.

---

[57] CAC, Jacob Papers, JACB 1/9.
[58] CAC, Churchill Papers, CHAR 20/48/18.
[59] Morton, *Atlantic Charter*, p.77.
[60] CAC, Churchill Papers, CHAR 20/48/21 & 22.
[61] Morton, *Atlantic Charter*, p127; Mass Observation cited in Toye, R., *The Roar of the Lion*, (Oxford University Press, 2013), p.113.

On his return, it fell to Churchill to defend the Charter. He presented it as a vital step in establishing a common rapport and policy with the President. In a point which he was to repeat in his later public broadcast, he told the War Cabinet that it was significant that Roosevelt should have agreed to a declaration which 'in his (the President's) phrase referred to *the final destruction of Nazi tyranny*'.[62] He reported that he felt he had got on 'intimate terms' with Roosevelt, that the President's two sons were in uniform and a strong family influence for war, and that Roosevelt himself was determined that the United States should come in, but was being held back by fear of defeat or delay in congress. 'The President had said that he would wage war, but not declare it, and that he would become more and more proactive. If the Germans did not like it, they could attack American forces'. When Churchill had felt it necessary to warn the President that, 'he would not answer for the consequences if Russia was compelled to sue for peace and, say, by the Spring of next year, hope died in Britain that the United States were coming into the war', Roosevelt had made it clear that he would look for an incident (presumably the sinking of an American ship).[63]

In the absence of minutes of the meetings with Roosevelt, it is not possible to know how much of this was wishful thinking or exaggeration on Churchill's part. Writing later, he recalled that the President had favoured including a statement that the 'naval and military conversations had in no way been concerned with future commitments other than as authorised by Act of Congress', and that he had talked Roosevelt out of this on the grounds that it would be a gift for German propaganda and would be discouraging to neutral and defeated nations.[64] If true, this suggests a more cautious policy on the part of the President than that which Churchill chose to present in the immediate aftermath.

The Prime Minister did not broadcast to the public until ten days after Attlee's reading of the Charter. When he did so, on Sunday 24 August, he deliberately invoked the divine service held exactly two weeks before, in a speech which used biblical language to denounce the 'barbaric fury of the Nazis', to describe Hitler as 'a devil', and to contrast this with his conviction that we had the chance to play our part in a 'great design, the end of which no mortal can foresee', and in which 'we had the right to feel that we were serving a cause for the sake of which a trumpet has sounded from on high'. He described the

---

[62] TNA, CAB 65/19, WM (41) 84.
[63] TNA, CAB 65/19, WM (41) 84.
[64] Churchill, *The Second World War*, Vol. III, p.387.

Atlantic Meeting as symbolizing 'the marshalling of the good forces of the world against the evil forces which are now so formidable and triumphant and which have cast their cruel spell over the whole of Europe and a large part of Asia'.

By choosing to broadcast on a Sunday, and by deliberately using such religious imagery and moral language, Churchill was reaching out to the American audience, hoping to exploit a common Christian heritage and what he felt to be a shared sense of English-speaking values. He made this explicit when he said that the Atlantic Meeting, 'was bound to be important because of the enormous forces at present only partially mobilized but steadily mobilizing which are at the disposal of these two major groupings of the human family: the British Empire and the United States, who fortunately for the progress of mankind, happen to speak the same language, and very largely think the same thoughts, or anyhow think a lot of the same thoughts'. Later in his text he addressed the issue of American entry to the war head on, saying that it was Hitler's plan to divide and conquer, picking off his enemies 'one by one', before concluding a few paragraphs later that 'by the mercy of God', the United States still retained, 'the power to marshal her gigantic strength, and in saving herself to render an incomparable service to mankind'.[65]

The text of the Charter and the broadcast were both part of the grand narrative that Churchill created, with Roosevelt's blessing, to bind the British and the Americans together in a common and righteous cause. The problem with this big picture was that it immediately raised lots of potentially awkward questions about detail and interpretation. Churchill had referred by name in his broadcast to a whole host of occupied and threatened European nations. On 26 August Chaim Weizmann sent a telegram to Lord Moyne, the Colonial Secretary, conveying the 'shock reaction' among American Jewry to the 'Prime Minister's failure to mention Jews among peoples awaiting restitution and liberation after destruction of Nazi tyranny'.[66] In November, Churchill received via the Governor of Nigeria a message to him from the *West African Pilot* newspaper, which had published a leading article seeking clarification on whether the Charter applied to coloured races in the colonial Empire, and asking 'Are we fighting for security of Europeans to enjoy the four freedoms while West Africa continues on pre-war status?'[67]

---

[65] Rhodes James, *Complete Speeches*, Vol. VI, pp 6473-6477; CAC, Churchill Papers, CHAR 9/152 & CHAR 9/182.

[66] CAC, Churchill Papers, CHAR 9/182/239.

[67] CAC, Churchill Papers, CHAR 20/45/25.

The Nigerian letter had been prompted by reports of Churchill's remarks in the House of Commons on 9 September 1941, in which the Prime Minister had struck a rather different tone about the Atlantic Charter from his earlier broadcast. He had told the House that the joint declaration did 'not try to explain how the broad principles proclaimed by it are to be applied to each and every case which will have to be dealt with when the war comes to an end, and that it would not be wise to be drawn into 'laborious discussions on how it is to fit all the manifold problems'. Moreover, it did not supersede or 'qualify' the existing statements of policy that had been made about the development of constitutional government in India, Burma or other parts of the British Empire. Indeed, 'At the Atlantic Meeting we had in mind, primarily the restoration of the Sovereignty, self-government and national life of the States and nations of Europe now under the Nazi yoke'.[68]

It was this speech that prompted an article by George Strauss in the left-wing newspaper *Tribune* entitled 'Churchill must not make the peace' denouncing the Prime Minister's 'disappointing' and 'alarming' comments. 'We had hoped that he would use the occasion to clarify those of its [the Charter's] many phrases which can be interpreted in a variety of ways, and that he would confound the fears so widely expressed that the Charter envisaged no real social progress. But he did neither'.[69]

Hannen Swaffer, writing in *People*, thought it an 'admirable Charter', but warned that he had heard 'hundreds of pious platitudes' in his life, and invariably 'the forces of Wealth and Power and Privilege have got to work – and that has been the end of them'. He felt that Churchill had seen the Blitzed towns and the 'stalwartness' of the people, and that it was 'impossible to believe that he will forget what is owed them', but feared that the establishment might stop him.[70]

Richard Toye in his book *Churchill's Empire* has shown how the raising and dashing of expectations created by the Atlantic Charter led to immediate problems with nationalist leaders in Africa, Burma and India, and concludes that, 'By putting his name to the Atlantic Charter, Churchill had unleashed expectations that he could not control'.[71] Others, like John Charmley, have identified his obsession with an American alliance as his most 'serious blind spot'.[72] So, by agreeing to those clauses of the Charter which opposed territorial changes that did not accord with the wishes of

---

[68] Rhodes James, *Complete Speeches*, Vol. VI, pp.6480-6481.
[69] CAC, Churchill Papers, CHAR 20/29B/122.
[70] CAC, Churchill Press Cuttings, CHPC 19.
[71] Toye, R., *Churchill's Empire*, (Macmillan, 2010), pp.212-216.
[72] Charmley, J., *Churchill: The End of Glory*, (Hodder & Stoughton, 1993), p.466.

the people, and which respected the rights of all peoples to choose their own form of government, had he simply walked into an American trap aimed at undermining the British Empire?

If so, then he did it with his eyes open. After all, he had claimed that it was the British who had drafted these clauses. Moreover, having spotted the American attempt to impose free trade and remove Imperial Preference, it seems inconceivable that he did not think about the implications of the other clauses on the Empire. He rejected a call for the Charter to be endorsed in the House of Commons on the grounds that there would certainly be 'amendments and demands for explanations of particular phrases' stating that its provisions 'must be regarded as a rough and ready guide in a war emergency'.[73] This echoes his earlier telegram to Attlee, and confirms that he wanted to keep the focus on general principles rather than specifics.

Even Leo Amery, who as Secretary of State for India suddenly found himself fighting hasty rear-guard actions in India and Burma to damp down the nationalist expectations stoked by the declaration, wrote in his diary that: 'We shall no doubt pay dearly in the end for all this fluffy flapdoodle. But if meanwhile under cover of it our two democratic dictators have really got down to business, we must be content to accept it as the price of victory'.[74]

It was more important for Churchill and for Britain to be seen as noble allies of the United States than as 'Old World' reactionaries. Nor can this have been an isolated view; otherwise he would have faced more concerted opposition from the War Cabinet and from Cadogan, who were all party to the final text. In August 1941, the ongoing battle in the Atlantic, the need for material aid to sustain Britain in North Africa, the deteriorating situation in the Far East, and the huge psychological value of American intervention all pointed towards the overriding value of achieving an American alliance.

The problem was that there was no alliance, and it was not just the general public who felt deflated. Cadogan describes high level frustrations surfacing as early as 25 August with Beaverbrook, just back from the United States, 'thumping the table and saying P.M. must do something "dramatic"'.[75] Given that Churchill had broadcast in the most dramatic terms just the day before, it is difficult to see what more he could be expected to do. Three days later he telegraphed to Hopkins:

---

[73] CAC, Churchill Papers, CHAR 20/26/51.
[74] CAC, Amery Papers, AMEL 7/35.
[75] Dilks (ed), *Cadogan Diaries*, p.402.

I ought to tell you that there has been a wave of depression through Cabinet and other informed circles here about President's many assurances and no commitments and no closer to war etc. I fear this will be reflected in parliament. If 1942 opens with Russia knocked out and Britain left again alone, all kinds of dangers may arise. I do not think Hitler will help in any way. Tonight he has 30 U-Boats in line from the eastern part of Iceland to northern tip of Ireland. We have lost 25,000 tons yesterday (27th) and today (28th) but he keeps clear of 26th meridian. You will know best whether anything more can be done. Should be grateful if you could give me any sort of hope.[76]

In private, Churchill admitted his personal frustrations in a letter to his son, Randolph, reporting that while the meeting had been 'by no means unfruitful', establishing a 'deep and intimate contact of friendship' with the President, he was 'deeply perplexed to know how the deadlock is to be broken', and feared that Roosevelt was moving with public opinion rather than leading and forming it.[77]

Churchill must take some of the blame for stoking the high British expectations. But he cannot be blamed for taking an opportunity to engage with Roosevelt or for issuing the declaration. It was the top priority of the British government to ally themselves to the United States. To fail to take the opportunity or to argue over points of detail would have been to risk damaging relations. Instead, he had done everything he could to exploit the opportunity provided by the Atlantic Meeting. At Roosevelt's request, and in the knowledge that there would be collateral damage to his Imperial policy, he had agreed the mission statement for the Anglo-American alliance. In the short term he had gained the goodwill of the President, and a better understanding of American thinking and military personalities, but little else. The Americans would continue to inch towards war. After the attempted sinking of the USS *Greer* in September, the President did finally authorise his navy to implement the plans discussed in Newfoundland and begin escorting convoys, but even further incidents in the Atlantic like the U-boat attack on the USS *Kearney* and the sinking of the USS *Reuben James* failed to act as a causus belli, and it would take the Japanese attack on Pearl Harbor in December, to bring the United States fully into the conflict. This did not stop the British from continuing to try and milk the last drops of publicity from the Atlantic Meeting with the production of specially designed Christmas cards.[78]

---

[76] CAC, Churchill Papers, CHAR 20/42A/35.
[77] CAC, Churchill Papers, CHAR 1/362/28-32.
[78] CAC, Martin Papers, MART 3.

Churchill's personal investment in the Atlantic Charter stands in very marked contrast to his handling of the promised treaty with Russia, where he was happy to let Anthony Eden take the lead in the negotiations. The Foreign Secretary visited Moscow in December 1941, and bore the brunt of the increasingly frustrating discussions thereafter. The Russians made it very clear that their primary interest was in *realpolitik* not principle. They wanted the British to recognise the Russian borders as they had existed in June 1941, immediately prior to Hitler's invasion, and incorporating those territories which the Soviet Union had been able to annex while allied to Nazi Germany: namely the Baltic States, and parts of eastern Finland and eastern Poland. These demands were in clear conflict with the Atlantic Charter and its clause about self-determination. The British immediately found themselves caught between the wishes of Washington and those of Moscow.

After consulting with the Americans, Eden produced a compromise draft, incorporating President Roosevelt's suggestion that 'any persons wishing to emigrate from the territories which the Soviet government propose thus to reoccupy shall be given the opportunity to do so'. His paper to the War Cabinet noted that it would be difficult to persuade Stalin to agree to such a concession, and, warned presciently that, 'even if he does, it has the disadvantage that any attempt on our part to implement it in practice is bound to arouse Soviet ill-feeling and resentment without achieving any satisfactory results'. Moreover, there was a bigger hurdle, in that the British could not acknowledge any future Russo-Polish border, having given an undertaking to the Poles not to recognise any territorial changes effected to their borders since August 1939.[79] Nevertheless, the War Cabinet endorsed Eden's approach and the Russian Foreign Minister, Molotov, was encouraged to visit London en route to the United States in order to settle the matter face to face.[80]

Molotov arrived on 20 May, initiating five days of tortuous negotiations. Churchill was conspicuous largely by his absence. He did chair the very first meeting with the Soviet delegation on the morning of the 21st at which he noted that the 'Soviet draft political Treaty was not at all free from grave difficulties', and that, 'It could be argued that it contravened the spirit of the Atlantic Charter', and it would not be endorsed by President Roosevelt. He did not want a document that emphasised differences between the three countries.[81] It was probably

---

[79]   TNA, CAB 66/23, WP (42) 144.
[80]   TNA, CAB 65/30, WM (42) 44.
[81]   TNA, CAB 66/24, WP (42) 218.

with relief that he then handed over the detailed discussions to Eden, Cadogan and the Foreign Office team. The fact that this was handled at Foreign Secretary level was clearly important in protecting Churchill from what seemed a very real prospect of failure, but his hands-off approach stood in marked contrast to his dealings with the Americans, where he was clearly leading from the front. As Elisabeth Barker put it, in her book *Churchill and Eden at War*, 'Churchill gave more weight than Eden to partnership with America, Eden more weight than Churchill to partnership with Russia. Both were changeable, but this difference between them was constant'.[82]

The deadlock was ultimately broken when the Russians, acting on instructions from Stalin, agreed to accept a revised British treaty that made no mention of borders or territories, and under which the two countries pledged themselves to twenty years of mutual assistance. The question of Poland had been put into abeyance. This was a huge relief to Eden, welcome news to Churchill, and was quickly endorsed by the Cabinet. Cadogan's role in drafting the text means that he was a co-author of both the Charter and the Russian Treaty, though the two documents have little else in common: one was a principled declaration of common ground between would-be allies, while the other was a rather forced recognition of practical reality signed by mutually suspicious parties. Both constrained Britain's role in the post-war world.

But Churchill undoubtedly felt the necessity of a Soviet treaty in 1942. Militarily, the Russians were now engaging vast German armies on the Eastern Front, thereby saving the United Kingdom from the renewed threat of invasion and protecting the northern flank of the British armies in the Middle East from German attack through the Caucasus. In Britain, such was the popular support for the brave defence being put up by the Russians, that it was deemed wise for Clementine Churchill to become the head of the Red Cross Aid to Russia Fund.[83] As the summer months approached, with their long hours of Arctic daylight, Churchill and the Chiefs of Staff were already worrying about whether the convoys to the northern Russian ports of Archangel and Murmansk could be maintained against increased German bombers and U-boats.[84] At the War Cabinet meeting of 18 May Churchill made an eloquent appeal for their continuation, stating that 'it was our duty to fight these convoys through, whatever the

---

[82] Barker, E., *Churchill and Eden at War*, (Macmillan, 1978), p.233.
[83] Soames, M., *Clementine Churchill*, (revised edition, Doubleday, 2002), pp.360-363.
[84] See for example TNA, CAB 65/30, WM (42) 48.

cost. The Russians were engaged in a life and death struggle against our common enemy'.[85] But short of pledging to respond in kind if the Germans bombed Russia with poison gas, which was also discussed in Cabinet at this time, there was little else Churchill could promise.[86] The Russians and, increasingly, the British public, press and parliament were pressing for a 'Second Front now' in Western Europe. This he was not yet willing or able to give, and in its absence the treaty assumed a greater significance.

The Atlantic Meeting may have raised expectations for an immediate American entry in August 1941, but viewed from Washington those expectations were clearly unrealistic. Only congress could declare war, and Roosevelt knew that it was not yet prepared to do so. His strategy was to proceed measure by measure: amendment of neutrality laws, destroyers for bases, extension of the draft, lend lease and defence of the Atlantic. The Atlantic Charter was an important step in this process. The Charter did provide a foundation stone for the Anglo-American alliance. It marked the first coming together of the political and military leaders of Britain and the United States and was a clear assertion of their common values and their intention to work together. Churchill, for all his impatience, realised that there was no point in the Americans asserting principles for the post-war world unless they were prepared to play a role in enforcing the settlement; and so he knew that the Charter brought them one step closer to war.

Churchill kept the original of his first typescript draft of the Atlantic Charter, complete with handwritten annotations in red ink. For many years after his death it was displayed in a glass frame on the wall at Chartwell, his beloved home in Kent. It had to be taken down when it started to fade, and is now stored away from the light in an acid-free folder and box in the secure strong room of the Churchill Archives Centre.[87] The fact that it was kept and displayed is a reflection of the iconic status that the Charter came to assume in the post-war world. It is now held up as one of the founding documents of the United Nations Organization (those nations that later subscribed to the principles set forth in the Charter became known as the United Nations and gave their name to the international organisation that was finally created in June 1945). For Churchill, the vindication of the Charter came not in August 1941 but later, through its identification with the birth of

---

[85] TNA, CAB 65/30, WM (42) 64.
[86] TNA, CAB 65/30, WM (42) 51.
[87] CAC, Churchill Archives Centre, WCHL 13/2 & 3.

the Anglo-American 'Special Relationship', the creation of the United Nations, and the concept of the good war. It played a role in setting the scene and creating the right narrative to underpin the Allied war effort. Churchill, with his eye for history and drama foresaw some of this. He touched on it in his speech to parliament on 9 September 1941 when he said: 'Although the principles in the Declaration, and much of the language, have long been familiar to the British and American democracies, the fact that it is a united Declaration sets up a milestone or monument which needs only the stroke of victory to become a permanent part of the history of human progress'.[88] The Charter was as much a piece of theatre as diplomacy, and, if not its author, Churchill was certainly its impresario.

On one level, Churchill's responses to the invasion of the Soviet Union and the Atlantic Meeting seem very different. In his dealing with the Russians he was reactive and pragmatic and prepared to delegate the negotiations to Cripps and Eden. Contrast this with his personal mission to meet President Roosevelt; travelling thousands of miles, at considerable personal risk, for little immediate tangible benefit. There is no doubt that the difference in approach reflects the higher priority being placed on an American alliance, as it was not known how long the Russians might last, and British planners had long since concluded that an ultimate Allied victory depended on the United States entering the conflict. What is also clear is that this was in accord with Churchill's own preference; one that we now take for granted but which was not universally shared in Britain, where public support for Stalin and the Soviet Union remained strong for the rest of the war. He was already a firm believer in the closer union of the English-Speaking Peoples and remained an opponent of communism. The ideals of the Charter would have appealed to his romantic nature. The historian in him would have appreciated their value in putting the Allies firmly on the right side of history, while the politician undoubtedly saw their propaganda value.

Yet, at this point in the conflict, there are perhaps more similarities than differences in his approach to his two potential allies. In both cases he acted decisively and quickly, and largely on his own initiative. His guiding focus, common to both, was the best means of obtaining victory, and in this he showed himself to be flexible and prepared to subjugate any ideological concerns to the immediate business of winning the war.

He did not know how long the Russians would hold; he did not know how long the Americans would wait. He had embraced the

---

[88] Rhodes James, *Complete Speeches*, Vol. VI, p.6481.

Devil and crossed the deep blue sea. He had shown himself willing to travel, politically and ideologically, in order to start constructing his Grand Alliance, but there was also very little doubt that his personal preferences and priorities lay in the West with the United States. However, it was also clear that the American and Soviet attitudes to the post-war settlement, and especially to the fate of the Balkan and East European countries that bordered on Russia, were going to be very different. At the moment these problems were hypothetical, and subordinated to the need to obtain military victory, but as the war progressed Churchill would inevitably find himself caught between the contrasting attitudes of his two allies. Not least because the exiled governments of occupied countries like Greece and Poland were shortly to be numbered among the twenty-six original signatories to the Atlantic Charter.[89]

Did the defeated nations have the right to determine their own form of government? Should Poland be forced to cede territory to the Soviet Union against her will? How might a policy of assigning spheres of influence in Balkan countries be reconciled with the clauses opposing territorial aggrandisement and interference? These are problems which Churchill cannot have fully anticipated in 1941, and we will follow some of the repercussions in future chapters.

Churchill was clearly aware of the challenges posed by implementation of the Atlantic Charter, and of the inherent tensions between some of its clauses and the likely results of the British treaty with Russia, but in the short term he knew he needed both. His heart yearned to bring the Americans into the conflict; his head knew that he had to keep the Soviets there.

---

[89] TNA, PREM 3/485/9.

Chapter 5

Do or Die?

How did Churchill survive the fall of Singapore?

In October 1988 Denis Kelly, a former literary assistant to Sir Winston Churchill, wrote to Martin Gilbert, the historian and Churchill biographer. A copy of the letter survives in the small collection of Kelly's papers at the Churchill Archives Centre. He began:

> You tell me you are writing a book about the Second World War. Here is what Churchill told me about it. I have been careful to distinguish between what he said and my now subsequent comments. All that he told me was in private conversation, with no-one else present, at lunch or dinner. I can give you no dates except that it took place at Chartwell between 1947 and 1957.

Kelly then relates how he put the question to Churchill: 'What were the biggest mistakes in the Second World War? Immediate answer. "Losing Singapore and letting the Russians into Europe."'[1]

Of course, this letter is problematic. It was written years after Kelly's relationship with Churchill had ended, and years after the supposed dinner conversations had taken place. Moreover, as Kelly admits, there were no witnesses, and, as Duff Cooper so memorably put it in the title of his memoirs, *Old Men Forget*. Old men can also exaggerate, and here there was scope for invention or exaggeration by both Churchill, who was talking to Kelly with the benefit of hindsight after the war had ended, and by Kelly, who was remembering a conversation that had taken place thirty or forty years previously. Yet, if we accept that

---

[1] CAC, Kelly Papers, DEKE 1.

some such comment was made to Kelly by Churchill at some point, it hints at the significance that Churchill put on the loss of Singapore. This chapter will look at why the episode was so damaging, before considering its aftermath and the strategy deployed by Churchill to survive the resulting crisis.

The immediate period after the Japanese attack on Pearl Harbor on 7 December 1941 should have been a time of personal triumph for Churchill. The United States was now finally an ally and ultimate victory seemed possible. Just a week later, he travelled to the United States to stand shoulder to shoulder with Roosevelt and the American people. He stayed as a guest in the White House; told the two Houses of the American Congress that, 'if my father had been American and my mother British, instead of the other way round, I might have got here on my own'; and delivered his famous 'Some chicken, some neck speech' to the Canadian parliament in Ottawa. He was feted and celebrated, and helped negotiate the genesis of the Anglo-American military alliance, with the creation of the new Combined Chiefs of Staff Committee in Washington DC. Yet he returned to Britain in mid-January 1942 to face a darkening scene and a veritable storm of criticism. After the Atlantic Charter meeting he had hoped for an 'incident' that would bring the United States into the war. The irony was that Pearl Harbor was the worst possible such incident, exposing the weakness of the British position in the Pacific, while also temporarily removing the American Pacific Fleet; the one substantial naval force in the theatre, which Churchill had been relying upon to provide cover for British vulnerability. As David Day has pointed out, the British were correct in their assumption that the Japanese would not risk exposing their flank by attacking Singapore while the United States Fleet was at Hawaii, but failed to foresee that, 'The pre-emptive strike on Pearl Harbor was the obvious but totally unexpected solution to the Japanese predicament'.[2]

The small island of Singapore was the key to the British position in the Pacific, the lynchpin of her Empire in the East, and the Japanese knew it. At twenty-seven miles long from east to west and thirteen from north to south, it is comparable in size and shape to England's Isle of Wight, though crucially – as we will see – without the cliffs.[3]

---

[2] Day, D., *The Great Betrayal*, (Oxford University Press, paperback edition, 1992), pp.344-345.

[3] Mace, M. & Grehan, J. (eds), 'Lt General Arthur Percival's Despatch on Operations, 8 Dec 1941 – 15 Feb 1942' (War Office, 1948)' in *Despatches from the Front. The Commanding Officers' Reports from the Field and at Sea. Disaster in the Far East 1940-1942. The Defence of Malaya, Japanese Capture of Hong Kong, and the Fall of Singapore*, (Pen & Sword, 2015), p.275.

Located almost on the Equator, at the tip of the Malay Peninsula, its significance in 1941 lay in its role as the main British naval base in the Pacific Theatre; a strategic hub at the intersection of the Indian Ocean, the South China Sea and the Pacific Ocean, from which it was intended that British naval power should dominate and defend the sea lanes linking Britain's global interests in Australia, New Zealand, China, Hong Kong, India and Burma.

In March 1924, Churchill had written a newspaper article vigorously defending the decision to build a naval base at Singapore, and attacking socialist Prime Minister Ramsay MacDonald's attempts to abandon or defer the project as part of the wider British disarmament policy. The article carried the subtitle 'Abandonment A Long Step Towards Imperial Disintegration'. In it, drawing on his experience as the former First Lord of the Admiralty, Churchill made the case that the dawn of the oil age in naval construction necessitated the building and maintaining of refuelling stations around the globe if British dominance of the high seas was to be retained. Unless such a base was built at Singapore it would be impossible for Britain to send a strong fleet into the Pacific Ocean, and if Britain could not do this then it had sacrificed the power to come to the aid of Australia and New Zealand, the 'two great democratic communities ... united to us by the strongest ties of sentiment and interest'.[4] Churchill was prepared to leave the final decision of the siting of this base to the experts, who had recommended Singapore. He was not interested in the geography or in the detail; he was interested in the principles of keeping a global navy, maintaining a presence in the Pacific Ocean, and binding together the Empire and Commonwealth, and particularly the English-speaking democracies.

It can and has been questioned whether Churchill's actions in the 1920s were consistent with these writings. In 1926, in his role as Chancellor of the Exchequer (the Minister in charge of British finance) he drove through cuts to the naval expenditure on the new base, thereby reducing its capability to house a full fleet.[5] True, it was Churchill's job at the time to scrutinise military spending, and at that point there seemed little prospect of a war with Japan. But, from the outset, both in Churchill's thinking and in terms of wider British strategy, there had been a clear disconnect between the importance being attached

---

[4] CAC, Churchill Papers, CHAR 8/200B.
[5] For an overview, see Farrell, B., 'Churchill and Imperial Defence: Putting Singapore in Perspective' in Farrell, B. (ed), *Churchill and the Lion City: Shaping Modern Singapore*, (National University of Singapore, 2011), pp.36-55.

to Singapore as a centre of British power, and the resources needed to make that vision a reality.

Prior to 1940, the Admiralty had ranked the maintenance of Singapore as second only in priority to the security of the British homeland, and above that of the Eastern Mediterranean. The logic was clear. Lose control of the Suez Canal and shipping could still reach the Empire in the east via the much longer Cape route. Lose Singapore, and all shipping to and from the Far East would be threatened, and communications with Australia and New Zealand would be severed. Moreover, it was assumed that the French navy would help defend the Mediterranean, allowing the British greater flexibility to reinforce the Pacific.

Yet, as we have seen, by 1941, this strategy had changed. The Nazi domination of Western Europe, the ever-present threat of invasion, and the U-boat stranglehold over the Atlantic was keeping the strongest British naval forces in home waters. Any additional capacity was now being used to escort the Arctic convoys, taking military supplies to Stalin's Russia via the northern ports of Archangel and Murmansk, or was engaged in the military operations in the Mediterranean, where success depended on denying the Italians control of the sea, and in holding supply lines through Gibraltar, Malta, and Alexandria. Moreover, the assumption that the French fleet would be on hand to help in the Mediterranean, had become a fear that it might turn hostile, creating an additional need for strong British naval forces to guard against this risk. Churchill's attack on the French fleet at Oran, and his promotion of offensive operations in North Africa and Greece, had therefore come at the price of reinforcements for the Pacific. The Prime Minister had consistently overruled his Chiefs of Staff, preferring to allocate finite resources to the Middle East, where fighting was already taking place, rather than the Far East, where it might yet be avoided. He made it clear, as late as 20 October 1941, that he did not believe the Japanese would go to war with Britain and the United States, and after the Atlantic Meeting he was confident of maintaining a united front with the President.[6] Even if the worst were to happen, the American British Canadian staff talks in the spring of 1941 had seemed to confirm that British interests in the area would be protected by the American Pacific Fleet, even though that fleet would operate from Hawaii rather than Singapore.

The British Commander in Chief in the Far East from November 1940 to December 1941 was Air Chief Marshal Sir Robert Brooke-Popham.

---

[6] TNA, CAB 69/8, DO (41) 66.

He was told that Singapore would have to be defended by air power, and garrisoned to withstand a siege of 180 days' duration, until reinforcements could arrive by sea. It was also made clear to him that nothing was to be done to seek a war with Japan, while everything was to be done to encourage co-operation with the American navy.[7] On paper this might have looked sound, but in practice it relied on a number of assumptions that simply could not be met. To hold Singapore by air power meant holding the whole of Malaya, as if the Japanese gained airfields on the peninsula they would be able to subject Singapore island to constant air attack. It followed that defending the airfields entailed trying to find the ground troops to hold the whole peninsula. As with the navy, the Royal Air Force and the British army were already overstretched by their commitments at home and in the Mediterranean. In August 1940, the number of first-line aircraft needed to defend Singapore had been estimated at 336; the actual strength in December 1941 was 158, of which some were obsolete. There was a token naval force, and by December this had been supplemented by the battleship HMS *Prince of Wales* and the older battlecruiser HMS *Repulse,* but without air protection such ships were vulnerable. The army also appeared stronger on paper than it really was. Lieutenant-General Percival, commander of the British army in Malaya, later estimated his total forces during the entire Singapore campaign at some 125,000 including non-combatant support troops. Yet he never had them all available at the same time, some arrived very late, and it was a non-cohesive force composed of British, Australian, Indian and Malay troops, many of whom lacked jungle warfare training, and had no tanks and few armoured vehicles. Moreover, in defending the whole Malay Peninsula, they were defending an area the size of England, and, as Percival pointed out, it was the army 'that had to bear practically the whole weight of the Japanese attack with little air or naval support'.[8] There were simply not enough resources to go around.

Churchill's assumptions about Singapore were based on what he had read, not what he had seen. In his wartime communications he often referred to Singapore island as a 'fortress'. It was no such thing. The naval base had large guns to defend against seaborne attack, but

[7] Mace & Grehan (eds), 'Air Chief Marshal Sir Robert Brooke-Popham's Despatch on Operations, 17 Oct 1940-27 Dec 1941' in *Despatches from the Front*, pp.2-6.

[8] Mace & Grehan (eds), 'Air Chief Marshal Sir Robert Brooke-Popham's Despatch on Operations, 17 Oct 1940-27 Dec 1941' pp.34-39, appendices p.78 & p.84. 'Lt General Arthur Percival's Despatch on Operations, 8 Dec 1941 – 15 Feb 1942', in *Despatches from the Front*, p.175 & pp.316-317.

no defences had been constructed on the northern or western shores of the island. General Wavell had been appointed in December 1941 as the Supreme Allied Commander for the newly created American-British-Dutch-Australian (ABDA) area in South-East Asia, thereby replacing Brooke-Popham as the theatre commander with overall responsibility for the region. But even he failed to appreciate the full enormity of the deficiencies in Singapore's defences until it was too late. It was only in his telegram of 21 January 1942, as the British prepared to retreat into the city, that Wavell reported to the Prime Minister, 'I did not realise myself until lately how entirely defences were planned against seaward attack only'.[9] This perplexed Churchill, who struggled with this issue when it came to writing about the episode in his history. In one of his unpublished notes to his literary team, he posed the question, 'How can we explain them not fortifying the Gorge. Nobody thought of it in time. In Wavell's telegrams he only just found out how it had been neglected. He had been Commander-in-Chief India for a year'.[10] His use of the word 'Gorge' is of course revealing, and clearly demonstrates his lack of personal knowledge of conditions on the ground in Malaya; the banks of the Straits of Johore being relatively flat, twenty-seven miles long, and fringing narrow waters that were only too easy for the enemy to cross. This highlights a weakness in Churchill's ability to grasp and direct the Singapore campaign; he had never travelled east of India, and, unlike the centres of British power in the Mediterranean, he could not visualise the terrain.

According to Denis Kelly, Churchill admitted that once the war had begun, 'There was a veil over my mind about the Japanese War. All the proportions were hidden in the mist'.[11] Certainly, he could not have anticipated the Japanese attack on Pearl Harbor, but it is clear that both he and Roosevelt knew that the situation was deteriorating. In a letter of 15 October 1941, Roosevelt had told Churchill that 'the Jap situation is definitely worse & I think they are headed North – however in spite of this you & I have two months of respite in the Far East'.[12] Roosevelt was almost exactly right, but, by the time of the attack on Pearl Harbor, it was already too late. Britain was politically unable to abandon Singapore for fear of alienating Australia and New Zealand, but was also militarily unable to hold the island. A successful

---

[9] CAC, Churchill Papers, CHAR 20/68B/138.
[10] CAC, Churchill Papers, CHUR 4/255A/119.
[11] CAC, Kelly Papers, DEKE 1.
[12] CAC, Churchill Papers, CHAR 20/20/38.

defence could only have been contemplated if it had been reinforced much more fully, much earlier. But this would have meant diverting scarce resources at a time when Britain was not at war with Japan, and at a time when priority was being given to the defence of the British Isles and offence in the Mediterranean.

The issue of sending a naval force to Singapore had been repeatedly discussed. Robert Menzies, the Australian Prime Minister, had called for the despatch of a nucleus of five capital ships in August, and a meeting in September between Duff Cooper and senior military and diplomatic figures in the region had 'stressed the propaganda value of one or two battleships'.[13] By October, the accession of a more hard-line government in Japan had led the Foreign Secretary, Anthony Eden, to the same conclusion, and at Defence Committee meetings on 17 and 20 October it was Churchill who proposed sending HMS *Prince of Wales*. He argued that the mere presence of such a capital ship would have a powerful deterrent effect on Japan, and endorsed Eden's suggestion that it should call in on Cape Town en route to advertise its coming. The naval experts were opposed, arguing that the ship would be of more use in the Western Mediterranean, while Singapore would be better defended by a larger squadron of older ships.[14] But with Attlee backing Churchill and Eden, the politicians got their way. Previously, Churchill had opposed the Chiefs of Staff and blocked reinforcements to Singapore, now he overruled them to send one fast capital ship. Ironically, he did it not because he thought there would be war, but because he thought it would deter war. It was to have been sent with an aircraft carrier, but damage to HMS *Indomitable* left the *Prince of Wales* and the *Repulse* without air cover and dangerously exposed to attack from the skies.

The Prime Minister may have been influenced by his recent journey across the Atlantic. He had been impressed by the *Prince of Wales*. To him, like Singapore itself, the ship was a symbol of British power. In the case of both, he overestimated their defences, and underestimated his enemy.

While the British commanders in Singapore were being careful not to do anything to antagonise the Japanese, the Japanese were consolidating a new position in French Indo China that brought their planes within bombing range of Malaya and Singapore. While the British continued to hope that the American Pacific Fleet would act

---

13 CAC, Churchill Papers, CHAR 20/41/105; Mace & Grehan (eds), 'Air Chief Marshal Sir Robert Brooke-Popham's Despatch' in *Despatches from the Front*, p.28.

14 TNA, CAB 69/2, DO (41) 65; CAB 69/8, DO (41) 66.

as a deterrent to Japanese aggression in the Pacific, and might be able to sail to the rescue of Singapore, the Japanese were planning their audacious assault on that very fleet at Pearl Harbor. Their first attacks on Singapore came in the early hours of Monday 8 December, local time, and were designed to coincide with the bombing of the US Pacific Fleet at Hawaii (which was eighteen hours behind Singapore and so hit on the morning of 7 December).

The Japanese quickly overran the advanced British airfields and established air superiority. On the morning of 10 December their planes found and sunk *Repulse* and *Prince of Wales*. By the end of January all British armed forces had been withdrawn into Singapore. Such was the speed of events, that by the time Churchill focused on Singapore, its doom was probably sealed. But this was not something that he could easily admit. The idea of an Imperial 'fortress' was still ingrained, and he could not face the fact that a large British-led army could be so quickly defeated by an Asiatic force. On 27 December, he told the new Australian Prime Minister, John Curtin, that he refused to share his view on the 'danger of early reduction of Singapore' and pledged to defend it 'with the utmost tenacity'.[15] He was not alone in believing that Singapore might be held. He had sent out Conservative politician, Duff Cooper, as the Cabinet's representative, the Minister Resident in the Far East. On 18 December 1941, Cooper wrote a letter for the Prime Minister, summarising the situation as he saw it. It concluded that 'Unless the unforeseen happens – such as a successful enemy landing on the island itself – I have no doubt of our ability to hold out for three or four months, or even indefinitely provided we can get reinforcements and, later, food supplies'[16]. The despatch of this letter was delayed, and Duff Cooper was able to add a codicil on 20 December, in which he stated that:

> So long as we hold Singapore it will be easy to rectify the set-backs we have hitherto experienced. But if we lose it, owing to our attaching excessive importance to North Africa, we may find that we have won the war in Europe only to start it all over again in Asia with all the cards in the hands of the enemy.[17]

Advice like this, from his appointed expert on the spot, must have encouraged Churchill in reinforcing Singapore. On 14 January 1942, in response to increasingly alarmed telegrams from Curtin in Australia, he

---

[15] CAC, Churchill Papers, CHAR 20/47/97-99.
[16] CAC, Norwich Papers, DUFC 3/7.
[17] CAC, Norwich Papers, DUFC 3/7.

sent a three-page telegram summarising the proposed reinforcements for Singapore: the British 18th Division was being despatched from the United Kingdom, existing divisions were being reinforced, the two Australian Divisions were being withdrawn from the Middle East, and there were plans to increase the air strength with eight fighter squadrons, eight bomber squadrons, and additional torpedo bombers and flying boats.[18] In the event, most of this would arrive too late or not at all. It was sent to meet the demands of Britain's allies with the approval of the Chiefs of Staff, but without the required three months that they had insisted upon just months before in May.

Churchill was determined that Singapore be defended for as long as possible, and to the bitter end if necessary. Wavell was meant to receive his orders directly from the newly established British and American Combined Chiefs of Staff Committee in Washington DC, but this did not stop Churchill bombarding him with telegrams. On 20 January, he wrote:

> I want to make it absolutely clear that I expect every inch of ground to be defended, every scrap of material or defences to be blown to pieces to prevent capture by the enemy and no question of surrender to be entertained until after protracted fighting among the ruins of Singapore City.[19]

Then again on the 10 February:

> The 18th Division [which was newly arrived from Britain] has a chance to make its name in history. Commanders and Senior Officers should die with their troops. The honour of the British Empire and of the British Army is at stake. I rely on you to show no mercy to weakness in any form. With the Russians fighting as they are and the Americans so stubborn at Luzon, the whole reputation of our country and our race is involved. It is expected that every unit will be brought into close contact with the enemy and fight it out.[20]

On 11 February, he told President Roosevelt, 'We have 106,000 men in Singapore Island, of which nearly 60,000 are British or Australian, 40,000 being British. I am very glad Wavell is there today. The battle must be fought to the bitter end, regardless of consequences to the city or its inhabitants'.[21] The following day he informed the American leader that, 'A fierce battle is raging at Singapore and orders have been given to

---

[18] CAC, Churchill Papers, CHAR 20/68B/80-82.
[19] CAC, Churchill Papers, CHAR 20/68B/124.
[20] CAC, Churchill Papers, CHAR 20/70/9.
[21] CAC, Churchill Papers, CHAR 20/70/12.

fight it out'.[22] He was desperate to avoid a humiliating defeat while his allies were fighting so hard. A surrender was not the way he wanted to mark the start of the 'special relationship'. Churchill's deliberate use of such dramatic and archaic language reveals much about his emotional response to the unfolding crisis. This was a battle about empire, race and national pride. He believed that the British troops were superior to the Japanese, and that it was essential that we prove to our new Russian and American allies that we were their equal in taking on the enemy.

But there was to be no great last stand. The Japanese crossed the Straits of Johore on 8 February, and Percival surrendered a week later on the 15th. Far from holding out for 180 days, Malaya had fallen in sixty-eight and Singapore island in just a week. There is no doubt that Singapore's loss was a huge catastrophe. Churchill recognised it as 'the worst disaster and largest capitulation in British history'[23]; an enormous defeat for the whole apparatus of British political and military power, and one which was compounded by the speed with which it had all happened. Images of British officers walking into captivity under white flags were beamed around the world.

Churchill had been slow to realise the full gravity of the situation, and the sinking of the *Prince of Wales,* the pride of the British fleet, which had so recently carried him across the Atlantic, clearly came as a devastating personal and political blow. It was followed by the humiliating images of General Percival's surrender. There is no doubt that he felt it keenly. Here was an act of national shame which was incompatible with his grand narrative for the inherent superiority of British and Imperial troops. It is a view that was perhaps best articulated in the broadcast he had made just a few months earlier after the fall of Crete in April 1941:

> Military defeat or miscalculations can be redeemed. The fortunes of war are fickle and changing. But an act of shame would sap the vitals of our strength and deprive us of the respect which we now enjoy throughout the world, and would especially rob us of the immense potent hold we have, during the last year gained by our bearing, a potent hold upon the sentiments of the people of the United States.[24]

To Churchill, Singapore was just such an act of shame, occurring just at the moment when America had finally entered the war, and when

---

[22] CAC, Churchill Papers, CHAR 20/70/30.
[23] Churchill *The Second World War*, Vol. VI, p.81.
[24] CAC, Churchill Papers, CHAR 9/181B/180.

Britain most needed to impress her new ally, and to honour her promise to defend Australia and New Zealand.

General Sir Alan Brooke, who had just replaced Dill as Chief of the Imperial General Staff, found himself repeatedly forced to defend the conduct of the army against 'most unpleasant remarks by various ministers in connection with defeats of our forces!', later adding that, 'These were very difficult times for me in the Cabinet and Winston was the worst offender'.[25] But Churchill's view was echoed by other members of the inner circle. Alexander Cadogan's diary entry for Saturday 31 January 1942 read, 'We've retreated into Singapore island. That must surely be indefensible against the air. Coming on top of our loss of Benghazi, most depressing. I'm afraid our soldiers seem very incapable'. By Monday 9 February he was prepared to be even more scathing, 'Our generals are no use and do our men fight? ... As P.M. says, what will happen if Germans get a footing here [Britain]? ... . Poor Winston v. desperate'.[26] Seen in this context, Singapore was the culmination of a series of retreats and defeats that had begun in Norway and France in 1940, and continued in Greece and the Middle East in 1941.

Nor was it an isolated defeat. As Cadogan's diary infers, the final days of Singapore coincided with a renewed offensive by Rommel in the North African desert. The port of Benghazi was retaken by the German general, and the Egyptian border threatened once again. Then, on 12 February, the powerful German battlecruisers *Scharnhorst* and *Gneisenau*, along with the cruiser *Prince Eugen*, slipped undetected from their moorings at Brest and made their way brazenly up the Channel to safety in Germany without being sunk, having only belatedly been detected and attacked by the Royal Navy and RAF. It seemed that Britain was being outsmarted in each theatre. Public opinion was outraged. Cadogan felt it to be, 'the blackest day, yet of the war'.[27] Churchill later conceded that, 'It was certainly not strange that public confidence in the Administration and its conduct of the war should have quavered'.[28]

After almost two years at the helm, Churchill knew that this defeat had the potential to cause him real damage; in the short term to his running of the British war effort, and in the longer term to his legacy as a successful war leader. Whatever the tactical failings of the military

---

[25] Danchev & Todman (eds), *Alanbrooke Diaries*, p.226.
[26] David Dilks (ed), *Cadogan Diaries*, p 430, & pp.432-433.
[27] Dilks (ed), *Cadogan Diaries*, p.433.
[28] Churchill, *The Second World War*, Vol. IV, p.71.

commanders on the ground, and he clearly thought there were several, he had 'to take upon himself the full responsibility for the political decisions which had governed the size of our forces in Malaya at the outbreak of hostilities'.[29]

It was the Prime Minister who had ignored General Dill's objections in April 1941, in order to prioritise the Mediterranean over the Far East.

It was the Prime Minister who now stood accused of misleading the Dominion governments of Australia and New Zealand. After all, had he not persuaded them to send their troops to the defence of the Middle East on the understanding that the Japanese would not be able to threaten their homelands; on the promise that Singapore would be held as a strategic hub, through which the British would be able to reinforce the Allied presence in the Pacific?

It was the Prime Minister who had promised the British people and parliament that he would wage war until final victory, assuming a personal control over the direction of the war effort by making himself Minister of Defence, but who now had to explain a further major defeat and capitulation.

Indeed, Churchill now found himself criticised from all sides. To the Prime Minister of Australia, John Curtin, the loss of Singapore was always going to be 'an inexcusable betrayal', and viewed from Australia and New Zealand, Britain should have done more to secure Singapore's defence.[30] Yet as the War Cabinet noted on 16 February, as soon as Singapore had fallen, 'In retrospect, it now seemed a pity that we had sent the 18th Division'.[31] Churchill was simultaneously vulnerable to the charges of not having done enough to reinforce Singapore, and of having only sent reinforcements when it was too late for them to be effective. The same was clearly true of the *Prince of Wales*. Not only had the Prime Minister insisted on the ship's despatch, but he had also chosen to publicise the fact, as a deterrent to Japan and a reassurance to Australia and New Zealand.

Churchill told the War Cabinet of the 'grievous loss' caused by the sinkings on the evening of 10 December, which, 'coming on top of the disaster which the Americans had sustained at Pearl Harbor, entirely changed the balance of naval forces in the Pacific', and meant 'we might have to take a lot of punishment in this area'. But he then spoke of the significance of the American entry into the war, the German defeats on the Eastern Front, and the turning of the tide in Libya (not knowing that it would shortly turn again). 'These developments far outweighed the

---

[29] TNA, CAB 65/29, WM (42) 9.

[30] CAC, Churchill Papers, CHAR 20/69A/6-8.

[31] TNA, CAB 65/25, WM (42) 21.

Churchill emerging from 10 Downing Street, May 1940. Behind him is Brendan Bracken, disliked by many in the establishment, as one of the new Prime Minister's myrmidons. (Churchill Archives Centre (CAC), CSCT 5/4/15)

ACTION THIS DAY

PRIME MINISTER'S PERSONAL MINUTE

10, Downing Street,
Whitehall.

S q/S for War
C.I.G.S.

SERIAL No. M. 523/1

S.O. 2
an on this

1.   Naturally we all wish to make an end in Abyssinia. Let me have a short account of the position. How many troops have we still operating from the Sudan and Kenya in Abyssinia and on the L. of C.

            (a) ration strength
            (b) fighting strength

S.O. 11 must provide this.

Air Ministry will provide by midday

MoS a

setting forth the principal formation, by brigades or columns. What is the total number of transport vehicles assigned to these forces? What is the Air Force strength in personnel, and in Squadrons, and in effective machines? What is the number of troops and transport now being moved northwards? Where is the Duke of Aosta, and what is the number of troops under his control? What is their condition, and what are the prospects of reducing him? When can this be expected? When do the rains come, and how do they affect the problems?

M.t.3.c
to provide
a note by midday

MoS b

2.   What are the remaining forces in the Sudan and in Kenya that have not crossed the Abyssinian frontier (on

Action This Day! This simple red label came to epitomise Churchill's whole approach to waging war. (CAC, MISC 55/5)

The sinking of the French fleet at Mers-el-Kebir on 3 July 1940 marked a turning point for Churchill: the Rubicon had been crossed, and a new war strategy was now needed. (Historic Military Press)

Leading from the front at a meeting with General Sikorski at Downing Street in August 1940, but the picture also captures some of those who wrestled with the fall of France, including (at top of steps) Lord Halifax (in spotted tie), Clement Attlee (moustache) and Arthur Greenwood (light suit). Archibald Sinclair and Desmond Morton watch on from behind the railings. (CAC, CHPH 12/F1/38)

'A great hour to live': Churchill and President Roosevelt seated side by side on the deck of HMS *Prince of Wales*, Sunday, 10 August 1941. (CAC, CSCT 5/4/40)

'"Good old Winnie", they cried. "We thought you'd come and see us. We can take it. Give it 'em back".' This photograph was taken in Bristol in April 1941. It captures Churchill's defiant spirit during the German bombings. (CHPH 12/F1/50)

COPY NO: _1_

M O S T   S E C·R E T

NOTE: This document should not be left lying about and, if it
is unnecessary to retain, should be returned to the
Private Office.

P R O P O S E D   D E C L A R A T I O N

B. ~~ALTERNATIVE VERSION - i.e. VERSION "A"~~
~~INCORPORATING NEW PARAGRAPH PROPOSED BY~~
~~CABINET IN ABBEY TELEGRAM NUMBER:- 31.~~

       The President of the United States of America and the
Prime Minister, Mr. Churchill, representing His Majesty's
Government in the United Kingdom, being met together, deem it
right to make known certain common principles in the national
policies of their respective countries on which they base their
hopes for a better future for the world.

       First, their countries seek no aggrandisement,
territorial or other;

       Second, they desire to see no territorial changes
that do not accord with the freely expressed wishes of the
peoples concerned.

       Third, they respect the right of all peoples to choose
the form of government under which they will live; and they
wish to see self-government restored to those from whom it
has been forcibly removed.

       Fourth, they will endeavour, with due respect to their
existing obligations, to further the enjoyment by all peoples
of access, on equal terms, to the trade and to the raw
materials of the world which are needed for their economic
prosperity.

       Fifth, they support fullest collaboration between
Nations in economic field with object of securing for all
peoples freedom from want, improved labour standards, economic
advancement and social security.

       Sixth, they hope to see established a peace, after the
final destruction of the Nazi tyranny, which will afford to
all nations the means of dwelling in security within their own
boundaries, and which will afford assurance to all peoples
that they may live out their lives in freedom from fear.

       Seventh, they desire such a peace to establish for all nations
safety on the high seas and oceans.

       Eighth, they believe that all of the nations of the
world must be guided in spirit to the abandonment of the use
of force. Because no future peace can be maintained if land,
sea or air armaments continue to be employed by nations which
threaten, or may threaten, aggression outside of their
frontiers, they believe that the disarmament of such nations
is essential pending the establishment of a wider and more
permanent system of general security. They will further the
adoption of all other practicable measures which will lighten
for peace-loving peoples the crushing burden of armaments.

Private Office.
August 12, 1941

Copy No.1 of the proposed *Atlantic Charter* declaration, complete with Churchill's
faded annotations, 12 August 1941. He claimed the first draft as 'a British production
cast in my own words'. (CAC, WCHL 13/2)

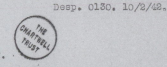

```
┌─────────────────────────┐
│    MOST SECRET          │
│  CIPHER TELEGRAM        │
└─────────────────────────┘
```

SERIAL No. T 206/2

MOST SECRET.

From:- The War Office.

To:- C.-in-C., S.W. Pacific.

Desp. 0130. 10/2/42.

MOST IMMEDIATE.

62733   Cipher (M.O.1) 10/2.

        CLEAR THE LINE. Following Personal from Prime Minister
to General Wavell.

        I think you ought to realise the way we view the
situation in Singapore. It was reported to the Cabinet by the
C.I.G.S. that Percival has over 100,000 men of whom 33,000 are
British and 17,000 Australian. It is doubtful whether the
Japanese have as many in the whole Malay Peninsula, namely
five divisions forward and a sixth coming up. In these
circumstances defenders must greatly outnumber Japanese forces
who have crossed the Straits and in a well-contested battle they
should destroy them. There must at this stage be no thought of
saving the troops or sparing the population. The battle must be
fought to the bitter end at all costs. The 18th Division has a
chance to make its name in history. Commanders and Senior Officers
should die with their troops. The honour of the British Empire
and of the British Army is at stake. I rely on you to show no
mercy to weakness in any form. With the Russians fighting as
they are and the Americans so stubborn at Luzon, the whole
reputation of our country and our race is involved. It is
expected that every unit will be brought into close contact with
the enemy and fight it out. I feel sure these words express
your own feeling and only send them to you in order to share your
burdens.

C. 4. (Telegrams)   Copies to:-

                              S. of S.
                              C.I.G.S.
                              Col. Jacob (10 copies)

                              The King.

'It is expected that every unit will be brought into close contact with the enemy and fight it out.' Churchill's telegram to General Wavell regarding Singapore, 10 February 1942. (CAC, CHAR 20/70/9)

Churchill and Stalin at their first meeting in August 1942. It was not all smiles, and Churchill later likened his mission to 'carrying a large lump of ice to the North Pole'. (CAC, BRDW I Photo 5)

Churchill in the Western Desert with General Dorman-Smith (far left) and General Auchinleck (right), August 1942. Both generals are about to be sacked. (CAC, CHPH 12/F1/80)

With General Giraud, the President and General de Gaulle at the press conference in Casablanca, January 1943. 'It was then that the President suggested, as if it were a happy thought that had just entered his mind, that we might call this the "Unconditional Surrender" Meeting.' (CAC, CHPH 1A/F3/1)

The British Prime Minister spent Christmas Day 1943 recovering from pneumonia at General Eisenhower's villa in Carthage. His illness seems to have been induced as much by mental frustration as physical exhaustion. He is shown flanked by Eisenhower and General 'Jumbo' Wilson. (CAC, KINNA 1/4)

A show of Cabinet solidarity as Churchill returns to Britain after his extended period of illness in January 1944. The Prime Minister is shown shaking hands with Clement Attlee, while Anthony Eden, Sir John Anderson and Lord Woolton look on. (CHPH 1A/F3/21)

Churchill being cheered by troops, c1944. Such occasions were almost as important for his own morale as for those he was visiting. (CAC, CSCT 7/6)

The infamous percentages agreement, 9 October 1944, ticked top right by Stalin. This was horse trading at the highest level, by which Churchill hoped to strengthen bilateral relations with the Soviet Union and preserve the British Empire's dominance in the Mediterranean. (CAC, CHUR 4/356/173)

With Greek Regent, Archbishop Damaskinos of Athens. On meeting him, Churchill seems to have undergone his own immediate Damascene conversion, writing in the most glowing terms about this 'magnificent figure' who 'impressed me with a good deal of confidence'. (CAC, BRDW I Photo 1)

2,633

(218)

CENTRE OF PUBLIC OPINION   12th June, 1945.

Questionnaire No.42.

REPORT ON QUESTION NO.3

"Whom would you like to see as Prime Minister

following the General Election?"

RESULT

CHURCHILL..............	48%	
EDEN....................	18%	
ATTLEE.................	13%	
BEVIN..................	5%	
CRIPPS.................	4%	
MORRISON..............	4%	
SINCLAIR..............	1%	
GREENWOOD.............	1%	
OTHERS................	2%	
Don't Know...........	4%	
	100%	

'Whom would you like to see as Prime Minister following the General Election?'
Churchill would have been pleased by what he read, but it should have asked which
party people were going to vote for. (CAC, CHAR 2/548B/218)

With Clementine in his constituency on polling day, 5 July 1945. She felt he should have retired but he was not ready 'to be put on a pedestal'. (CSCT 5/5/141)

immediate consequences of the position in the Far East, serious as they were'.[32] Two days later, in a telegram to the Prime Minister of Australia, he asserted that the 'Accession of United States as full war partners makes amends for all and makes the end certain'.[33] He defended his actions again to Curtin in a telegram of 19 January, in which he 'took the fullest responsibility for the main priorities and general distribution of our resources' since becoming Prime Minister, and confirmed that he 'deemed the Middle East a more urgent theatre'.[34] Such arguments also formed a key part of his defence to parliament in January.[35] His confidence in himself and his strategy remained. General Brooke, a not uncritical observer of Churchill, noted in his diary for 16 February, the day after the fall of Singapore, that the Prime Minister was 'on the whole in a very good mood', and later added, 'This was typical of Winston, in a real crisis he was always at his best, and stood all the heavy shocks without flinching'.[36] Yet some of that Churchillian bravura may have been for show. According to Gerald Pawle, whose information would have come from Churchill's aide Commander Thompson, 'he asked a senior naval officer point-blank what he considered were the views of the rank and file of the country. Did they accept what they read in the Press, or were they really prepared to support him in the bad days?'[37] Whatever the answer, he now needed to quell the opposition at home and abroad, restore confidence, and reassert his authority.

Let us look then at how Churchill managed the unfolding crisis at home. The sinking of HMS *Prince of Wales* and HMS *Repulse* was reported in *The Times* of 11 December, which warned that 'searching questions will be in the minds of everyone; and public opinion will not be satisfied unless it has the assurance that the Government have faced them unflinchingly and drawn the necessary conclusions from the answers to them'.[38] The newspaper articulated the widely held belief that lessons had not been learnt from previous operations in Crete and that the two ships-of-war had been doomed without adequate fighter support. Churchill was aware that the sinkings and the sudden Japanese advance was likely to create demand in the House of

---

[32] TNA, CAB 65/20, WM (41) 126.
[33] CAC, Churchill Papers, CHAR 20/46/91.
[34] CAC, Churchill Papers, CHAR 20/68B/116-117.
[35] *Hansard*, House of Commons Debate, Vol. 377, cc359-383, 21 January 1942.
[36] Danchev & Todman (eds), *Alanbrooke Diaries*, p.230.
[37] Pawle, *The War & Colonel Warden*, p.163.
[38] *The Times*, Issue 49106, 11 December 1941, *The Times* Digital Archive 1785-2011 (Gale); accessed June 2017.

Commons for discussion, and by the 12th he was already anticipating that, 'If there was strong criticism, this should be resolutely dealt with'. Knowing that he was about to depart for his vital conference talks with Roosevelt in the United States, he told his Cabinet colleagues that any such debate should be held in secret session, with arrangements that, 'a Labour critic would be answered by a Labour Member, a Liberal critic by a Liberal and so forth'.[39] His was a national government and it was vital that it spoke with one voice.

By the time Churchill arrived back from North America in January, and against the backdrop of the worsening position in the Far East, it was clear that discontent in press and parliament was growing. The latest Pacific reverses had provided a focus for concerns about policy and strategy that had been simmering for some time, perhaps inevitably after two years of war and hardship. Sir Charles Wilson, later Lord Moran, Churchill's doctor, recalled travelling with the Prime Minister, on the train back to London on the final leg of his return journey on 17 January. Having expressed his satisfaction on the 'good job of work' done with the President, and his confidence that, 'the House will be pleased with what I have to tell them', Churchill opened the morning papers to be confronted with a public opinion that 'seemed to be baffled by the way things had gone wrong'. 'He put down the *Manchester Guardian* with an angry gesture. "There seems to be plenty of snarling," he said in a tired voice'.[40]

Some of this snarling was soon coming from influential and therefore potentially damaging sources. The former Australian Prime Minister Robert Menzies published a letter in *The Times* on 21 January voicing his belief that Australia deserved better representation in the running of the war, either in a new Empire Cabinet, or on a controlling body for the Pacific theatre, or through a permanent representative on the British War Cabinet.[41] Then William Beveridge, Master of University College, Oxford, and an influential social reformer (soon to unveil his Beveridge Report), unleashed a broadside that accused Churchill of failing to learn the lessons of 1916. The Prime Minister should adopt the policy introduced by Lloyd George in the last war of having a War Cabinet composed solely of Ministers without departmental responsibility. He should employ only the best people, regardless of party concerns and personal loyalties. He should reorganize key government departments, and he

---

[39] TNA, CAB 65/20, WM (41) 127.
[40] Moran, *Struggle for Survival*, p.24.
[41] *The Times*, Issue 49139, 21 January 1942, *The Times* Digital Archive 1785-2011 (Gale); accessed June 2017.

should relinquish his post as Minister of Defence, to create 'time for all his essential tasks of initiative, judgement, foresight and co-ordination'.[42] Such a comparison with the First World War would have set Churchill's alarm bells ringing. Similar criticisms of Asquith's Cabinet, combined with a munitions shortage and the failure of the Dardanelles operation, had cost Churchill his job at the Admiralty in 1915, and ultimately led to Asquith's fall as Prime Minister in 1916. Yet, as we have seen, the lesson that Churchill had taken away from those events was the need to concentrate executive power not to dilute or relinquish it.

Beveridge's intervention had been timed for maximum impact before the key discussion in the House of Commons. Churchill had already decided to hold this in order to head off criticism. He now determined to call the bluff of his detractors by demanding a Vote of Confidence in his government. On 27 January, he stood in the House of Commons and announced a three-day debate on the war, in which 'Any member will be free to say anything he thinks fit about or against the Administration or against the composition or personalities of the government, to his heart's content...'. He admitted that there would be more bad news from the Far East, and that 'Wrapped up in this bad news will be many tales of blunders and shortcomings, both in foresight and action'. Then he dealt with some of the charges that he felt might be levelled against him. It had been necessary to concentrate against Rommel in the Middle East; it would have been wrong to countenance a 'Second Front now' which might have led to 'another and far worse Dunkirk'; and 'while facing Germany and Italy here and in the Nile Valley we have never had the power to provide effectively for the defence of the Far East'. It had been government policy to avoid war with Japan 'until we were sure that the United States would also be engaged'. He refused to offer up 'scapegoats to public displeasure', promised that Singapore would 'be fought to the last inch', and declared that he would not put any obstacle in the way of the return of Australian troops to their homeland. It was a bravura performance that ended with a clever reminder to his audience of the complexities of the international scene, and of the fact that they only enjoyed the luxury of being able to criticise, because his government had brought them successfully through the threat of invasion:

I must confess to feeling the weight of the war upon me even more than in the tremendous summer days of 1940. There are so many fronts which

---

[42] *The Times*, Issue 49143, 26 January 1942, *The Times* Digital Archive 1785-2011 (Gale); accessed June 2017.

are open, so many vulnerable points to defend, so many inevitable misfortunes, so many shrill voices raised to take advantage, now that we can breathe more freely of all the turns and twists of war.[43]

His intention was to lance the boil and prevent discontent from festering and developing into a more serious and coherent opposition, particularly as things might well get worse in Singapore. To this end, it had been decided not to move the Vote of Confidence until the second day of the debate, thereby allowing everyone, including supporters of the government, to voice reasonable criticism without fear of disloyalty on the first.[44] This was a calculated and managed gamble. Churchill had seen how quickly the House had turned against Neville Chamberlain after Narvik in May 1940, and was keen to head off any possibility, however unlikely, of a repetition. Yet, it had been the debate over Norway, and some of the powerful speeches made within it, that had led directly to Chamberlain's fall, and so he knew he risked opening a Pandora's box.

In the ensuing first day of debate, many criticisms were certainly made. Frederick Pethick-Lawrence, serving as the official leader of the opposition (while the Labour Party leaders were in the Government) and representing Edinburgh East for the Labour Party, complained that 'a smokescreen had been put over events in the Pacific', and asked why the *Prince of Wales* and *Repulse* had been sent without air cover. Major Arthur Henderson, representing Kingswinford for Labour, said that there was 'a good deal of dissatisfaction in the ranks of the workers of this country', and called for the creation of a Minister of Production. This was taken up by the Liberal MP for Wolverhampton East, Sir Geoffrey Mander, who argued among other things that there should be 'one individual Minister in charge of the three production Departments', as 'We have failed in production'. Sir Herbert Williams, Conservative member for Croydon South, wanted a restructured War Cabinet and the Prime Minister removed from his position as Minister of Defence, arguing, 'I do not want to change the Prime Minister. I want, as somebody said, a changed Prime Minister'. He predicted dire consequences for Churchill if changes were not made, arguing that 'Within a measurable period of time, however, it will not be this Government that will crash, but he himself will crash, and he will have brought the trouble on himself'.[45]

[43] *Hansard*, Vol. 377, cc359-383, House of Commons Debate, 27 January 1942.
[44] TNA, CAB 65/25, WM (42) 10.
[45] *Hansard*, Vol 377, cc359-383, House of Commons Debate, 27 January 1942.

Churchill was banking on the fact that he retained the backing of the three major political parties, that his own personal standing in the country and on the international stage meant that there was no alternative Prime Minister, and that he could face down his opponents with a strong parliamentary performance. In the short term his strategy was successful. While the debate included a lot of criticism, the opposition lacked leadership, ranged across too many issues to be effectively focused, and, with very few exceptions, was not specifically directed against the Prime Minister, whom most speakers still sought to defend. Sir Geoffrey Mander summed up the prevailing attitude with a typically British cricketing analogy, 'On the front bench we have a splendid captain but a mixture of first, second and third elevens'.[46]

Churchill won his Vote of Confidence by four hundred and sixty-four to one. The concerns and criticisms of most ordinary backbench members of parliament were superseded by the need to appear loyal and patriotic, but a significant level of dissent and disquiet had been exposed. Yet the victory was not quite as absolute as the figures might suggest. The full membership of the House of Commons was 615.[47] Some were no doubt on active service, but many had stayed away or abstained, and Churchill was rattled enough to complain to one of his coalition partners, Liberal Party Leader Archibald Sinclair, about the failure of six of the twenty Liberal members to actively support the government.[48] The question for the Prime Minister was what would happen if things did not improve?

Of course, they did not improve. Singapore was not to be fought to the last inch, and faced with the perfect storm of defeat in the Far East, reverses in the Middle East, and embarrassments in the Channel, Churchill quickly and quietly shelved his refusal to 'offer up scapegoats' and set about a major reconstruction of his government. He had learned the lessons of 1915 and his aim was now to regain the initiative by making changes on his own terms, before they were forced on him by public opinion and parliament.

One of the main criticisms in press and parliament was of failures in production and supply. Churchill had hitherto resisted the creation of a Minister of Production, a single super Minister in the War Cabinet, to help co-ordinate the activities of the Ministry of Supply, the Ministry of Aircraft Production and the Admiralty in producing equipment for the armed services, and charged with improving cooperation across

---

[46] *Hansard*, Vol 377, cc359-383, House of Commons Debate, 27 January 1942.
[47] *Whitaker's Almanack 1941*, p.296.
[48] Churchill, *The Second World War*, Vol. IV, p.63.

government. He may have feared the creation of a powerful Cabinet rival. When the issue had been raised a year earlier, he had claimed that such change would undermine Cabinet government and be a step towards a 'Dictator country'.[49] He had preferred to delegate to Cabinet committees composed of the ministers with the authority to act, while using Professor Lindemann and his statistical unit to liaise with the relevant departments and maintain a watching brief, drawing the 'attention of the Prime Minister to short-falls in programme or dangerous running down of stocks'.[50] Yet, at the Atlantic Meeting in August, the American military leaders had made clear their frustrations at having to deal with so many different and sometimes competing departments over requests for British military supplies. President Roosevelt had appointed one man, the business leader Donald Nelson, to supervise the whole field of American production; making him Chairman of the US War Production Board and Director of Priorities. While the January meetings in Washington had set up new Anglo-American Combined Raw Materials and Shipping Adjustment Boards with committees in London and Washington DC.[51] With failure in the Far East as a catalyst, Churchill now bowed to all these pressures and announced the creation of a new ministry.

While this move was likely to be popular at home and abroad, his choice of minister to fill this new role was much more difficult. Churchill initially appointed Lord Beaverbrook, who had served both as Minister of Aircraft Production and then as Minister of Supply, initially making him Minister of War Production. Beaverbrook accepted and served very briefly, from 4-19 February, before resigning. His official reason was ill health, citing his asthma, which Churchill later explained away as masking a probable nervous breakdown.[52] The reality was more complex. By 19 February, the pressure of events and the resulting worsening political situation at home was forcing Churchill to push through a more radical reconstruction of his government. In particular, he was coming under pressure to find a role for Sir Stafford Cripps, the newly returned Ambassador from Moscow.

A famously austere figure, Cripps was almost the anti-Churchill. Tall, lean, ascetic, teetotal and vegetarian, he was a practising Christian socialist who looked to the Soviet Union as our natural ally rather than the United States. He had also been thrown out of the Labour Party

---

49 CAC, Churchill Papers, CHAR 9/146A/5-13.
50 Nuffield College, Cherwell Papers, F43/8a.
51 Churchill, *The Second World War*, Vol. IV, p.55; TNA, CAB 65/25, WM (42) 8.
52 Churchill, *The Second World War*, Vol. IV, p.66.

for his pro-communist views. The arrival of Russia in the conflict had massively raised his public profile and popularity, and after his return to Britain on 23 January, his reputation had been further enhanced by a successful press conference and BBC broadcast. The confidence debate in January had included calls for his inclusion in the War Cabinet. Churchill's later history of this episode damns Cripps with faint praise, claiming that Leftists and their press credited him with doing more 'than any living man' to bring Russia into the war, and that some on the extreme Left appeared to regard him as worth running as an alternative Prime Minister. He claimed to be bringing Cripps within the fold, because he liked and admired him, acting entirely on the merits of the case. But this was more about politics and silencing a potential focal point for opposition. He did not want to give Cripps the powerful new Production portfolio. Instead he first offered him the subordinate position of Minister of Supply, made vacant by Beaverbrook's initial promotion. When Cripps declined, clearly holding out for something more, and faced with a resurgence of criticism over the fall of Singapore and the *Scharnhorst* escape, Churchill brought him into the War Cabinet as Lord Privy Seal (previously held by Attlee), and made him Leader of the House.[53]

Up to this point the office of Leader of the House had been held by Churchill himself. The role involved organising government business in the Commons, and ironically Churchill's relinquishment of the office is also a testament to his mastery of it. It was a clever way of making Cripps responsible for presenting the Cabinet line in parliament, and therefore less able to criticise it (ultimately, he would resign from the role and serve out the war as Minister of Aircraft Production). Moreover, it showed Churchill responding to the criticism that he was overburdened and setting aside some of his responsibilities, without giving up what was really important to him. Cadogan wrote at the time that 'He will not give up Ministry of Defence', and Churchill was very clear when writing his history that, had he been deprived of it, he would not have remained an hour in office.[54] The whole nature of his war premiership rested on his direct contact with the military Chiefs of Staff and his ability to keep control of both policy and strategy. In his speech to parliament after the Cabinet reconstruction, he chose to downplay the significance of his dual role, arguing that there was nothing he could not do as Minister of Defence which he could not do as Prime Minister, and stressing that it was his practice to leave the

---

[53] Churchill, *The Second World War*, Vol. IV, p 56, p.63 and pp.69-70.
[54] Dilks (ed), *Cadogan Diaries*, p.434; Churchill, *The Second World War*, Vol. IV, p.80.

Chiefs of Staff alone, subject to his 'general supervision, suggestion and guidance'.[55] One can only imagine that his Chiefs would have seen this as an important qualification, given the level of such supervision, suggestion and guidance.

Beaverbrook opposed the plan to promote Cripps. It was a rare moment, as he found himself in agreement with the Labour members of the Cabinet, who saw Cripps as a renegade from their Party. But when Churchill chose to appease Attlee by making him Deputy Prime Minister, a role he had effectively been playing already by chairing the Cabinet when Churchill attended the Atlantic Meeting, this was a step too far for Beaverbrook and he stormed out of the Cabinet. Some have implied that he was lining himself up for a possible succession if Churchill lost office, but it seems more likely he recognised that he was the focus of considerable hostility within the Cabinet and parliament, and felt he could do more to promote himself and his causes, like aid to Russia, from outside.[56] Indeed, though Beaverbrook was one of his closest confidants, Churchill may have seen this as an opportunity to distance himself from a minister who was hated by the Labour Party and had become politically divisive, and whose 'very strong personal antagonisms' with Ernest Bevin, the Minister of Labour, would surely only have worsened had he become Minister of Production.[57] Clementine Churchill, for one, was not sad to see him go, regarding him as a disruptive influence in her husband's government, advising him to, 'Try ridding yourself of this microbe which some people fear is in your blood- Exorcise this bottle imp… '.[58] One senses that Churchill found it much harder, viewing both Beaverbrook as an old friend and as a counterweight to the socialists in his government. As we will see, the 'Beaver' would remain an influential voice in Downing Street.

Beaverbrook's departure allowed Churchill to install Oliver Lyttelton, another close colleague and Conservative, as the new Minister of Production. Lytellton was an experienced businessman, who had already served in the wartime government as President of the Board of Trade and as Resident Minister in the Middle East; a trusted pair of hands, he was more acceptable to the Labour members of the coalition.

---

[55] *Hansard*, Vol. 378 cc 27-176, House of Commons Debate of 24 February 1942; CAC, Churchill Papers, CHAR 9/154B/246-252.
[56] See Moran, *Struggle for Survival*, pp.25-30; Churchill, *The Second World War*, p.55.
[57] Churchill, *The Second World War*, Vol. IV, pp.66-68; Schneer, *Ministers at War*, pp.133-136.
[58] CAC, Baroness Spencer- Churchill Papers, CSCT 1/26; cited in Soames, M., *Clementine Churchill*, p.351.

At the end of this exercise, Churchill was left with a slightly smaller War Cabinet of seven instead of eight. He was forced to accept the loss of Beaverbrook, chose to drop Labour Minister Arthur Greenwood in place of Cripps, and demoted Kingsley Wood from the War Cabinet while keeping him as Chancellor of the Exchequer. Attlee was now Deputy Prime Minister, but was also given the Dominions Office and the immediate responsibility of dealing with the troublesome Australians. Eden remained Foreign Secretary; Bevin remained Minister of Labour. Sir John Anderson and Oliver Lyttelton, both of whom lacked a political base and were entirely dependent on the Prime Minister's patronage for their position, were now running the key home affairs and production briefs. Churchill had kept the balanced political division of his coalition, while maintaining his control. It is noticeable that he had deliberately ignored the advice of Beveridge and others to create a War Cabinet of high ranking individuals free from departmental responsibility. His first Cabinet of May 1940 had been constructed largely of such figures, and ever since, as he had grown into the role, he had sought to move away from this policy, and now argued that those in the War Cabinet needed to be able to act as well as talk. No doubt this was true, but the policy had the additional advantage of keeping political rivals busy and focused on specific areas, while he concentrated on the central strategy.

Further down the political chain, he used the opportunity to remove the last remnants of the old regime. The Secretary of State for War, David Margesson, who had served as Chamberlain's Chief Whip, was replaced with the civil servant James Grigg. While Lord Hankey, the former long-serving Cabinet Secretary, whose criticisms of the government had helped create the atmosphere of discontent, was removed as Paymaster General.[59]

The episode is illustrative of a different side of Churchill, and one that is often overlooked, namely that of the tactical politician. The deteriorating situation in the Far East generated real discontent in the House of Commons, which, if mishandled, could easily have escalated. Leo Amery described the mood of the House in February 1942 as 'formidable'. After the fall of Singapore and the escape of the German ships from the Channel, Churchill had faced calls for another debate. Amery noted that 'It was quite clear from the whole tone and temper of the House that if he had adhered to his original policy and flatly refused a Debate the House would have brushed him aside'.[60]

<hr>

[59] Churchill, *The Second World War*, Vol. IV, pp.68-75; Schneer, *Ministers at War*, p.132.
[60] CAC, Amery Papers, AMEL 7/36.

In the event, Churchill's changes to his government meant that the opposition dissipated. He used the crisis to tighten his control, while appearing to make concessions.

Churchill the tactician and conciliator was also evident on the international stage, where the fallout from defeat in Singapore had prompted a crisis in relations with Australia. The sudden loss of British and American naval dominance in the Pacific exposed Australia to attack. The war was suddenly in her back yard, and, not surprisingly, her government was not prepared to sit back and let Britain decide her fate. Prime Minister Curtin had caused consternation in London by publishing a New Year's message on 27 December that spoke of Australia looking to America for the 'shaping of a plan, with the United States as its keystone', and 'free from any pangs as to our traditional links of kinship with the United Kingdom'.[61] Having ordered the withdrawal of the two Australian Divisions from the Middle East, the Australian Prime Minister then bombarded Churchill with telegrams, urging Allied naval concentration against the Japanese, requesting that Australia be included in the newly created South Western Pacific Theatre and placed under the protection of the American fleet, demanding a voice in Pacific Strategy, a seat on the British War Cabinet, and calling for the reinforcement of troops already fighting in Malaya. His telegram of 6 January, which would have reached Churchill in America, spoke of the 'overwhelming views of the Australian people on their right to be heard' and criticised a strategical approach that was 'not well conceived'.[62]

Things had reached a low by 18 January when Curtin sent a frank telegram complaining that, 'As far back as 1937 the Commonwealth Government received assurances that it was the aim of the United Kingdom Government to make Singapore impregnable', implied that Australia had been misled over 'the conception of the Empire and local defence', and ended with a strong assertion of their right to respond by making their own policy.[63] When erroneous information reached him that the Defence Committee (Operations) had considered abandoning Singapore, Curtin wrote in the most forthright terms that it,

> would be regarded here and elsewhere as an inexcusable betrayal. Singapore is a central fortress in the system of Empire and local defence…

---

[61] Black, D., 'Biography of John Curtin', website of the John Curtin Prime Ministerial Library, http://john.curtin.edu.au/resources/biography/details.html, accessed June 2017.

[62] CAC, Churchill Papers, CHAR 20/68A/3-5, 12, 36-38, & 58.

[63] CAC, Churchill Papers, CHAR 20/68B/107-108.

we understood that it was to be made impregnable and in any event it was to be capable of holding out for a prolonged period until the arrival of the main fleet. ... On the faith of the proposed flow of reinforcements we have acted and carried out our part of the bargain. We expect you not to frustrate the whole purpose by evacuation.[64]

Much Cabinet time in January 1942 was given over to discussing the Australian position. Sir Earle Page, a senior Australian politician, was in London and invited to attend War Cabinet meetings. It was Page who told Curtin of the proposed evacuation, though in fact the Defence Committee had agreed to prioritise the defence of Singapore and had only been discussing hypotheticals. Page's presence clearly annoyed General Brooke who accused him of wasting time.[65] Yet, whatever Churchill's true feelings, and one suspects he regarded the Australian demands as an unwelcome complication, the Prime Minister deliberately chose the path of conciliation.

Churchill and Roosevelt had agreed to the creation of two complementary political bodies to help co-ordinate the war against Japan; a Far East Council in London and a Pacific Council in Washington DC. Australia and New Zealand, as Commonwealth countries, were to be represented from London. When Curtin objected, believing that the real decisions would now be made by the President and Combined Chiefs in America, Churchill argued that 'the wisest course was not to oppose their wishes' (this did indeed prove wise, as the Americans ultimately refused and the Australians had to join the Council in London).[66] He also agreed that an accredited Australian representative should have the right to attend War Cabinet discussions and be heard on the formulation and direction of policy relating to Australia, and he extended identical rights to Canada, South Africa and New Zealand.[67]

Moreover, 'It went without saying that the Australian troops and air squadrons serving overseas must move homewards to the defence of their own country, now that danger threatened it. But effect could only be given to this process very gradually'.[68]

Churchill clearly could not risk a public rupture with Australia at this juncture. The Allies, already on the defensive, needed to present a united front against Japan. He did not want to encourage anti-British sentiment in Australia, which might drive the country closer towards

---

[64] CAC, Churchill Papers, CHAR 20/69A/6-8.
[65] Danchev & Todman, *Alanbrooke Diaries*, p.221.
[66] TNA, CAB 65/25, WM (42) 10.
[67] TNA, CAB 65/25, WM (42) 11.
[68] TNA, CAB 65/29, WM (42) 11.

the United States, and he did not want British public opinion focusing on Imperial disintegration. When he spoke in parliament on 27 January he reported the positive measures he had taken, and affirmed again that, 'We shall not put any obstacle to the return of the splendid Australian troops'.[69]

Yet this did not stop him trying to do exactly that. When it became clear that Singapore was lost, Churchill's focus moved immediately to the defence of Burma. He wanted to divert the Australian troops which Curtin's government had recalled from the Middle East. The Australian Prime Minister had made it clear that they should be returned to Australia, but Churchill sent the convoy to Rangoon on his own authority, confident that his subsequent appeal, endorsed by President Roosevelt, would have to be accepted by the Australians.[70] Instead, he was faced with an unambiguous refusal. Curtin accused him of exceeding his authority, adding to the dangers of the troops, and ignoring the vulnerability of Australia, adding that he had already exposed the Australian forces to conflict in Greece, Malaya and Singapore, all 'without adequate air support'.[71] Confronted with these cutting words Churchill acquiesced and confirmed that the convoy would return to Australia after refuelling at Colombo. He took full responsibility for his action.[72] Ultimately, Curtin did allow Australian troops to remain in Ceylon.[73]

There is no doubting Churchill's own determination to wage war, and he expected everyone around him to share this conviction and to conform to his view of national honour. Whether at Calais, Dunkirk, Crete, Tobruk, Hong Kong or Singapore he exhorted British and Imperial troops to fight till victory or death. He believed in their innate superiority, certainly against the Italians and the Japanese, and felt that success ought to be obtained providing there were sufficient troops on the ground. He was prepared to move heaven and earth when necessary to divert ships, troops and equipment around the globe to get the required numbers in place, but failed, perhaps wilfully, to appreciate the adjustments and delays needed to train, co-ordinate and deploy a modern, multi-national, multi-service force in difficult foreign theatres.

---

[69] *Hansard*, Vol 377, cc569-690, House of Commons Debate, 27 January 1942.
[70] CAC, Churchill Papers, CHAR 20/70/66.
[71] CAC, Churchill Papers, CHAR 20/70/115.
[72] CAC, Churchill Papers, CHAR 20/70/117.
[73] David Day, *The Great Betrayal*, p.355.

Singapore illustrates the limitations of Churchill's power. He could not have foreseen or prevented many of the events that led to the Japanese success. Yet it was also partly a crisis of his own making, as it flowed directly out of his strategy to prioritise other areas, and his decision to rely on the Americans. There is no doubt that it damaged him, both at home and abroad, eroding the political capital that he had accrued in 1940 and weakening the bonds of Empire. He needed to reassert his authority. Yet, his response reminds us how tactical and effective he could be in a real crisis. By suppressing his natural instincts to engage in argument and recrimination, by facing down his critics, by taking responsibility while also restructuring and offering concessions, he avoided the attempts to force a change in his role or his strategy. But it would count for nothing, if his troops could not fight. He needed a victory.

His questioning of events at the time and afterwards suggest that Churchill's confidence in Britain's ability to fight had taken a knock. In the case of the *Prince of Wales*, he could also put names and faces to many of the dead. These were the young officers whose wardroom he had shared, with whom he had watched *That Hamilton Woman*, and been so proudly filmed and photographed only four months before. According to his doctor, it was it was these ghosts that were still haunting Churchill's dreams in 1953.[74]

---

[74] Moran, *Struggle for Survival*, p.101.

Chapter 6

Leadership or Interference?

Why did Churchill sack General Auchinleck?

Colonel Jacob must have been exhausted. As a military assistant to the Minister of Defence, and a member of Churchill's inner circle, he was no stranger to long hours and important errands. But now, after a sleepless night waiting for messages from London, he found himself in the full August heat of the Egyptian desert, hot and dusty after an uncomfortable plane journey from Cairo, standing outside the caravan that formed the field headquarters of General Sir Claude Auchinleck. The 'Auk' was the British Commander-in-Chief in the Middle East, but had temporarily taken direct command of the Eighth Army. He was about to lose both jobs.

'I felt as if I were just going to murder an unsuspecting friend', was how Jacob described his mission to his diary. After the usual exchange of formalities and pleasantries, he handed over the message that he was bearing. The general 'opened it and read it through two or three times in silence. He did not move a muscle, and remained outwardly calm, and in complete control of himself'.[1]

The date was Saturday, 8 August 1942. The letter was from the Prime Minister. The key line was that the War Cabinet had now decided that the moment had come for a change.[2] Auchinleck was being relieved of the Middle Eastern command that he had held for just over thirteen months. Churchill remained in Cairo, feeling it easier for all concerned to wield the knife in writing. He did meet with the general the following day for an hour of conversation at the British Embassy that 'was at once

---

[1] CAC, Jacob Papers, JACB 1/16.
[2] Letter cited in Churchill, *The Second World War*, Vol. IV (1951), pp.421-422.

bleak and impeccable'.[3] For those in the inner circle, like Jacob, this turn of events was no surprise. Churchill had come to Egypt because he was frustrated at previous failures to defeat the enemy in North Africa, was depressed by Auchinleck's refusal to mount an offensive, and was desperate for 'a more vigorous handling of matters'.[4] He was obsessed with obtaining a decisive victory in the Middle Eastern theatre and in defeating the German Commander, General Rommel. When Jacob returned to Cairo to report on his difficult mission, the Prime Minister responded with: '"Rommel, Rommel, Rommel, Rommel", he cried, "'what else matters but beating him?"'[5].

But why did it matter so much in August 1942?

When Churchill had dismissed Wavell and appointed Auchinleck in June 1941, his decision to change the commander had not signified a change in his approach. From the beginning, Auchinleck found himself facing the same barrage of calls for action that had been fired at his predecessor. Churchill was not prepared to accept, after all of Wavell's early gains against the Italians, that the British should be back defending the Egyptian border, while the Germans under Rommel held Libya and threatened Cairo. Stung by defeat in Greece and the German domination of the Balkans, he wanted to show the Russians that Britain was engaged with the enemy and demonstrate to the Americans that the Mediterranean was a worthwhile theatre for their resources. British success would deter Vichy France, Spain or Turkey from joining Germany and Italy, and prove to the people of Britain and the wider Empire and Commonwealth that his policy of waging war could still deliver victory. He had worked hard to contain rising discontent after Singapore, but nationalist agitation was growing in India. While the bombing of Germany might be gradually increased, the Middle East was the only theatre where offensive action could be contemplated.

The Middle Eastern theatre also remained the crucible in which British international prestige might be irrevocably broken. The British were not optimistic about the ability of the Russians to hold, and feared that Hitler's next move might come through the Caucasus against the Iranian and Iraqi oil fields, on which the British war effort depended. If Rommel could be defeated, it would free up the troops needed to meet this new threat. If not, the British could face a two-pronged attack in

---

[3] Churchill, *Second World War*, Vol. IV, p.423.

[4] TNA, CAB 65/31, WM (42) 101.

[5] CAC, Jacob Papers, JACB 1/16.

Egypt from the north and west. What quickly became clear was that the Prime Minister and his new commander had different responses to this dilemma. Churchill favoured gambling everything on a decisive victory in the Western Desert, while the Russians still held and Turkey remained neutral. His general felt the need to secure both flanks.

Auchinleck's difficulties were compounded by British naval losses in the Mediterranean, which allowed his enemy to be reinforced, by the aggressive character of Rommel's leadership, and by the superiority of German tanks, guns and tactics. When he did launch an offensive in November 1941, managing to relieve the garrison that had been doggedly holding out in Tobruk since April, it had immediately prompted a swift counterattack by Rommel that had checked the British forces in the middle of the Libyan Desert at Gazala. In an ominous foreshadowing of future events, Auchinleck had been forced to remove General Cunningham from his command of the Eighth Army and intervene in the battle himself. In the end, the operation, codenamed *Crusader* marked a limited British advance and success, but not one that was conclusive or secure enough to help Churchill as he struggled with the international and domestic reaction to the loss of the British Empire in the Far East.

It can have come as a surprise to no-one then that hardly had the desert dust settled on *Crusader*, before Churchill was cabling Auchinleck again. On 26 February 1942, under the guise of asking the general for his intentions, the Prime Minister made his own wishes very clear: 'According to our figures you have substantial superiority in the air, in armour and in other forces over the enemy. There seems to be danger that he may gain reinforcements as fast or even faster than you. The supply of Malta is causing us increasing anxiety, and anyone can see the magnitude of our disasters in the Far East. Pray let me hear from you'.[6] The aim was clearly to prod Auchinleck into renewed activity, but instead the cable elicited a lengthy response in which the general explained why he did not feel able to take the offensive for several months. There was much in this response that Churchill would not have wanted to hear: the enemy had just been reinforced, it would take time to rectify the inferiority of the British tanks in terms of mechanical reliability and gun-power, as it would the German lead in training and leadership, and the British would not have a numerical superiority in tanks before June. To 'launch a major offensive before then would

---

[6] CAC, Churchill Papers, CHAR 20/70/128.

be to risk defeat in detail and possibly endanger safety of Egypt'.[7] To the Prime Minister, it must have seemed like Wavell and 1940 all over again.

Unfortunately for Churchill, Auchinleck was a careful military commander who was not to be pushed into precipitate action by political considerations. Claiming that news of Auchinleck's proposed delay 'had come as a shock to him', Churchill took the matter to the Defence Committee, but not before drafting a ferocious reply to his Middle Eastern Commander 'in which he poured abuse on him for not attacking sooner'.[8] He was ultimately talked out of sending it by the Chiefs of Staff, helped by new Cabinet addition, Oliver Lyttelton, who as the former Minister Resident in the Middle East, recently returned from Cairo, was able to give chapter and verse on some of the technical difficulties being encountered in the Western Desert.[9]

Blocked in the Defence Committee, Churchill was not prepared to let the matter rest. His blood was up, and he now tried another tack by asking Auchinleck to return home 'for consultation at your earliest convenience'. Again, he was frustrated. The general refused to delegate his authority and leave the Middle East at such a crucial time. Incensed, Churchill replied in the strongest terms, regretting 'extremely' Auchinleck's inability to come home. He accused Auchinleck of endangering Malta, where an early British offensive might help lift the Italian blockade of the beleaguered island, and claimed that it would 'be thought intolerable' that the 635,000 men on his ration strength sat by while the Germans launched another counterstroke on Russia. The claim that the Middle Eastern command was bloated by too many support personnel who did not fight was a recurring Prime Ministerial complaint, no doubt strengthened by the scale of the surrender of Singapore. After stating that it would give him 'the greatest pain to feel that mutual understanding had ceased' he announced that he was sending out Sir Stafford Cripps and the Vice Chief of the Imperial General Staff, General Nye, to discuss the situation.[10] Auchinleck again refused to take the hint, and simply replied that he would welcome the visit.[11]

The issue flared up again a few weeks later, when Auchinleck once more raised the possibility of delaying his offensive, even offering to transfer troops to India in the light of the new threat from the Far

---

[7]   CAC, Churchill Papers, CHAR 20/71A/9-12.

[8]   Danchev and Todman (eds), *Alanbrooke Diaries*, p.235.

[9]   TNA, CAB 69/4, DO (42)7.

[10] CAC, Churchill Papers, CHAR 20/71B/164.

[11] CAC, Churchill Papers, CHAR 20/71B/168.

East. Faced with the possible loss of Malta, and a further defeat in the Mediterranean, Churchill cabled that the fall of the island would be 'a disaster of the first magnitude to the British Empire and probably fatal in the long run to the defence of the Nile Valley'. He urged Auchinleck to 'attack the enemy and fight a major battle if possible, during May; and the sooner the better'. He warned him, with information drawn from decrypted German signals, that the enemy might be planning an attack on him in early June.[12] When Auchinleck's Middle Eastern Defence Committee responded by saying that they did not consider the fall of Malta to be necessarily fatal to the security of Egypt, and welcomed the prospect of an enemy attack as perhaps 'the best thing that could happen' given British defensive preparations, Churchill replied that, 'We are determined that Malta should not be allowed to fall without a battle being fought by your whole army for its retention'. He added that, 'the very latest date for engaging the enemy which we could approve is one which provides a distraction in time to help the passage of the June dark-period convoy'.[13]

Even when forced to confirm his intentions to obey these orders, Auchinleck asked that the offensive not be publicised, insisting that 'owing to the narrowness of our margin of superiority over the enemy, both on the land and in the air' success could not be 'regarded as in any way certain'. Churchill accepted that there could be 'no safe battles' and confirmed he would feel 'even greater confidence' if Auchinleck took direct command at the front, as he had done in the closing stages of *Crusader*. He also urged him to move troops from his northern front in Syria. But Auchinleck demurred.[14] The battle lines had been drawn, both in the Western Desert, and between London and Cairo.

In the end, it was Rommel who moved first. His attack on the British positions at the end of May, though checked initially, quickly took advantage of poor dispositions by General Ritchie, the new Eighth Army Commander. These left the British forces exposed to attack: too far forward, and too isolated from one another, to make a concerted defence. Away from the action, Auchinleck's reports to Churchill were initially positive. On 1 June he cabled that, 'there is no shadow of doubt that Rommel's plans for his initial offensive have gone completely awry and that this failure has cost him dear in men and material'. A week later, he was prepared to admit, 'We know we have had heavy losses, but so has the enemy and so far he has little to show for it

---

[12]   CAC, Churchill Papers, CHAR 20/75/3.
[13]   CAC, Churchill Papers, CHAR 20/75/8-10 & CHAR 20/75/11-12.
[14]   CAC, Churchill Papers, CHAR 20/89.

strategically'. The true seriousness of the situation was revealed when Ritchie ordered a withdrawal towards Egypt. Tobruk was exposed, along with the road towards Cairo. In response to alarmed telegrams from Churchill, Auchinleck first confirmed that Tobruk would be held, but was then forced to backtrack and to admit it might fall.[15] The surrender followed on the 21 June, providing the general with the most unwelcome birthday present.[16]

Churchill was in Washington meeting with President Roosevelt when the news came through. It must have been a moment of agonising personal humiliation. According to Brooke, on what was his very first visit to the White House, the confirmation was hand-delivered by the American Chief of Staff, General Marshall. He later claimed that, 'Neither Winston nor I had contemplated such an eventuality and it was a staggering blow'.[17] While Churchill would later write that, 'At home we had no inkling that the evacuation of Tobruk had ever entered into the plans or thoughts of the commanders'.[18] This was not strictly true. Auchinleck had made it clear to the Chiefs of Staff earlier in the year, after raising the siege of Tobruk, that it would not be his intention to try and hold it should similar circumstances occur in the future, as he no longer regarded it as strategic asset. The defences had accordingly been partly dismantled and neglected. His error was that, in the last few days, he had gone back on this and reassured the Prime Minister and the War Cabinet that the port would be held. The result was that the speed of its fall came as a real shock, for which the Prime Minister, President, parliament, press and public were all unprepared.

For Churchill, Tobruk was a symbol. When Rommel had first advanced, it had withstood his siege for over eight months. Now it had fallen to enemy attack within a matter of hours. He was also conscious that in a desert war, largely fought over country devoid of life, where obscure ridges and depressions routinely gave their names to engagements, Tobruk was a powerful and internationally recognisable name, and one that would now be added to the roll call of British failures, from Narvik to Singapore. One beneficial result was the aid immediately offered by President Roosevelt, which ultimately manifested itself in the form of Sherman tanks and 105mm self-propelled guns. These would help bring victory in the desert, though not in time to help Auchinleck. The more poisonous legacy

---

15 CAC, Churchill Papers, CHAR 20/89.
16 Roberts, A., *Masters and Commanders*, (Allen Lane, 2008), p.3.
17 Danchev & Todman (eds), *Alanbrooke War Diaries*, p.269.
18 Churchill, *The Second World War*, Vol. IV, p.372.

was a further undermining of the relationship between Churchill and his theatre commander. By 30 June, Winston was all for flying out to the Middle East himself. It fell to Brooke to talk him out of it, before confiding to his diary that, 'I cannot imagine anything more trying than Winston descending on one in the middle of a serious battle!!'[19]

Auchinleck was also clearly shaken by the scale of Ritchie's defeat. On 23 June, he sent a message to Brooke offering to resign and suggesting General Alexander as his replacement, writing that 'there is no doubt that in a situation like the present, fresh blood and new ideas at the top may make all the difference between success and stalemate'.[20] There was no possibility of accepting this in the height of battle, though it may have been seen by Churchill. The following day the general cabled the Prime Minister announcing his decision to retreat to a more defensible position well within the Egyptian border. His telegram used the terms 'deeply regret', 'severe blow' and 'heavy defeat'. Both the politician and the general were left trying to come to terms with what had happened. Alamein was less than two hundred miles from Cairo, where evacuations had now commenced. On 3 July, the War Cabinet heard presentations from Brooke and Eden, outlining the contingencies that had been developed by the military and political authorities for the loss of Egypt.[21] The whole British position in the Middle East and, with it, Churchill's main offensive strategy, were now threatened with annihilation.

Recovering from his initial shock, the crisis now brought out the best in Auchinleck. He flew to the front and took over from General Ritchie, sacking yet another Eighth Army commander, and assuming personal control over the battle, as Churchill had wanted him to do from the beginning. He pulled the British and Imperial forces back to El Alamein, where the passage of Rommel's advancing armour was restricted to a narrow corridor between the sea and the Qattara depression. There, he fought a well-orchestrated battle that brought his enemy to a standstill. In an historical analogy that Churchill might in other circumstances have appreciated, the historian, and my predecessor as Keeper of the Churchill Archives, Correlli Barnett, likened this victory to Wellington's repulse of Napoleon at Waterloo, while ruefully noting that 'for Auchinleck there was no Blücher with forty thousand fresh men to come up on the flank and turn defeat into rout'.[22]

---

[19] Danchev & Todman (eds), *Alanbrooke Diaries*, p.275.
[20] Barnett, C., *The Desert Generals*, (2nd edn, Allen & Unwin, 1983), p.180.
[21] TNA, CAB 65/27, WM (42) 85; TNA, CAB 65/31, WM (42) 85.
[22] Barnett, *The Desert Generals*, p.217.

There was no way that Churchill was going to compare the first Battle of El Alamein to a second Waterloo, nor his Commander-in-Chief to Wellington, but he did later grudgingly admit that, 'Auchinleck, once in direct command, seemed a different man from the thoughtful strategist with one eye on the decisive battle and the other on the vague and remote dangers in Syria and Palestine'.[23] Immediately before the battle, he sent some typically last-minute Churchillian advice, urging Auchinleck that 'all uniformed personnel in the Delta and all available loyal man-power' be 'raised to the highest fighting condition'. His figure for the men on the ration strength had now swollen to over 700,000, of whom, 'Every fit male should be made to fight and die for victory'.[24] The familiar refrain was that, 'Egypt should be defended just as drastically as if it were Kent or Sussex".[25] His backing for his general in the field was also slightly barbed, 'Whatever views I may have about how the battle was fought or whether it should have been fought a good deal earlier, you have my entire confidence and I share your responsibilities to the full'. It was a line that was repeated in a telegram of 28 June in which Auchinleck was urged not to vex himself 'with anything except the battle. Fight it out wherever it flows. ...We are sure you are going to win in the end'.[26] A few days later, in words that would have stunned any listening Chiefs of Staff, he told the House of Commons that it was his policy not to worry his generals:

> They have to fight the enemy. Although we have always asked that they should keep us informed as much as possible, our policy has been not to worry them but to leave them alone to do their job. Now and then I send messages of encouragement and sometimes a query or a suggestion, but it is absolutely impossible to fight battles from Westminster or Whitehall. The less one interferes the better.[27]

His interpretation of 'sometimes' would seem to be very wide, and his meaning of 'battle' perhaps very narrow, though once conflict was joined he did show more restraint in contacting Auchinleck directly. More worrying perhaps for the general was his decision to remove a paragraph stating that, 'On general grounds one sh[oul]d be chary

---

[23] Churchill, *The Second World War*, Vol. IV, p.385.
[24] CAC, Churchill Papers, CHAR 20/89.
[25] CAC, Churchill Papers, CHAR 20/89.
[26] CAC, Churchill Papers, CHAR 20/89.
[27] CAC, Churchill Papers, CHAR 9/155/202-203.

of removing Commanders in the field when they h[a]v[e] met w[ith] misfortune'. It implied he may have been keeping his options open.[28]

In the immediate term, his personal telegrams show him harrying others to try and maximise support for the fighting front. He pressed the Ministry of Supply and the War Office over the desert worthiness of tanks, he chased the Chief of the Air Staff over the availability of heavy bombers, and he urged the First Sea Lord to return British battleships to Alexandria. His War Cabinet secretariat were kept busy chasing the progress of reinforcements and supplies, while he took a particular interest in the transit of the American Sherman tanks, though they could not arrive in time to influence the outcome of this battle. He also chose this moment to urge the creation of a Jewish force that might play a role in Palestine, criticising the intransigence of his own officials in the military and Colonial Office for their bias in favour of the Arabs, and suggesting that it might be necessary to make an example of some anti-Semites in high places.[29] There was no doubting his level of personal engagement.

Churchill and Auchinleck were briefly united in fighting the first battle of El Alamein. But once the fighting had ended, in an uneasy stalemate and entrenched positions, the old divisions between Prime Minister and Commander-in-Chief quickly resurfaced. Churchill wanted the offensive resumed: Auchinleck remained wary of defeat and wanted time to build up his forces. The threat of a Russian collapse and a new German front in the Near East hung over them both, but they continued to respond in opposite ways. Auchinleck favoured building up troops throughout his theatre to cope with both threats, while Churchill told him bluntly that, 'The only way in which a sufficient army can be gathered in the northern theatre is by your defeating or destroying General Rommel and driving him at least to a safe distance. ...if you do not succeed in defeating and destroying Rommel, then there is no possibility whatever of making a sufficient transference to the north and we shall continue to be entirely dependent on the Russian front holding'.[30]

In the aftermath of Singapore, Churchill's prestige hinged on success in the Middle East. Yet, as Cadogan confided to his diary on 19 June, there was now a growing fear that 'we are out-generalled everywhere'.[31]

Lord Wedgwood, the veteran Liberal and Labour politician, wrote to Churchill on 4 June, commenting that, 'The fault cannot lie in our

---

[28] CAC, Churchill Papers, CHAR 9/155/243.
[29] CAC, Churchill Papers, CHAR 20/67/6.
[30] CAC, Churchill Papers, CHAR 20/89.
[31] Dilks (ed), *Cadogan Diaries*, p.458.

men. It must be higher up. I don't think the War Office have frowned enough on surrender'.[32] This would certainly have struck a chord. When the fall of Tobruk was debated by the War Cabinet a month later, on 6 July, Churchill was all in favour of drawing up proposals 'defining the conditions which must be satisfied before any General Officer in the field was justified in surrendering'.[33] On 3 July, Julian Amery, the son of Cabinet Minister Leo Amery and an officer just returned from the Middle East, used his connections to secure an interview with the Prime Minister, lobbying him on the subject of poor equipment and bad morale in the Western Desert, and urging him to make a personal visit. It was an intervention that incensed Brooke, cutting as it did across the normal chains of communication and command, causing the general to dismiss Amery as a 'young brute' and 'bar lounger'.[34] But there was another junior officer with even greater access: Churchill's only son Randolph was serving as an officer in the Middle East. He prepared some extensive unofficial briefing notes for his father, including assessments of the main personalities and issues. Among other things, and, in a tone that was generally critical of the army, it praised the theatre air commanders, Tedder and Conyngham, claimed that 'the average officer of the RAF has an incomparably superior war mind to the average army officer', reported the 'widespread' view that Auchinleck's Chief of the General Staff, General Corbett, was a 'blockhead', and recommended the appointment of an Eighth Army Commander with a better understanding of both tank and desert warfare.[35]

But these private communications were nothing when compared to the storm of criticism that erupted in the public arena in response to the fall of Tobruk. Churchill complained both at the time and afterwards about the 'nagging and snarling' by press and parliament, accusing his critics of feeding enemy propaganda and undermining Britain's reputation throughout the world.[36] It was especially awkward for him to have to read some of the British newspaper comment while in Washington, and to see it start to influence American opinion. The left-wing *Tribune* of 26 June 1942 put the blame for military failure firmly at Churchill's door:

> But the fact must be faced. Words may marshal men for battle. But they do not win them. As a maker of speeches Churchill is supreme. It is

---

[32] CAC, Churchill Papers, CHAR 20/62/47.
[33] TNA, CAB 65/27, WM (42) 86.
[34] Danchev & Todman, *Alanbrooke Diaries*, pp.276-277.
[35] CAC, Churchill Papers, CHAR 20/65/88-97.
[36] Gilbert, *The Churchill Documents*, Vol.17, p.906.

time, however, that he gave place to men who can win battles. It is clear that the central direction of the British war effort is at fault. That central direction is Churchill.

On the subject of his replacement, it concluded:

If no other name springs to the lips it is because nothing can grow in the blighting shades of his oppressive ego. It is time to cut down the tree and let in the light.[37]

While he might have been able to dismiss this, given the political leanings of the *Tribune* and its regular criticism of his leadership under the editorship of long-term Labour critic Aneurin Bevan, he would have struggled to ignore the more coded warning in *The Times* of 29 June, which argued that:

MR CHURCHILL returns to face a week of questioning and criticism and even personal attack. He will have no difficulty in discomfiting those few who wish to overthrow his leadership or his Government, but the hope must be that he will do something much more than that, or rather something very different. Public opinion is prepared for uphill fighting in the present stage of the war but not for faults and deficiencies that it believes to have been preventable.[38]

Within the House of Commons, the 'shrill voices' of a minority were now accompanied by a 'glum attitude' on the part of the majority, and Churchill later reflected that a normal party government 'might well have been overturned at this juncture'.[39] At the end of June, a byelection for the parliamentary seat of Maldon in Essex, not very far from Churchill's own constituency, provided dramatic proof that all was not well. Caused by the death of the incumbent, the Conservative Sir Edward Ruggles-Brise who had held it since 1922, the election was not contested by the main opposition Labour and Liberal parties, who were part of Churchill's national coalition, and should have been an easy victory for the government candidate, who was defending a sizeable majority. Instead, the supposedly safe seat fell to the independent Tom Driberg, a journalist and another prominent critic of the way the war was being run.

---

[37] CAC, Churchill Press Cuttings, CHPC 20.
[38] CAC, Churchill Press Cuttings, , CHPC 20.
[39] Churchill, *The Second World War*, Vol. IV, p.351.

At the beginning of July, while the battle was still raging in the Middle East, Churchill found himself facing another vote of no confidence in parliament. This was the second since the beginning of the year, and, unlike January's, which had been called by the government to face down its opposition, this was a genuine challenge brought by disaffected MPs. As Leo Amery noted in his diary, 'This is the first time that Winston has been directly challenged. Hitherto it has always been in the form of praising him but criticising his colleagues'.[40]

It is true that the motion was easily defeated, by 475 to 25. It is also true that some of the opponents were particularly clumsy in the way they chose to make their case. John Wardlaw-Milne, a Conservative MP, and the proposer of the motion of censure, famously lost the attention of the House with his suggestion that, because of his royal status and despite lacking all relevant experience, the Duke of Gloucester should be given a role as Commander-in-Chief of the Armed Forces. However, such incompetence should not obscure the fact that the debate represented a groundswell of discontent which Churchill knew he could not ignore.

The Prime Minister chose to give the closing speech on 2 July, and was once again forced to sit on the government front bench listening to the criticism of his direction of affairs. This time some of the attacks were both very personal and highly effective, and were made by more substantial political opponents. Aneurin Bevan declared that 'the Prime Minister wins Debate after Debate and loses battle after battle'. He accused Churchill of an outdated 'Maginot minded' approach to warfare, of thinking in medieval terms and of failing to appreciate more modern concepts, such as the role of dive bombers and transport planes. In an attack on the Prime Minister's preferred strategy he argued that the long range bomber was 'not a decisive weapon of war', and called instead for the better integration of the air force with the army and the navy, so that air power could be used in support of ships and troops. He urged the creation of a small War Cabinet of strong men with no departmental interests to act as a 'clamp' on a Prime Minister who 'often mistakes verbal felicities for verbal inspiration', and he advocated a drastic purge of the highest levels of a British army that was riven by class prejudice. In his conclusion, he contrasted the stubborn Soviet defence of Sebastopol (which ironically was about to fall) with the surrender of Tobruk after just twenty-six hours, and demanded a 'Second Front Now' to help the 'lion-hearted Russians'.[41]

---

[40] CAC, Amery Papers, AMEL 7/36.
[41] Gilbert, *The Churchill Documents*, Vol.17, pp.839-850.

Leslie Hore-Belisha, formerly Secretary of State for War under Chamberlain, flung Churchill's own words back at him: quoting Winston's 17 November 1938 speech against appeasement, in which he had called on members of his own party to vote against the government, in order to 'make them act'. He went on to recite many of Churchill's more confident recent predictions of victory in the desert, before stating, 'when I read that he had said we are going to hold Egypt, my anxieties became greater than they otherwise would have been. ...How can one place reliance in judgments that have so repeatedly turned out to be misguided?'. 'In 100 days we lost our Empire in the Far East', he concluded, before asking, 'What will happen in the next 100 days?'[42]

For a Prime Minister who presented himself as a war leader, who saw himself as a defender of the British Empire, and who was clearly identified with a strategy of fighting in the Mediterranean, this was all wounding material. In the end, he carried the day without giving up his powerbase as Minister of Defence or making further concessions, having only just restructured his Cabinet in February, but he must have been conscious that both his position and his room for manoeuvre were weakening. He knew that many of those parliamentarians who had hitherto supported him were becoming privately restless. The fall of Chamberlain had demonstrated how quickly the political landscape could alter. Further defeats would inevitably lead to an escalation of discontent. He needed a victory to defuse the domestic political situation, and he continued to gamble on the Middle East as the only theatre where this could be delivered. He had lost confidence in Auchinleck's ability to deliver it, but time was running out, and press, parliament and public might now lose confidence in him. He had to be seen to act.

It is hardly surprising then that, by late July, Churchill had decided he needed to review the position in the Middle East for himself. The final straw, or at least the excuse he gave the War Cabinet, was a telegram from Auchinleck delaying any further offensive until September. In front of his colleagues, he spoke about the possibility of appointing a new Eighth Army Commander, thereby allowing Auchinleck to 'once more concern himself with the duties of Commander-in-Chief'.[43] Behind the scenes, he may well already have been contemplating the Auk's removal.

This sacking of Auchinleck was subsequently presented by Churchill as a decisive turning point in the war. In his narrative, it allowed him to

---

[42] Gilbert, *The Churchill Documents*, Vol. 17, pp.878-887.
[43] TNA, CAB 65/31, WM (42)101.

install General Alexander as the new theatre commander with General Montgomery (following the death of first choice, General Gott) as head of the Eighth Army; thereby paving the way to victory at the Second Battle of El Alamein.

Supporters of Auchinleck have long argued that he was badly treated by Churchill, both at the time of his dismissal, and later, when Churchill came to write his version of events. The Churchill Archives Centre has a small collection of correspondence between Correlli Barnett and Major-General Eric Dorman O'Gowan, who as Major-General Dorman-Smith served as Auchinleck's personal Chief of Staff during the first Battle of El Alamein, and was dismissed alongside his boss a few weeks later. He was considered by many to be a controversial character, given to unorthodox views and outspoken opinions, whose influence Brooke saw as a contributory factor in Auchinleck's downfall.[44] O'Gowan certainly did not pull his punches in retirement. When, in the fourth volume of *The Second World War*, Churchill published the message he had sent to Attlee on 6 August 1942, claiming that there was no confidence in Auchinleck's command, and referring to the removal of Dorman-Smith and other officers, he found himself facing litigation. In a dispute that was settled out of court, O'Gowan managed to win a clarification, with Churchill forced to concede in later editions that his published remarks should not be taken as 'imputing personal blame to any individual'. The controversy raised questions about Auchinleck's dismissal that were taken up by Correlli Barnett in his book *The Desert Generals*.[45]

O'Gowan believed that, 'the first Battle of El Alamein, the Battle for Egypt, was indeed the turning point of the war for Britain; had we then lost Egypt I cannot see how a successful recovery could be expected, certainly there could not have been a landing in North West Africa'. At its conclusion the Germans were so sewn up that they could neither hope for success in a renewed offensive nor take the necessary decision to pull out, they had lost the initiative and their fate was sealed. He felt that 'Churchill's incessant nagging did not help, but only created a lack of confidence' in Auchinleck, and he accused the former war leader of blackening the reputations of honest soldiers in his later published account: 'Not before in British history has a P.M. displayed quite such cattish meaness'.[46] There was much

---

[44] Danchev & Todman, *Alanbrooke Diaries*, p.224.

[45] Churchill, *The Second World War*, Vol IV, pp.415-417; Barnett, *Desert Generals*, pp.234-235; Reynolds, *In Command of History*, pp.356-360.

[46] CAC, Barnett Papers, BRNT 2, (letters from O'Gowan to Barnett, 27 May 1958; 3 July 1958; 12 July 1958; 14 July 1958).

more in a similar vein. It was ammunition that Barnett was able to deploy in print to support his thesis that the first Battle of El Alamein was the real turning point in the desert campaign, the moment at which Rommel was decisively halted and weakened, and at which 'Auchinleck had saved the Middle East, with all that this implied for the general course of the war'.[47]

With the benefit of hindsight, there is clearly much truth in this. The Allied position at El Alamein was strong and easy to defend and reinforce, while Rommel was weakened with over extended supply lines. But that is not how it appeared at the time, to either Churchill or Auchinleck. The British had been defeated at Gazala, Tobruk had fallen, and Egypt was in danger. El Alamein was the last real defensive position before the Nile Delta. Auchinleck had managed to rally the British forces, but his attempted counter attack had ended in a stalemate. Twice he had tried to take the offensive, and twice he had been thwarted. Twice he had been forced to sack his choice of Eighth Army Commander, first Cunningham and then Ritchie, and even Barnett and O'Gowan both agree that Auchinleck made mistakes in his choice of subordinates. By promoting Ritchie beyond his abilities, above more experienced commanders, and by bringing Dorman-Smith with him from Cairo and imposing him as a personal Chief of Staff on the existing structures of the Eighth Army, Auchinleck had sowed the seeds of discontent in his own ranks.[48] O'Gowan's letters refer to Auchinleck's disagreements with several of his subordinate commanders, as well as his problems with the press.[49] None of this would have mattered with victory, but, as Churchill and his party discovered when they arrived in Cairo, the Eighth Army did not feel itself to have been victorious and the atmosphere was rife with recriminations.

Jacob, who knew many of the senior officers and met with some of them socially, recorded that, while, 'There is a universal respect for General Auchinleck as a big man, and a strong personality. ... Nevertheless, he has not created a coherent Army, and most of the criticisms and explanations which people give are directed to matters which are his immediate concern'. While misfortunes were not universally attributed to inferior equipment, 'All are agreed, however, that faulty leadership and bad tactics were the principal causes of

---

[47] Barnett, *The Desert Generals*, p.217.
[48] Barnett, *The Desert Generals*, p.130 & pp.181-182.
[49] See, for example, CAC, Barnett Papers, BRNT 2, (letter from O'Gowan to Churchill, 3 July 1958).

our defeat'. Even allowing for the inevitable bias, given Jacob's role as a member of the Prime Minister's party, morale in the desert was clearly not high.[50] Churchill wrote to Clementine from Cairo that, 'This splendid army, about double as strong as the enemy, is baffled and bewildered by its defeats'.[51]

Seen from Churchill's perspective, Auchinleck was a Commander who had to be driven to take the offensive, who had refused to engage and consult, who had argued against strategic priorities identified by the Chiefs of Staff and War Cabinet, who did not seem able to maximise the use of the considerable resources that were being prioritised for the Middle East, who had failed to hold Tobruk despite promising to do so, and who had already offered to resign, thereby implying that he had lost confidence in himself. Nor was Churchill acting in isolation. His decision to remove Auchinleck was taken after full consultation with Brooke. Field Marshal Jan Smuts, the Prime Minister of South Africa, whose advice Churchill greatly valued, was summoned to Cairo. The views of experts on the spot like the British Ambassador, Sir Miles Lampson, or the Resident Minister in the Middle East, Richard Casey, were sought.[52]

But the decision must also be seen in the context of grand strategy and of relations with both Russia and the United States. Churchill could not afford to be defeated in the Middle East, but nor did he want to be diverted from it. Yet both Moscow and Washington were reluctant converts to his Mediterranean war.

On 8 April, the notoriously frail Harry Hopkins, friend and emissary to President Roosevelt, arrived in London and delivered a letter from his boss to Winston Churchill. Dated 23.00 hours on 3 April, and written out by hand on green White House paper, it read:

> What Harry and Geo. Marshall will tell you about has my heart & mind in it. Your people & mine demand the establishment of a front to draw off pressure on the Russians, & these peoples are wise enough to see that the Russians are today killing more Germans & destroying more equipment than you and I put together. Even if full success is not attained, the big objective will be.
>
> Go to it! Syria and Egypt will be made more secure, even if the Germans find out about our plans.

---

50 CAC, Jacob Papers, JACB 1/16.
51 CAC, Baroness Spencer-Churchill Papers, CSCT 2/31; cited in Soames, *Speaking for Themselves*, p.466.
52 CAC, Jacob Papers, JACB 1/16.

Best of luck. Make Harry go to bed early, and let him obey Dr Fulton, U.S.N. [US Navy], whom I am sending with him as super-nurse with full authority.[53]

Though couched in the President's informal style, this short and simple message was about grand strategy at the highest level. It marked the opening shot in what would become a long and complex war of words between the Americans and British on the nature and timing of a second front in Western Europe. The President, almost certainly deliberately, had given little warning of the arrival of Hopkins and Marshall, or of the subject they wished to discuss (though as Andrew Roberts has shown British sources in Washington had been able to tip Churchill off[54]). Roosevelt knew from their previous talks in the White House in January that Churchill favoured joint action in the Mediterranean, where American involvement in French North Africa would help the British position in Egypt and Libya. He also knew that the American Chiefs of Staff remained wary of entangling the United States in what they regarded as a peripheral and imperial conflict, and he now questioned how a Mediterranean strategy would help ease pressure on the Russians.

General George Marshall, the US Chief of Staff, favoured a frontal assault on Germany through France. The secret memorandum that he and Hopkins handed over outlined his plan for future operations in Western Europe. Whereas Churchill's previous directives had asserted the primacy of the Middle Eastern theatre, this began with the unambiguous statement that 'Western Europe is favoured as the theatre in which to stage the first major offensive by the United States and Great Britain. By every applicable basis of comparison, it is definitely superior to any other. …Through France passes our shortest route to the heart of Germany'. In eleven pages of typescript it proposed the combined British-American landing of forty-eight divisions on the continent in 1943. This was to be preceded by the build-up of forces and the heavy raiding of the French coast, and was accompanied by contingency plans for a possible 'emergency' landing in France in 1942 in the event of either a Russian or German collapse on the Eastern Front; to take the pressure of an ally or seize the advantage from the defeat of an enemy.[55]

---

[53] CAC, Churchill Papers, CHAR 20/52/29.
[54] Andrew Roberts, *Masters and Commanders*, pp.132-133.
[55] CAC, Churchill Papers, CHAR 20/52/30-73.

While Marshall shared and debated this document with the British Chiefs of Staff, Churchill moved quickly to circulate it to the three service ministers and to Eden and Attlee. Meanwhile, the American visitors were extended every courtesy. Brooke's diary confirms that, in contravention of the President's orders, Hopkins and Marshall were exposed to the full force of late night Churchillian hospitality at Chequers.[56] They were also invited to attend staged meetings of both the Defence Committee and the full War Cabinet.[57]

The problem facing the British was that they could not afford to reject the American plan and alienate the President. As Hopkins said, when he spoke at the Defence Committee meeting on 14 April, 'if public opinion in America had its way, the weight of American effort would be directed against Japan'.[58] Yet if implemented in full, it would mean that all British and American effort would be focused on a return to France. British reinforcements and American supplies to the Mediterranean would have to be curtailed, with the result that all there might be lost, while the British were also relying on some American activity in the Far East to prevent further Japanese incursions towards India. There was a real fear at this point that, between them, the Germans and Japanese could close both ends of the Suez Canal and bring the British Empire to its knees, hence Auchinleck's wariness about his 'northern front' in Turkey and the Caucasus.[59]

Moreover, it was clear from US data, that in the event of an 'emergency' invasion of France in 1942, the Americans were expecting the British to provide most of the air and naval support and would only be able to provide a maximum of eleven divisions, four parachute battalions and ten Anti-Aircraft regiments, of which, because of transport constraints, only three and a half divisions might be guaranteed.[60] Even allowing for the concentration of the Wehrmacht on the Eastern Front, and for the inclusion of all British troops in the United Kingdom, the British experience against German troops in Norway, France and Greece, would suggest that this was nowhere near enough. And how were American forces to get to Britain and then to France? Marshall admitted to the Defence Committee that 'the main difficulties would be found in providing the requisite tonnage, the landing craft, the aircraft and the

---

56 Danchev & Todman, *Alanbrooke Diaries*, p.247.
57 TNA, CAB 65/26, WM (42) 47; CAB 69/4, DO (42) 10.
58 TNA, CAB 69/4, DO (42) 10.
59 Tamkin, N., 'Britain, the Middle East and the "Northern Front", 1941-1942', *War in History*, Vol.15, No.3, 2008, pp.322-323.
60 CAC, Churchill Papers, CHAR 20/52/30-73.

natural escorts'.[61] Portal, Chief of the British Air Staff warned that the fighter force of this country might be wiped out in just two months, if involved in constant operations over the continent without American support.[62]

From the British perspective, this meant that no landing in force could realistically be contemplated in 1942, and that losses would be incurred in other theatres during the long delay while forces for a cross-Channel assault were built up in the United Kingdom.

Yet Churchill led his colleagues in 'cordially accepting the plan', noting 'that there was complete unanimity on the framework' and that, 'The two nations would march ahead together in a noble brotherhood of arms'. His one and important caveat, and a justification he would use for reopening the issue, was that 'it was essential to carry on the defence of India and the Middle East'.[63] But, as we have seen, this did not stop him from interpreting defence as offence and simultaneously pushing Auchinleck to take action in the Western Desert. Indeed, he now needed a victory there more than ever to demonstrate to the Americans the value of his Mediterranean strategy, and to eliminate Rommel while American reinforcements and supplies could still be diverted to Cairo.

Ironically, it was the subsequent British defeat in the desert, and the fall of Tobruk, that prompted the immediate despatch of American tanks and guns to the theatre, and started to draw the Americans away from France and into the Mediterranean. While the United States wanted the decisive battle fought in Western Europe, it was not in their interest to see a complete collapse of the British in the Middle East, as this would have given the enemy control of the Suez Canal and the oil fields in Iraq and Iran, strengthening their front against Russia, and possibly bringing Turkey, Spain, Portugal and Vichy France into the conflict on their side. Nevertheless, the American army still favoured a Europe first policy, and, in response to his President's desire to see US ground forces in action, General Marshall now advocated a limited operation to establish a beachhead in Northern France in the autumn of 1942.

After returning from his meetings at the White House in June, Churchill reported to the War Cabinet on 7 July that, 'It had been agreed in Washington that should continental operations in 1942 prove impracticable, we should immediately consider what could be done

---

[61] TNA, CAB 69/4, DO (42) 10.
[62] TNA, CAB 69/4, DO (42) 10.
[63] TNA, CAB 69/4, DO (42) 10.

elsewhere'. There then followed a long discussion of future possible operations. Brooke criticised it in his diary as 'a dreadful exhibition of amateur strategy by Cabinet Ministers!', while Cadogan's journal recorded that it had been 'very depressing' and blamed the Chiefs of Staff for having no ideas and opposing everything. He quotes Churchill as saying, 'We'd better put an advertisement in the papers, asking for ideas'.[64] Needless to say, the official minutes give only little hints of these divisions, and the diary entries remind us that this meeting was taking place at a time of considerable stress, immediately after the confidence vote in the Commons, with the latest merchant convoy PQ17 to Russia dispersed and under heavy attack, heavy losses being suffered in the Atlantic, and with the battle in the desert hanging in the balance.

Churchill's preference, now endorsed by his colleagues, was for an operation against French North Africa, not least because 'a threat to Rommel's rear might cause the Axis considerable embarrassment'. He felt that, 'the President had always expressed the keenest desire to carry it out'. The Prime Minister also favoured an operation to take northern Norway, 'carried out if possible in conjunction with the Russians' which the Chiefs of Staff deemed impracticable.[65] Brooke was certainly not prepared to consider British operations in the Arctic.[66] Norway apart, it is clear that Churchill and the Chiefs of Staff were already in broad agreement on the strategy for the second half of 1942, and particularly on the need to resist demands for some form of early Second Front in Europe. Seen from Churchill's perspective, it was important to be able to demonstrate a united front to the Americans. He now despatched a telegram to Roosevelt, opposing the idea of a French lodgement, on the grounds that it would curtail the bomber offensive against Germany, absorb too much energy, and ruin the chances of a larger successful operation in 1943, and stating, 'I am sure myself that GYMNAST [codename for operation in North Africa] is by far the best chance of effecting relief to the Russian front in 1942'.[67]

Matters came to a head when General Marshall returned to London in July. The Chiefs of Staff argued against his plan for an autumn landing on the Cherbourg peninsula, and then, working with the Prime Minister, presented a united front to the War Cabinet, who dutifully expressed themselves opposed to the American plan for 1942 and in

---

[64] Danchev & Todman, *Alanbrooke Diaries*, p.277; Dilks (ed), *Cadogan Diaries*, p.461.
[65] TNA, CAB 65/31 WM (42) 87.
[66] Danchev & Todman, *Alanbrooke Diaries*, pp.267-268.
[67] TNA, CAB 65/31 WM (42) 88.

favour of multiple landings on the North African coast.[68] It was the Americans who now blinked. Rather than risk a breach so early in the alliance, Marshall and Roosevelt agreed to delay French operations and give priority to the Mediterranean. In this, they were almost certainly influenced by their own need to divert increasing resources to the Far East.

So far so good for Churchill. But he was fighting this battle on several fronts. Pressure for an intervention in France was also coming from Moscow. A recurring refrain in the parliamentary confidence debates of January and July was the need for a 'Second Front Now' in order to help the Russians, and this had the backing of powerful figures like Lord Beaverbrook, who, freed from the shackles of collective government responsibility, could now use his control over sections of the press to advance this agenda. Maisky, the Soviet Ambassador, lunched with Beaverbrook on 16 July and felt he aspired to the premiership and was using 'Churchill's reluctance to open a second front immediately, to create a situation in the country such that Churchill will have to go'.[69]

It was a problem that was compounded by the sudden suspension of the merchant convoys carrying essential military supplies to Russia by the northern route, sailing into the ports of Archangel and Murmansk. When faced on 4 July with the possibility of an attack by the powerful German battleship *Tirpitz*, operating out of a Norwegian Fjord, the Admiralty had ordered the PQ 17 convoy to scatter. The individual ships were then picked off by German aircraft and submarines. By the time of the Defence Committee meeting on the evening of Friday 10 July it was being reported that, of the thirty-six ships which had originally sailed, sixteen were probably lost, two had turned back, and two others were doubtful.[70] The final figure was just eleven survivals.[71]

The losses led to an anguished discussion about whether the sailing of further convoys could be justified. The meeting of the 10th decided to postpone the sending in the next sailing of six RAF squadrons with 1,900 men. At a subsequent meeting on the following Monday, Admiral Pound confirmed that 'no additional protective measures were possible' and refused to guarantee that a single ship would survive, owing to the improved German tactics. The convoys were the surrogate for a Second Front and Churchill made it clear that he thought it would be justifiable to sail the next one if even only half the

---

[68] TNA, CAB 65/31, WM (42) 94.
[69] Gorodetsky (ed), *The Maisky Diaries*, pp.450-51.
[70] TNA, CAB 69/4, DO (42) 14.
[71] TNA, CAB 65/31, WM (42) 96.

ships could get through, but, faced with this bleak prognosis from the First Sea Lord, he acquiesced, and the next sailing was cancelled.[72]

Two days later, the issue was the subject of a difficult dinner conversation between Churchill and Maisky in 10 Downing Street. Upon being told of the suspension of the convoys, the Soviet Ambassador immediately replied that it made the question of a second front more urgent. He recalled Churchill prioritising his worries as the battle in Russia, the situation at sea, and then the battle in Egypt.[73] Maisky would have been even less happy had he known that a factor in the decision to cancel the Russian convoys had been the need to withdraw naval forces from the Home Fleet to help with the next Malta convoy.[74] It suggested that the Prime Minister's actual priorities were quite the reverse, and that he remained focused on salvaging his policy in the Middle East.

On 23 July, Churchill received a terse telegram from Stalin accusing him of refusing to continue to send supplies via the northern route and of postponing a second front in Europe until 1943. The Prime Minister was clearly annoyed and told his colleagues that, 'he would not have received a message in these terms but for the stern fight which the Russians were putting up against the Germans', though viewed objectively Stalin's conclusions seem fairly accurate. The Cabinet was concerned that public opinion might 'get out of hand as regards the staging of a second front in Europe', and on 27 July they took the decision to resume the northern convoys in September.[75] Yet the relationship with the Soviets had clearly been damaged.

At the same time, the British continued to fear a Soviet collapse that would see German troops pouring into Iraq and Iran through the Caucasus. Churchill felt that the pressure this threat had put on both Wavell and Auchinleck, as successive Commanders in Chief in the Middle East, had distracted them from their primary function against Rommel, while Brooke viewed the area as being ultimately of more strategic importance than Cairo, and a potential major theatre of operations for 1943.[76] This gave the Prime Minister and his Chief of Imperial General Staff enough common ground during their stay in Cairo to agree to the creation of a separate Near East Command, centred on the British position in Palestine. They offered it to Auchinleck at the time of his dismissal, against the wishes of the War Cabinet, but

---

72 TNA, CAB 69/4, DO (42) 15.
73 Gorodetsky (ed), *The Maisky Diaries*, pp.447-450.
74 TNA, CAB 69/4, DO (42) 14.
75 TNA, CAB 65/31, WM (42) 95; TNA, CAB 65/31, WM (42) 96.
76 CAC, Jacob Papers, JACB 1/16; Danchev & Todman, *Alanbrooke Diaries*, p.290.

the general refused what would have been an obvious demotion. Ultimately, the attack through the Caucasus never materialised, but in 1942 it seemed a very real prospect and so exerted a considerable influence on British strategic thinking. It remained another factor pulling Churchill away from Europe and towards securing victory as quickly possible in the Western Desert.

A key question was whether the Russians would hold, and so it was at this juncture that Churchill seized the opportunity to visit Marshal Stalin. In August 1942, immediately after his dismissal of Auchinleck, he flew to Moscow from Cairo via Tehran, crossing the Caucasus mountains. The visit has been well chronicled elsewhere, and was never going to be an easy mission. Churchill later likened delivering the news that there was to be no immediate second front to 'carrying a large lump of ice to the North Pole'.[77] Nevertheless, he was clearly excited at the prospect of establishing a face-to-face rapport with Stalin, and was convinced that by speaking frankly he could win the Russian leader over to the advantages of Anglo-American action in North Africa.

At the second meeting of the visit, in Stalin's office in the Kremlin on 13 August, the British Prime Minister found himself exposed to the full repertoire of Stalin's scorn and insults, albeit filtered through the interpreter. The Russian Marshal, just like the Americans, wanted the landing of six to eight British and American divisions on the Cherbourg Peninsula.[78] Churchill must have found the jibe that that 'if the British would only fight they would find the Germans were not supermen' particularly galling, as it went to the heart of his own fears about recent British military performance.[79] Jacob was brought in late to take the minutes, and discovered that things were not going well:

> A desultory argument about the possibility of a second front and similar matters, was proceeding. ...Stalin appeared quite at home, and made his remarks in a very low, gentle, voice, with an occasional gesture of the right hand, and never looked the Prime Minister in the face.[80]

Thereafter things did get better, and the two leaders parted on amicable terms after a long and private dinner on their final evening together. Churchill came away convinced that only he could have delivered

---

[77] Churchill, *The Second World War*, Vol. IV, p.428.
[78] Churchill, *The Second World War*, Vol. IV, p.438.
[79] Pawle, *The War and Colonel Warden*, p.6.
[80] CAC, Jacob Papers, JACB 1/16.

such disappointing news.[81] But the Russians had not yielded in their demands for a second front, and had no real option but to grudgingly acquiesce in Churchill's North African strategy. Stalin had assured Churchill that the Caucasus's would be held, but, having viewed some of the Russian defences while flying over them at low altitude, Brooke was not convinced.

Having dealt with both allies and replaced Auchinleck, the British Prime Minister now had to deliver a victory in the Middle East. If he did not, then he would face renewed pressure from parliament, public opinion, the Russians and the Americans to alter his strategy. He could not risk sacking another commander in the field: he could not keep facing down votes of confidence. The political capital that he had built up in the summer of 1940 had now been expended. Further defeats might prove fatal.

Churchill's doctor later wrote that, 'In 1953 I asked Winston to pick out the two most anxious months of the war. He did not hesitate: "September and October, yes, 1942"'.[82] Writing this chapter has helped me realise why. On the surface, compared to the summer months of 1940, or to the first half of 1942, September and October would seem a fairly quiet period. But that was part of the problem. Churchill was at his best at the centre of the crisis and in the thick of the fray, yet after dismissing Auchinleck and facing down all calls for the Second Front in France, he now had no option but to wait. He was gambling on a British victory in the desert, and the prior form was not exactly good.

There are many, O'Gowan and Barnett among them, who have argued convincingly that the groundwork for success had already been laid by Auchinleck, and that it was achieved less as a result of a change in commander and more as a result of the increase in the quantity and quality of British armour, while Rommel was already seriously overextended and weakened.

Churchill did not subscribe to this view. During the first Battle of El Alamein he cabled Auchinleck, 'This is a business not only of armour but of will power'.[83] He could not deny the importance of armour, and much of his war was spent wrestling with the logistics of building, deploying and replacing tanks, planes and ships, but, he also believed that, if properly motivated and led, his forces could, should and would do great things. On 8 May 1942, when discussing Auchinleck's refusal

---

[81] Churchill, *The Second World War*, Vol. IV, pp.450-451.
[82] Moran, *The Struggle for Survival*, p.71.
[83] CAC, Churchill Papers, CHAR 20/89.

to take the offensive, he had told the War Cabinet, 'battles were not won by arithmetical calculations of the strength of the opposing forces'.[84] While Churchill recognised that Auchinleck had ability, and had twice prevented defeat by taking personal command of the Eighth Army, he felt him to be too cautious, and to have presided over a loss of confidence among his troops. Churchill believed in the importance of morale, and in this he was not alone. Eisenhower felt it to be, 'the greatest single factor in successful war... It breeds most readily upon success; but under good leaders it will be maintained among troops even during extended periods of adversity'.[85]

Will power and self-belief were what Churchill felt the army had lacked in Singapore and what were needed in the desert now. It was his job to try and instil them. To what extent his actions changed morale, and to what extent morale contributed to victory is impossible to quantify. His actions in reinforcing the desert army and in removing the responsibility for Iran, Iraq, Palestine and Syria from Alexander and Montgomery, so that they could concentrate exclusively on Rommel, were surely also influential in delivering success, but the decision to remove Auchinleck tells us much about Churchill's style and view of leadership.

Churchill believed in leadership from the front. That is why he undertook the hazardous round trip to the Middle East and Moscow, flying, sometimes across contested skies, in a converted Liberator bomber without a pressurised cabin that necessitated the use of oxygen when travelling at altitude. For a hands-on leader, who could not bear inactivity, it was a chance to take action. The trip was a welcome change of scene and break from routine, which he clearly relished, but it was also a chance to 'settle the decisive questions on the spot'.[86] It was about reasserting his authority on the domestic and international stage after a period of political weakness, and was a demonstration that was aimed as much at his political colleagues and international allies, as it was the rank and file of the Eighth Army and the propaganda machines of the enemy. He was sending a signal and staking his leadership on his chosen battleground.

His decision could only be vindicated by events. On the 19 August, he was back in Cairo when he received news of the disastrous raid in force, using commandoes and Canadian troops, on the French harbour

---

[84] TNA, CAB 65/30, WM (42) 59.

[85] Eisenhower, D., *Crusade in Europe*, (Heinemann, 1948), p.231.

[86] Churchill, *The Second World War*, Vol. IV, p.408.

of Dieppe.[87] It was an unfortunate, if timely, illustration of the risks that might befall any limited operation in France, of the type that both General Marshal and Stalin had urged, and must have reinforced Churchill's view that the right course for 1942 was still to fight and win in the Mediterranean and North Africa, rather than to risk rebuff against the Atlantic seawall.

General Montgomery did finally deliver a decisive victory over Rommel at the second Battle of El Alamein in November. In August, Churchill had complained that, 'a kind of apathy and exhaustion of the mind rather than the body has stolen over our troops which only new strong hands, and above all the gleam of victory can dispel'.[88] Now, in his annual address at the Mansion House, in a line that he added by hand, he used this same analogy, and proudly announced that, 'The bright gleam has caught the helmets of our soldiers, and warmed and cheered all our hearts'.[89]

After two and a half years of weekly audiences, the King was in a better position than most to appreciate the personal significance to Churchill of these momentous events. George VI wrote to his Prime Minister:

> I know that the elimination of the Africa Corps, the threat to Egypt, was your one aim, the most important of all the many other operations with which you have had to deal.[90]

The King's first draft had contained the deleted line, 'It was the lynch pin of all of our war strategy'.[91]

---

[87] Churchill, *The Second World War*, Vol. IV, p.457.
[88] CAC, Baroness Spencer-Churchill Papers, CSCT 2/31; cited in Soames, *Speaking For Themselves*, p.466.
[89] CAC, Churchill Papers, CHAR 9/189/59.
[90] CAC, Churchill Papers, CHAR 20/52/93.
[91] Royal Archives, PS/PSO/GVI/C/069/21.

Chapter 7

Masterstroke or Millstone?

Why did Churchill embrace
Unconditional Surrender?

There is no mistaking the moment at which the policy of 'unconditional surrender' was unveiled to the world. It happened on 24 January 1943. The setting was a press conference on the lawn of a villa of the Hotel Anfa, just outside Casablanca in Morocco. The President and Prime Minister were sitting side by side in the North African sunshine: Roosevelt in a light grey suit, black tie and armband in honour of his late mother; Churchill in a dark pin-striped three-piece suit with his trademark spotted bow tie, and his hat and cane balanced on his lap. The press conference took place under a blue sky, overlooking the crashing surf of the Atlantic on one side and a countryside of rich red soil dotted with white villas and green orange groves and palm trees on the other.[1] It all seemed far removed from the horrors of war.

According to the correspondent of *The Times* newspaper, it was this moment that President Roosevelt chose to speak:

> Of something which has always been in the hearts and minds of people but never before placed on paper. That was the determination that peace can come to the world only by the total elimination of German and Japanese war power'. Turning to the British correspondents, he told how that great American soldier General U.S. Grant had been nicknamed 'Unconditional Surrender' Grant. Unconditional surrender to-day, Mr Roosevelt explained with emphasis, meant unconditional

---

[1]   CAC, Jacob Papers, JACB 1/19.

surrender by Germany, Italy and Japan, and that meant a reasonable assurance of future world peace.

It did not mean, he explained with the same emphasis, the destruction of the populace of those countries, but the destruction of the philosophies in those countries based on fear and hate and the subjugation of other peoples. It was then that the President suggested, as if it were a happy thought that had just entered his mind, that we might call this the 'Unconditional Surrender' Meeting.[2]

Churchill responded with a vigorous 'Hear, Hear'. Yet according to his war memoirs, it was with 'some feeling of surprise' that that the Prime Minister heard the President make this momentous announcement.[3] It had certainly not been the main purpose of the meeting of the Allied war leaders that had just taken place, and was not mentioned in the official communique that was being released to the press. However, as we will see, the concept of unconditional surrender had certainly been discussed, and Churchill had played a central role in its birth, if not in its proclamation. Now it had grabbed the international headlines, and quickly became a central policy to which all the United Nations, were seemingly being committed. What role did Churchill play in its development, why was it proclaimed at Casablanca, and how did it impact on Churchill's war leadership? Was it a masterstoke of Allied policy making or a millstone around Anglo-American necks that would constrain future action?

The Casablanca Conference took place from 14-24 January and was attended by Churchill and Roosevelt and their respective Chiefs of Staff. Harold Macmillan, the newly appointed British Minister resident in Algiers, likened it to a meeting of two emperors of the later Roman period, the Emperor of the East and the Emperor of the West, and noted with some prescience that, 'The only sad thing about it was that the Russians could not attend. If we had had the Red Emperor as well, it would have made the thing perfect'. He also described the atmosphere as 'a mixture between a cruise, a summer school and a conference'.[4] It is certainly clear from the contemporary accounts that Churchill was enjoying a further escape from the confines of Whitehall, but the sunshine and the smiles masked the fact that all was not well,

---

[2] CAC, Hankey Papers, HNKY 13/8.
[3] Churchill, *The Second World War*, Vol. IV, p.615.
[4] Macmillan H., *War Diaries: Politics and War in the Mediterranean 1943-1945*, (Macmillan, 1984), pp.8-9.

and that the new Anglo-American allies were wrestling with some serious problems.

The meeting took place in the immediate aftermath of the first joint Anglo-American military operation; the landings in November 1942 on the coast of French North-West Africa at Casablanca, Oran and Algiers. This was not an attack against Nazi Germany or Fascist Italy, but rather an operation against neutral Vichy France. In the words of General Eisenhower, who commanded the assault, 'we were invading a neutral country to create a friend'.[5] The hope was that the Allies would be welcomed as liberators, and that French North Africa would rise up and make common cause with the United Nations. This did not happen. At Oran, where memories of the sinking of the fleet were still raw, the invasion was bitterly resisted. Elsewhere, the Allied occupying forces faced hostility and non-cooperation, while the Germans gained time to reinforce. Meanwhile, Hitler used the move to terminate the last vestiges of French independence.

This left the President and the Prime Minister wrestling with the political implications of occupying French territory. This was not straightforward. In the war to date, the British had tended to back General de Gaulle and his Free French, while the Americans had always recognised Petain's Vichy regime. Roosevelt had formed a poor opinion of de Gaulle, reinforced by his unannounced seizure of the small French islands of Saint-Pierre and Miquelon off the North American coast in December 1941.

General Eisenhower had sought to bolster the North African invasion with deals aimed at winning over the local Vichy leaders and their forces. It was a policy that had proved very controversial with audiences at home in both Britain and America, where there was much opposition to collaboration with former fascist sympathisers and fellow travellers. Feelings ran particularly high in the case of Admiral Darlan, the former commander of the French navy who had become one of the most senior ministers in Petain's government. After his defection to the Allies, Darlan had been recognised by Eisenhower as High Commissioner of France for North and West Africa. This had understandably infuriated de Gaulle and his supporters. Perhaps unsurprisingly, Darlan had been assassinated, at which point the Americans had turned to General Henri Giraud. He had been captured during the battle for France in May 1940, but had managed to escape from German captivity earlier in 1942, and was neither a supporter of the Free French or Vichy, and was contemptuously dismissed by de

---

[5] Eisenhower, *Crusade in Europe*, p.98.

Gaulle as holding 'no position at all'.[6] The Allies wanted the various French factions to unite and work together as one authority, which they could recognise as temporarily representing France, now that France was occupied. Yet, as Churchill observed in a letter to Clementine, 'Many of these Frenchmen hate each other far more than they do the Germans'.[7]

In addition to these immediate objectives, the conference had also been called to look at future military strategy and to decide how to go forward together. This meant an immediate reignition of the debate about competing theatres and particularly the Mediterranean theatre versus a second front in France. It is clear from the British and American sources that Churchill and his Chiefs of Staff had prepared very thoroughly for the conference. Jacob's diary records his concern that the Americans might take offence at the sheer size of the British planning staff, which came complete with its own well equipped mobile headquarters, the converted passenger ship HMS *Bulolo*, which was moored in Casablanca Harbour.[8] Elliott Roosevelt, the President's son, later complained that the British staff officers seemed to outnumber their American counterparts two to one.[9] More importantly, the British arrived with a clear idea of what future joint strategy should be. Ian Jacob's diary records that:

> Our views were definite at any rate so far as the Mediterranean versus Northern Europe was concerned. The arguments in favour of exploiting success in North Africa by attacking 'the underbelly of the Axis' were, it seemed to us, overwhelming. The more we looked at Northern France the less one liked it with the forces likely to be available in 1943 in the UK. These forces would be small for a 'second front', & the rate at which they could be put ashore was severely limited by the lack of landing craft. The US had ceased to send any to the UK when TORCH [codename for the invasion of North Africa] took the field.[10]

The British knew, however, that the Americans still favoured a large-scale operation in Western Europe above further operations in the Mediterranean. True to his role as a prod, Churchill knew his mind. According to Jacob: 'He wanted the cleansing of the N. African shore to be followed by the capture of Sicily. He wanted the re-conquest

---

[6]   TNA, CAB 65/37, WM (43) 9.
[7]   Baroness Spencer-Churchill Papers, CSCT 2/32; Soames, *Speaking for Themselves*, p.475.
[8]   CAC, Jacob Papers, JACB 1/19.
[9]   Roosevelt, E., *As He Saw It*, (Duell, Sloan and Pearce, 1946), p.80.
[10] CAC, Jacob Papers, JACB 1/19.

of Burma, and he wanted the invasion of Northern France, on a moderate scale perhaps. ...he was indulging to the full in his usual pastime of having his cake and eating it – or trying to'. Yet, perhaps less characteristically, Churchill recognised that these complex issues would take time to work through, and advocated a policy of gradual persuasion by his team when dealing with the Americans, likening it to 'the dripping of water on a stone'.[11]

Visits by General Eisenhower and Alexander enabled the immediate North African strategy to be co-ordinated, and it was agreed that Alexander would shortly become Deputy Commander of the Allied forces in the theatre under Eisenhower. The protocols that would henceforth govern such joint commands were also worked through. The shotgun marriage of de Gaulle and Giraud proved harder to engineer. Roosevelt made it clear from the beginning of the conference that he wanted de Gaulle to attend and expected Churchill to be able to deliver him.[12] However, de Gaulle refused Churchill's initial invitations, arguing that while he would meet Giraud in French territory, he was reluctant to do so 'at a meeting of the Allies, who might press him to some compromise'.[13] It took a great effort by Eden and a further telegram from Churchill, endorsed by the War Cabinet and confirming the attendance of the President, to get the French General to reconsider. Churchill's cable made it very clear that, 'If with your eyes open you reject this unique opportunity, the consequences to the future of the Fighting French Movement cannot but be grave in the extreme'.[14] The Prime Minister knew that if de Gaulle became persona non grata with the Americans, then the British might have to abandon him. In the end, de Gaulle swallowed his pride and flew out for a symbolic photo-call and handshake with Giraud, which took place just before the final press conference on 24 January. It was preceded by an awkward meeting with Churchill, after which Churchill's doctor recorded the British Prime Minister's statement of amused exasperation about the Free French leader: 'His country has given up fighting, he himself is a refugee, and if we turn him down he's finished. Well just look at him! Look at him! ...He might be Stalin with 200 divisions behind his words'.[15] In a letter written to the King just after these events Churchill accused de Gaulle of being hostile to Britain and suggested that: 'The insolence with which he refused the President's invitation (and mine)

[11]   CAC, Jacob Papers, JACB 1/19.
[12]   Roosevelt, *As He Saw It*, p.70.
[13]   TNA, CAB 65/37, WM (43) 9.
[14]   TNA, CAB 65/37, WM (43) 11.
[15]   Moran, *Struggle for Survival*, p.81.

to come and make a friendly statement at Casablanca may be founded on stupidity rather than malice'.[16] When he came to publish this letter in his history *The Second World War* he had to admit to George VI that he was changing this text to read 'may not be founded on malice', as with the benefit of hindsight he no longer wanted to appear quite so rough on the French general.[17]

The initial Chiefs of Staff discussions proved difficult. Yet, with the help of Field Marshal Dill, who had flown in from the Combined Chiefs of Staff Committee in Washington, and knew the positions of those on both sides of the table, a consensus on future operations was reached by Monday, 18 January.[18] The next operations would be the capture of Sicily, while at the same time preparing forces and assembling landing craft in England 'for a thrust across the Channel in the event that the German strength in France decreases, either through withdrawal of her troops or because of an internal collapse'.[19] It seemed to be a complete acceptance of the British strategy and Brooke 'could hardly believe our luck'. Churchill had not been at the Combined Chiefs of Staff meetings, but was following their progress and had been working in tandem to secure these aims in his personal meetings and mealtime diplomacy with the President and his party. He was obviously delighted with the results and the minutes show that he immediately offered to enter into a treaty or convention with the United States to guarantee that, 'when Hitler breaks down, all of the British resources and effort will be turned towards the defeat of Japan'. Roosevelt replied that this was not necessary, among friends, but did indicate that efforts should be made to obtain the same engagement from Russia.[20]

In agreeing to the continuation of the Mediterranean strategy, the Americans were acknowledging that they did not have all of the resources to meet their existing obligations in North Africa, undertake their favoured offensives in the Pacific and simultaneously attack in France. Yet in committing to an attack on Sicily they were also, temporarily at least, further denuding any operation in France of such craft and thereby effectively shelving the plan for any quick offensive or lodgement across the Channel. The 'Second Front', at least in the terms that it was understood by the press and public in both Britain and America as an operation in force against the Germans in France,

---

[16] Royal Archives, PS/PSO/GVI/C/069/29.
[17] Royal Archives, PS/PSO/GVI/C/069/69.
[18] Danchev & Todman, *Alanbrooke Diaries*, pp.361-363.
[19] TNA, CAB 99/24.
[20] TNA, CAB 99/24.

had been put back yet again. It must have been very clear to all around the table that the Russians would not be pleased.

Casablanca marked a turning point because it introduced two new factors which altered Churchill's perception and strategy. The first was the arrival of the Americans on the battlefields in the West. This was something that he had been working tirelessly towards. The immediate effect was to greatly reinforce and strengthen his existing plans. The landings in French North Africa sealed Rommel's doom and opened the back door to Europe through Sicily and Italy. At the same time, the American Eighth Army Air Force was now building up in Britain and beginning to operate. Fifty-nine US bombers attacked Wilhelmshaven on 27 January 1943. It was the first American raid against German soil, and precursor of things to come on a much greater scale.[21] Churchill had endorsed a bombing offensive in 1940 as a way of taking the fight back to the enemy. The results had hitherto been limited by the resources available, and by the other calls on the bombers to support army and navy operations, but with the Americans now entering the fray, the tide of the air war was set to turn in 1943.

But it was also clear from the conference at Casablanca, and from the discussions that had preceded it in 1942, that American muscle came with a mind of its own. That mind ultimately favoured decisive action in France so that the war in Europe could be ended as quickly as possible, allowing United States forces to finish a job that they had already started in the Pacific. Even the joint bomber offensive, as it was accepted at Casablanca, was seen as a means of weakening Germany prior to invasion.[22] You can see Churchill adjusting to this new reality at the conference. It is discernible in his pledge to keep fighting against the Japanese, in his desire to help the President bring about the de Gaulle-Giraud reconciliation, and in his willingness (opposed by Brooke and ultimately rejected by the Americans) to consider smaller operations in France in 1943. He was throwing his hat in the ring with Roosevelt.

The other factor was Russian success. While Churchill and Roosevelt were meeting at Casablanca, the German Sixth Army was being destroyed at Stalingrad. The Anglo-Soviet Treaty negotiations in 1942 had illustrated the nature of Soviet ambitions in Eastern Europe. If these were achieved, there was the possibility that Stalin might seek a separate peace. Equally, there was the fear that he might seek further territorial gains in Europe. Either way, it made sense for the British

---

[21] Overy, *The Bombing War*, p.304.
[22] Overy, *The Bombing War*, p.303.

and Americans to be in Western Europe while the Russians were still fighting, and before they were too successful.

Stalin was indeed the spectre at the feast. The final conference communique, released after Churchill and Roosevelt had left Casablanca, was carefully worded so as not to offend the Russians, and to suggest to wider public opinion that the Anglo-American allies were meeting with full Soviet blessing. After confirming that the conference had reviewed the entire field of war and reporting that complete agreement had been reached, it carefully explained that Premier Stalin had been invited but had been unable to attend because of the great offensive taking place in Russia, that Churchill and Roosevelt had recognised the need to draw off pressure on the Russians, and that Stalin and Chiang Kai-Shek had been kept informed. Such words only served to highlight the Russian absence, and prompted the British War Cabinet to cable Churchill that, 'References to M. Stalin in communique seem to us dangerous unless previously agreed with him'.[23]

In neither the confidential military objectives, nor the public communique was there any mention of unconditional surrender. Nor, interestingly, is it mentioned in the diaries of those present like Brooke, Jacob and Wilson. What then was the origin of this headline-stealing concept and how did its birth relate to the main business which had been conducted at Casablanca?

When Churchill referred to unconditional surrender later in the war, and in its aftermath, he gave the impression that it was the spontaneous policy of President Roosevelt, announced at the press conference without his prior knowledge or consultation.[24] This may have been a genuine lapse of memory, or it may have been a deliberate decision, perhaps initially to let the President take the credit for the initiative, or later to distance himself from it, or indeed both. However, when he came to write his own history of the war, he was confronted by evidence of his own earlier involvement which he could no longer ignore.

According to Elliott Roosevelt, the phrase was his father's, but it was born the day before the press conference on the 23 January at a small lunch attended by the President, the Prime Minister, Harry Hopkins and himself. It seems to have arisen in response to a discussion about the press communique. According to Elliott, when Roosevelt proposed the phrase, Churchill 'munched a mouthful

---

[23] TNA, CAB 65/37, WM (43) 15.
[24] See for example *Hansard*, 18 Jan 1945, para 423-4; 21 July 1949, para 1593-1610, debate on War situation and Foreign Policy.

of food, thought, frowned, thought, finally grinned, and at length announced "Perfect! And I can just see how Goebbels and the rest of 'em 'll squeal!"'[25] The President then elaborated on his thinking, by speculating that it was just the thing for the Russians, before asking Hopkins to draw up a statement in time for the press tomorrow. That evening, after the final Chiefs of Staff meeting and a long session to finalise the text of the communique, Churchill raised his glass and proposed a toast to 'Unconditional Surrender'.[26]

Of course, this account is problematic. It was written after the event, and by the time it was published only Elliott and Churchill were still alive. In his own book, Churchill claimed that he could not recall the conversation, but admitted that the matter must have 'cropped up'.[27] Nor did unconditional surrender make it into the final press communique. Yet the account does illustrate that, while Brooke, Jacob and the other members of the British Chiefs of Staff delegation were immersed in planning future military operations with their American counterparts, Churchill and Roosevelt and their entourages were engaged in similar, if less structured, exercises on the political front. But unconditional surrender was not just on the menu as a dinner topic, it also found its way into the formal sessions, and it is clear from these that Elliott Roosevelt was wrong. The phrase was not born on the 23 January, as it had already been used by Churchill on the 18th.

The term surfaces at the first plenary meeting of the President, Prime Minister and their Chiefs of Staff on Monday, 18 January, in the form of an intervention from the British Prime Minister. It does so towards the end of the meeting, after the military strategy has been discussed and agreed, and once again in the context of how it might now be presented. After learning that agreements arrived at in the conference would be included in a paper, Churchill suggests that one should be given to Stalin. That prompts Roosevelt to bring up the subject of a press release and photograph. Churchill then:

> suggested that at the same time we release a statement to the effect that the United Nations are resolved to pursue the war to the bitter end, neither party relaxing in its efforts until the unconditional surrender of Germany and Japan has been achieved. He said that before issuing such a statement, he would like to consult with his colleagues in London.[28]

---

[25] Roosevelt, *As He Saw It*, p.119.
[26] Roosevelt, *As He Saw It*, p.119.
[27] Churchill, *Second World War*, Vol. IV, pp.614-616.
[28] TNA, CAB 99/24.

He then sent a telegram to the War Cabinet informing them of the intention 'to draw up a statement of the work of the Conference for communication to the press at the proper time' and asking for their views on the inclusion of a declaration of the 'firm intention' of the United States and British Empire to bring about the unconditional surrender of Germany and Japan. He added that, 'The omission of Italy would be to encourage a break up there,' and that the 'President liked this idea and it would stimulate our friends in every country'. The War Cabinet, with Attlee in the Chair, felt that it was wrong to exclude Italy, as this might be misunderstood in the Balkans and Turkey, presumably because suspicions would be aroused about the terms of any separate peace, and that at this stage it would be a mistake 'to make any distinction between the three partners in the Axis'. In their joint reply to Churchill, Attlee and Eden also made the additional point that 'knowledge of rough stuff coming to them' was more likely to undermine Italian morale.[29]

Writing in 1950, about Casablanca, Churchill referred to this correspondence but pointed out that no statement about unconditional surrender was included in the official communique, and suggested that in the 'pressure of business', and particularly with all the work that needed to be put into the de Gaulle-Giraud reconciliation, the matter was dropped and that he had no further discussions upon it until, 'with some feeling of surprise', he heard the President mention it to the press. This may be true, but Churchill had clearly raised the prospect and profile of unconditional surrender, and it is therefore important to consider what he meant by it.

Lord Hankey, the former long-serving Cabinet Secretary and minister whom Churchill had sacked in 1942, would later dismiss the unconditional surrender policy as 'a useful make-weight to the colourless communique'. His implication being that the Allies had so little they could actually announce, with all of the military decisions being obviously secret, that they introduced unconditional surrender as a deliberate headline grabbing exercise.[30] The fact that Churchill's intervention on 18 January was immediately preceded by Roosevelt's talking about the press statement and photograph certainly gives some credence to this, but the wider context of the discussions in that meeting suggests that Churchill may have been motivated by a number of factors.

He may have been following up on some of the informal conversations that he had already had with the President, using the

---

29 TNA, CAB 65/37, WM (43) 12.
30 CAC, Hankey Papers, HNKY 25/20.

forum of the plenary meeting to raise an issue he knew would appeal to Roosevelt. His offer of a treaty against Japan shows that he was keen to demonstrate that Britain was in the fight for the long haul and would go the distance in the Far East: the statement on unconditional surrender was another way of confirming this and demonstrating Anglo-American unity. It might also provide a framework, should Moscow endorse the concept, for getting the Russians to commit to entering the war against Japan. Meanwhile, the talk of Stalin and of the press, must also have focused his mind on how the agreed strategy would be seen by the Russians and by those strong elements of press and public who were agitating for the second front in France.

Ambassador Maisky had met with Eden on 26 January and voiced Russian concerns that the Germans were likely to try and split the united Allied front and test the ground for a compromise peace. He described how, 'Eden rose in agitation from his armchair and replied with uncharacteristic energy: "As long as Churchill is prime minister and I am foreign secretary, there will be no compromise with Germany"'. Yet, in his diary, Maisky gave private voice to his suspicion that the Allies were seeking to time a second front in France so that it came 'not too early and not too late'; delaying while the Russians broke 'Germany's backbone' but arriving in time to prevent the 'Bolshevization of Europe'.[31]

There were certainly elements of the press that interpreted unconditional surrender as a signal to the Kremlin. On 13 February 1943, the popular and influential British *Picture Post* magazine, with a circulation of nearly two million copies a week, published several pages of images relating to the Casablanca conference along with an accompanying article by Kingsley Martin. In his text, Martin, who was known for his pro-Soviet views, noted that the absence of Stalin as a 'disturbing fact' and argued that, 'if there had been the understanding and confidence that we should like between members of the United Nations, we may be sure that Stalin would have sent Molotov as his deputy with some experts to take part in the discussions'. He felt that the declaration of unconditional surrender was designed to counter the daily pronouncements emanating from Berlin which sought to assert that Europe 'was being opened to the tender mercies of Bolshevism'. It 'was meant to tell the world that from this anti-Bolshevik propaganda the Nazis have nothing to hope for and the Soviet [sic] nothing to fear'. He also questioned whether Stalin was starting to hint to the Allies that, unless there was some form of second front soon, Russia might

---

[31] Gorodetsky (ed), *The Maisky Diaries*, p.473 & p.475.

settle for pushing the Germans back behind the Curzon Line [in what had been eastern Poland] and halt its westward advance.[32]

The text of the official communique, the reservations expressed upon it by the British Cabinet, and the text of the Picture Post article are all revealing of the extent to which Stalin's absence figured in the minds of the politicians and the press at this time. While Maisky's discussion with Eden is proof of the mutual doubts and suspicions that were continuing to permeate Anglo-Soviet relations. After his visit to Moscow during the previous August, and having endured months of parliamentary and media campaigning for a second front, Churchill was well aware of the pressures. He had already said that a copy of the conference conclusions should be sent to Stalin, though he wanted it made clear that it expressed 'intentions and did not constitute promises'.[33] He must have known that Stalin would not have wanted to endorse the strategic military decisions, either as intentions or promises, and therefore have hoped that a broad statement of unconditional surrender might help paper across any cracks and reinforce the wider perception, if not the reality, of a united grand alliance.

If we accept Elliott Roosevelt's account of the lunch on 23 January, then concern about pleasing the Russians also seems to have been a factor in the President's approach. Broadcasting in the United States on 12 February after his return, Roosevelt was certainly very keen to stress that there was no room for the enemy to exploit divisions in the Allied ranks:

> In an attempt to ward off inevitable disaster, the Axis propagandists are trying all of their old tricks in order to divide the United Nations. They seek to create the idea that if we win this war, Russia, England, China, and the United States are going to get into a cat-and-dog fight.
>
> This is their final effort to turn one nation against another in the vain hope that they may settle with one or two at a time – that any of us may be so gullible and so forgetful as to be duped into making 'deals' at the expense of our Allies.[34]

The President also took the opportunity to forecast victory marches through the streets of Rome, Tokyo and Berlin. Unconditional surrender was part of a strong psychological message. After years of being on the defensive and responding to moves made against them,

---

[32] CAC, Martin Papers, MART 5: CAC, Kinna Papers, KNNA 1/7.

[33] TNA, CAB 99/24.

[34] CAC, Hankey Papers, HNKY 13/8.

the Allies were now taking the initiative and dictating the terms. It was a signal calculated to appeal to the general public and the troops in uniform, but one that was also aimed at intensifying resistance in occupied countries, and in encouraging neutral powers to choose the Allied side.

As a rallying cry, unconditional surrender also appeared consistent with the rhetoric that Churchill had been using since the beginning of the conflict. He had pledged to 'wage war' until victory, 'against a monstrous tyranny, never surpassed in the dark, lamentable catalogue of human crime'.[35] He had promised the blitzed citizens of Britain that he would 'Give it to 'em back', until 'the last vestiges of Nazi tyranny have been burnt out of Europe'.[36] His response to the German invasion of Russia had been to declare that, 'We will never parley, we will never negotiate with Hitler or any of his gang', and after the Atlantic Charter meeting he had sought to give hope to the occupied territories of Europe by promising them that, 'Help is coming; mighty forces are arming in your behalf. Have faith. Have hope. Deliverance is sure'.[37] On one level, unconditional surrender could be presented as an extension of his publicly stated and often repeated intention to fight until his enemies had been defeated and their ill-gotten gains returned. Yet, even at the height of the Battle of France he had not completely ruled out negotiation. Now that door seemed to be shutting.

Their position may have been hardened by the information that was now reaching Churchill and Roosevelt about the extent and nature of German and Japanese atrocities in the areas they controlled; and in particular, the beginnings of the Holocaust, a systematic and unprecedented campaign of genocide by the Nazis against the Jews. Churchill's Atlantic Charter broadcast in August 1941 may not have mentioned the Jews specifically, as Weizmann complained, but it had talked about a German policy of extermination and executions on the Eastern Front and of 'methodical, merciless butchery' on an enormous scale, which Churchill had labelled as a 'crime without a name'.[38] In October 1942, the Prime Minister had lent his support to a public meeting protesting against the massacre of the Jewish peoples in Eastern Europe, sending a letter that denounced these 'systematic cruelties' as 'vile crimes' that were 'amongst the most terrible events of history' and which placed an 'indelible stain' on those who perpetrated

---

[35] CAC, Churchill Papers, CHAR 9/139B/ 194.
[36] CAC, Churchill Papers, CHAR 9/176A/34.
[37] CAC, Churchill Papers, CHAR 9/151/122; CAC, Churchill Papers, CHAR 9/182B/18.
[38] CAC, Churchill Papers, CHAR 9/182B/173.

them.[39] It had been followed by a Joint Allied Declaration on 17 December 1942, protesting against 'this bestial policy of cold-blooded extermination'.[40] The meeting at Casablanca took place against this backdrop and no amount of sunshine would have been able to dispel the mounting horror and revulsion. Unconditional surrender was also about identifying and punishing the guilty.

Perhaps for Churchill, initially at least, it was also about trying to divide the enemy. His original suggestion had been that it be applied to Germany and Japan, but deliberately not Italy 'so as to encourage a break up there'.[41] This suggests that, having just approved a future military operation against Sicily, he might have been prepared to contemplate some form of negotiated peace with Italy to assist the military operations, though a condition would presumably have been Mussolini's removal. If so, this was not the view of his Foreign Secretary or wider War Cabinet, who wanted the Axis powers treated equally.

Finally, it can be safely assumed that Churchill and Roosevelt were both starting to think about the future. Given their shared experience of living through the First World War and its aftermath, it seems reasonable to assume that their conversations may have turned to the unsatisfactory nature of the subsequent peace settlement and the need to prevent history repeating itself. Last time the German army had been able to claim that it had been stabbed in the back by its politicians, and that it not been defeated: a myth that was integral to Hitler's own philosophy and a staple of Nazi propaganda. Unconditional surrender would prevent any such claim this time round.[42] In this, the President was also surely responding to domestic American criticism of the deal that had just been done with Darlan, and signalling that henceforth he would be following a more moral policy.

It has been suggested that, in accepting unconditional surrender, Churchill undermined his own strategy. If victory was to be achieved through a war of attrition, through bombing Germany into submission, supporting the Russians on the Eastern Front, fighting in the Mediterranean and seizing other opportunities as they presented themselves, then the end game was surely forcing the Germans to accept defeat and to seek terms.[43] After all, this was how wars were supposed to end. Lord Hankey compiled evidence in support of his opposition to the concept showing that between 1588 and 1919:

[39] Gilbert, M., *Churchill and the Jews*, (Simon & Schuster, 2007), p.192.
[40] Gilbert, *Churchill and the Jews*, p.195.
[41] TNA, CAB 65/37, WM (43) 12.
[42] Kimball, *Forged in War*, p.189.
[43] Reynolds, *In Command of History*, pp.323-324.

There were sixteen major wars. In only four or perhaps five cases was the victory so complete that we and our allies were in a position virtually to dictate the peace treaty… In fact, however, in practically every case except the Treaty of Versailles the peace treaty was negotiated.[44]

For both Churchill and Roosevelt, their heavy personal investment in the Casablanca conference at such a key moment in the war necessitated a big concept and a big headline. Unconditional surrender emerged from their formal and informal conversations, and drew consciously or unconsciously on the various concerns that they were facing at that moment. It provided a brutally simple statement of intent, but also served as a counterpoint to the Atlantic Charter. While the Charter had promised rights to victor and vanquished alike, the doctrine of unconditional surrender made it clear that the Axis powers would have no automatic right to decide how or when the Charter terms would be applied. This would be the prerogative of the victors. Of course, first the Allies had to win, and the announcement of 'unconditional surrender' also diverted attention from some of the difficulties that they were facing.

Churchill reported to parliament on 11 February, and used the occasion to address some of the current concerns about Allied strategy. He asserted that, 'We have to make the enemy burn and bleed in every way that is physically possible, in the same way as he is being made to burn and bleed along the vast Russian front from the White Sea to the Black Sea'. This was a recognition that the Russians were bearing the brunt of the fighting, but he accompanied it with a statement of the difficulties of bringing the Allied forces into action. The United States was having to cross oceans, and then there was 'the daring and complicated enterprise of landing on defended coasts and also the building-up of all the supplies and communications', all of which had to be accomplished in the teeth of heavy losses at sea from the ongoing U-boat campaign. It is clear that, without giving away the agreed strategy, he was emphasising the risks of the Second Front in France and the reasons for a likely delay. He was also careful not to state on which defended coasts the British and Americans might land. All he was able to promise was that it had been agreed in Casablanca 'to aid to the utmost in our power the magnificent, tremendous effort of Russia and to try and draw the enemy and the enemy's air force from the Russian front'.

---

[44] CAC, Hankey Papers, HNKY 13/8.

On unconditional surrender he sought to draw a distinction between what it meant for the enemy regimes and what it meant for their peoples: clarifying that while we would not 'stain our victorious arms by wrong and cruel treatment of whole populations', justice would be done 'upon the wicked and the guilty' and 'no vestige of the Nazi or Fascist power' or of the 'Japanese war-plotting machine' would be allowed to remain.[45] Roosevelt would echo these sentiments in his radio address of the following day. It suggests that both men were already aware of one of the principal criticisms of their new policy; namely that it would encourage resistance because it demanded that the peoples of enemy states, even if they overthrew their current rulers, would have to put themselves at the complete mercy of the victors.

That point was made in the House of Commons debate after Churchill had left the chamber by Richard Stokes, the Labour MP for Ipswich. He considered unconditional surrender to be, 'the most ill-judged name that could be given to any conference' and both a negation of the Atlantic Charter and contrary to Labour Party policy. He felt that the statement would only stiffen German resolve and that we had given 'something very delectable to Goebbels on a platter', whereas the 'object of our propaganda should be to shorten the war and not to lengthen it'.[46] Having got the bit between his teeth, this independent minded MP would not let the matter drop. A week later, when Attlee was dealing with questions for the Prime Minister, he asked whether Stalin had approved the declaration of unconditional surrender. When the Deputy Prime Minister responded with, 'I can hardly believe that anyone doubts Premier Stalin's attitude on the subject', Stokes argued that a Russian spokesman quoted in the *Manchester Guardian* had wanted to dispel the fear of total destruction from the minds of the Germans.[47] He further developed these ideas in a printed pamphlet entitled 'Unconditional Surrender! What does Stalin think?' In it he argued that:

> The declaration of 'Unconditional Surrender' made at Casablanca is the most dangerous utterance yet made by the President and Prime Minister and, if it is allowed to go unqualified, it will prolong the war by years. It is vitally important that it should be clarified, making clear to the German, Italian and Japanese people that we do not mean their total destruction and that the utterance meant the overthrow of their present rulers.

---

[45] *Hansard*, 11 February 1943, House of Commons Debate on War Situation, Vol 386, cc1453-1531.

[46] *Hansard*, 11 February 1943, House of Commons Debate on War Situation, Vol 386, cc1453-1531.

[47] *Hansard*, 17 February 1943, House of Commons, Vol 386, c1730.

He argued that in the Boer War, 'a similar declaration was made by Lord Milner which prolonged the war by two years. Imagine the amount of useless slaughter and suffering that will have to be endured in this war if this war goes on two years longer than it need!'[48]

The Boer War analogy was also made by Lord Hankey. As an archetypal establishment insider, credited with developing much of the machinery of modern Cabinet Government, Hankey was a very different type of critic. In April 1943, he was persuaded not to publish an article that made the same basic points as Stokes. He felt that if the principle was applied to the countries of Germany, Italy and Japan, rather than just the specific regimes of Hitler, Mussolini and Tojo, it would deter internal revolt as any successor government in the Axis countries would still have to accept unconditional surrender. Thus, the move had deprived our propaganda of a:

> useful means for promoting the separation of enemy peoples from their respective Governments and stimulating disillusionment. For we have now made it clear that we will not discriminate between good Governments, if they can be found, and the present corrupt factions. The effect may be to rally the enemy peoples behind their present leaders as the last hope of survival.

The enemy would be given 'the courage of despair'.[49] Hankey remained a convinced sceptic. Finally free to publish in 1949, he described unconditional surrender and war crimes trials as 'part of a philosophy of hate that grew up without our noticing it during the war. It must be banned for ever'. Writing at the beginning of the new Cold War between the former wartime Allies, he concluded:

> The only nation that gained any advantage from the policy of Unconditional Surrender was Russia, who, owing to the lengthening of the war, was able to overrun Eastern Europe and there to impose her own political system.[50]

It is unlikely that the opinions of either Stokes or Hankey caused Churchill much worry. Both were fringe figures. Though Stokes was right to raise a question mark over Stalin's attitude, and Hankey was correct that it would benefit Russia, allowing Stalin to dictate his own terms in Eastern Europe, while keeping the British and Americans

---

48 CAC, Hankey Papers, HNKY 13/8.
49 CAC, Hankey Papers, HNKY 13/8.
50 CAC, Hankey Papers, HNKY 25/20.

engaged in the West. Unconditional surrender may have sounded good in 1943, and supported Churchill's narrative of fighting on to final victory, but how would it work in practice?

The Allies did not have long to wait to find out. Italy was the first to fold. Mussolini was toppled by an internal coup in July 1943, just days after the Allied invasion of Sicily, the first part of Italy to be occupied. The King remained in place and a provisional government was established under Marshal Badoglio, a former army Chief of Staff who had resigned in 1940. It was not long before Badoglio started making secret peace overtures to the Allies through their diplomatic missions in Lisbon and Tangier. He was walking a tightrope. Faced with German troops in Italy, and more on the way, he had no option but to tell Berlin that his government would keep fighting. To Churchill and Roosevelt, it was not immediately clear what would happen next.

President Roosevelt cabled Churchill on 26 July, just after Mussolini's fall, stating that in the event of any overtures, 'we must be certain of the use of all Italian territory and transportation against the Germans in the North' and adding that, 'we should come as *close as possible* [my italics] to unconditional surrender followed by good treatment of the Italian populace'. Mussolini and his chief partners in crime were to be handed over, and no Allied officers were to agree to any general terms without the sanction of the President and Prime Minister.[51] 'As close as possible' suggested that there might be some small room for diplomatic manoeuvre, but when the President, possibly influenced by the likely effect of the bombing of Rome on his large domestic Italian-American electorate, suggested that the Italian capital be declared an open city (protected by international law from attack), Churchill replied: 'What will the Russians say? It would be taken as a proof that we were going to make a patched-up peace with the King and Badoglio and had abandoned the principle of unconditional surrender'. Moreover, the Allies would want to use Rome themselves as a base in due course.[52] This did not mean that Churchill did not want to act swiftly. He was concerned by what the Russians would say, and how this would impact on British and American public opinion, but he also feared what they and the Germans might do to exploit the emerging political vacuum in Italy. His telegram to Roosevelt of 5 August revealed his two fears. Firstly, that Italy had 'turned Red overnight' as the Communist partisans had seized their opportunity, and might succumb to 'rampant

---

[51] CAC, Churchill Papers, CHAR 20/116/22.
[52] CAC, Churchill Papers, CHAR 20/117/3-4.

Bolshevism'. Secondly, that the Germans were resolved to defend the country line by line. He wanted swift action to invade the mainland and forestall both, and was envisaging supporting the King and Badoglio, suggesting that 'we shall find little opposition, and perhaps even active co-operation, on the part of the Italians'.[53]

Badoglio wanted the Italians to be able to join the Allies in the fight against Germany. Eden pointed out that this was an offer to negotiate on terms and that we should insist on unconditional surrender. Churchill annotated Eden's minute 'Don't miss the bus', and replied that 'while they have to make the formal act of submission, our desire is to treat them with consideration… Merely harping on "unconditional surrender" with no prospect of mercy held out even as an act of grace may well lead to no surrender at all'. President Roosevelt had referred to 'honourable capitulation' and Churchill was in favour of this language being used.[54] It was agreed that there would be no bargain or plans in common, but that any actions against the Germans before the arrival of the Anglo-American forces would be regarded as a 'valuable service, and would render further co-operation possible against common foe. …and facilitate a more friendly relationship with United Nations'.[55]

The armistice was signed on 3 September but not announced until the 8th to coincide with major Allied landings in the bay of Salerno below Naples. The Germans immediately moved against Rome. Lord Hankey, speaking afterwards in the House of Lords, in remarks which were repeated in an American magazine, felt that insistence on unconditional surrender had contributed to an unnecessary delay. This could have been avoided through 'a better spirit of co-operation', and by treating Italy 'in the spirit of the prodigal son'. Unconditional surrender was a harsh and 'rather meaningless term, because there always have to be conditions. And these can always be imposed if the military situation permits and cannot be imposed unless the military situation permits'.[56] Speaking in the Commons two days earlier, Richard Stokes called unconditional surrender 'the most puerile bit of statesmanship ever forthcoming from responsible people'.[57]

On reviewing the process in January 1944, the British Joint Planning Staff recalled that 'Marshal Badoglio did his best to wriggle out of unconditional surrender', presumably referring to his attempts to insist

---

[53] Churchill, *The Second World War*, Vol. V, pp.89-90.

[54] Churchill, *The Second World War*, Vol. V, p.91.

[55] CAC, Churchill Papers, CHAR 20/117/46-47.

[56] *Hansard*, 23 September 1943. House of Lords Debate, Vol 129, cc111-161; CAC, Hankey Papers, HNKY 13/8.

[57] *Hansard*, 21 September 1943. House of Commons Debate, Vol 392, cc69-170.

first on the Italians being allowed to join the Allies and, secondly, on his attempt to secure the Allied protection of Rome. The first was refused and the second was cancelled when the Germans moved against the Italian capital. The planners also referred to the fact that the surrender instrument was subsequently modified by protocol, confirming further negotiation, but noted that, 'We can still safely claim that the Italians have accepted total defeat in writing, and we still have the freedom of action to bring this home to the Italian people in any way we think fit'.[58] Unconditional surrender was certainly a complicating factor in the armistice negotiations, one which limited the Allies own room for manoeuvre and which both Churchill and Roosevelt therefore chose to interpret as flexibly as possible. Yet there seems little evidence to suggest that it substantially slowed the surrender process. The real limiting factor for Badoglio was fear of the Germans and the timing of the Allied arrival. Anticipating the Italian armistice, Hitler had begun pumping troops into Italy, and Badoglio delayed first the signing and then the announcement until the Allied landings were imminent.

Achieving the unconditional surrender of Germany would clearly prove a much bigger challenge, and events in Italy must have focused minds on this. Moreover, it was at this point that doubts about the Russian attitude began to surface. The Soviet government had not been represented in Casablanca, and Stalin's agreement had been rather taken for granted. The issue seems to have surfaced at the first 'Big Three' meeting of Churchill, Roosevelt and Stalin at Tehran over dinner on the evening of 29 November 1943. Eden was there, and reported back to the Foreign Office that:

> Marshal Stalin spoke to the President last night (November 29th) about unconditional surrender. He said he thought this bad tactics vis-à-vis Germany and suggested we should work out terms together and make them generally known to the German people. Prime Minister agrees that this is a better suggestion.[59]

We know from Churchill's later published account that this dinner conversation was focused on the future of Germany. Indeed, he recounts how he stormed out of the meal when Stalin, egged on by Roosevelt and his son Elliott, joked about executing fifty thousand of the German officer corps.[60] Though he could not admit it in writing, Churchill knew

---

[58] TNA, CAB 121/92, JP (44) 5.
[59] TNA, CAB 121/92.
[60] Churchill, *Second World War*, Vol. V, p.330.

by this point that it was the Russians who had executed thousands of Polish officers in cold blood in the woods of Katyn in 1940.[61] Thus, while the official Allied line remained that this was a German atrocity, the reality lent credence to Stalin's jesting and must have left a bad taste. It also surely implied that any terms Stalin produced were unlikely to be lenient to the German people. The Russian leader made no secret of his desire to see the complete dismemberment of Germany, and it was at Tehran that Roosevelt brought forward his plan for splitting up the country.[62] Yet any retreat from unconditional surrender was now almost impossible. For in their joint meeting at Cairo, just days before the beginning of the Tehran Conference, the British and Americans had recognised it in writing as their supreme war objective.[63]

On 7 December Churchill read a despatch from the British Naval Attaché in Ankara, passing on the Turkish view that the Allies should 'publish Allied terms to Axis as even unconditional surrender entails conditions'. It argued that 'however severe the conditions might be the German front would collapse soon after they were known. It is the feeling that they have nothing to hope for that keeps them fighting'. In a clear reference to Stalin's comments at Tehran, Churchill annotated the page with a note for Eden stating, 'This tallies w[ith]what our friend said'.[64]

Then, just before Christmas 1943, through intermediaries in neutral Sweden, the Allies received what appeared to be a request from Himmler, the head of the German SS, asking for negotiations to clarify the meaning of unconditional surrender. This seemed to be another attempt to try and split the British and Americans from the Russians. Eden obtained the agreement of the War Cabinet to inform the United States and Soviet governments before replying that, 'we had nothing to say to Hitler, Himmler and those associated with him except that our terms were unconditional surrender'.[65] Churchill replied, agreeing with the approach, but still pondering on 'Stalin's suggestion at Tehran that "unconditional surrender" required some definition' and wondering about a public announcement by the three Allies 'which would undermine the present Nazi gang'.[66]

Eden had in fact already cabled Moscow and Washington on 17 December suggesting that the newly created European Advisory Commission, the body specifically intended to co-ordinate post-war

---

[61] Barker, *Churchill and Eden at War*, pp.248-250.
[62] TNA, PREM 3/193/5.
[63] TNA, PREM 3/193/5.
[64] TNA, PREM 3/193/5.
[65] TNA, PREM 3/193/5; CAC, Churchill Papers, CHAR 20/130/70.
[66] TNA, CAB 121/92.

Allied policy, might consider working out such terms. His message referred to the conversation at Tehran between Roosevelt and Stalin. When the reply came back saying that the President could not remember this conversation, Churchill tried to jog Roosevelt's memory, reminding him that it was before 'we began talking about the 50,000 and your compromise and my high falutin, and I finished up by no means certain that the Germans would be reassured if they were told what he [Stalin] had in his mind'.[67] Roosevelt's reply was unequivocal. He preferred to leave things as they were for the time being, 'as we really do not know enough about opinions within Germany itself to go on any fishing expedition there at this time'. Instead, he referred Churchill to the public announcement he had made on Christmas Eve confirming that, 'The United Nations have no intention to enslave the German people' and wanted them as 'useful and respectable members of the European family', but noting that we 'intend to rid them once and for all of Nazism and Prussian militarism and the fantastic and disastrous notion that they constitute the "Master Race"'. This was not far removed from his words after Casablanca, and it is where he now wanted the matter to rest.[68]

In London, the matter would not go back in its box that easily. On 7 January 1944, the members of the War Cabinet were circulated with a paper from the Joint Intelligence Sub-Committee which examined the effect of the unconditional surrender policy on German morale. It concluded that internal German propaganda was making very effective use of the concept, in convincing the German people that they 'will be held collectively responsible with their leaders for all crimes perpetrated', and it felt that some wider explanation of the policy might offer hope and encourage some withdrawal of support from the regime.[69] The matter was then referred to the Chiefs of Staff, who passed it to the Joint Planning Staff. From the military perspective, the planners felt it would be a 'cardinal mistake' to abandon the formula of unconditional surrender. It was both stimulating to Allied morale and essential that, this time, 'the German political and military leaders openly acknowledge total defeat' and were seen to do so by the German people.[70] This was endorsed by the Chiefs of Staff, but they also drafted a declaration to be issued by the three Allied leaders to reassure the German people about their future after surrender, and recommended

[67] CAC, Churchill Papers, CHAR 20/ 154/8-9.
[68] CAC, Churchill Papers, CHAR 20/154/35-36.
[69] TNA, CAB 66/45, WP (44) 10.
[70] TNA, CAB 121/92, JP (44) 5.

that it be issued before the American, British and Canadian forces returned to France, as this might weaken the morale of German troops.[71] Eden produced his own paper on 19 February agreeing that a joint pronouncement at the right psychological moment might be helpful, and circulating his own draft text.[72]

In the meantime, Churchill had waded into the debate with his own paper. It was written on 15 January in response to the original submission by the Joint Intelligence Sub-Committee, and was based on his knowledge of the President's position. He explained that his definition of unconditional surrender was that it meant that the Germans had no rights to any particular form of treatment, and that the Atlantic Charter 'would not apply to them as a matter of right'. However, he appended Roosevelt's remarks of 24 December, and, echoing his own comments at the time of the Italian surrender, confirmed that 'the victorious nations owe it to themselves to observe the obligations of humanity and civilisation'. That said, he felt that a frank statement about what was going to happen in Germany would not necessarily give the German people the reassurance the Intelligence sub-committee had been recommending. The country was likely to be disarmed and broken up, and Stalin had spoken at Tehran of requiring the forced labour of four million Germans to rebuild Russia, and of disposing of the German officer corps (though here he admitted that he was not sure how serious the Russian leader had been in that part of the conversation).[73]

The matter was finally brought to the War Cabinet on 13 March, where Churchill steered a discussion that decided 'no advantage would be gained by the adoption of any of the formulae proposed at this time'.[74] A stalemate had been reached. Unconditional surrender was a gift for German propaganda, but the terms of any conditional surrender were likely to be dictated from Moscow.

Churchill endorsed unconditional surrender because Roosevelt wanted it and he needed to please Roosevelt. As a concept it sounded good, and fitted well with his vocabulary of victory over tyranny and terror 'however long and hard the road may be'. In an atmosphere of mutual distrust, it was a public guarantee to the Soviet Union. As a piece of psychological theatre, it marked a turning point in the war,

---

[71] TNA, CAB 66/46, WP (44) 83.
[72] TNA, CAB 66/47, WP (44) 125.
[73] TNA, CAB 66/45, WP (44) 33.
[74] TNA, CAB 121/92.

illustrating that the Allies were now on the offensive. Like the Atlantic Charter, it was developed quickly, an example of the President and Prime Minister making policy in the moment, and was the product of largely informal discussions without input from expert advisers and committees. It was convenient, even essential, as propaganda, but more problematic as policy.

Once it had been publicly announced, it was almost impossible for Churchill to retreat from it, especially while Roosevelt remained so committed. Yet it is clear from the internal debates that Churchill had reservations. The contemporary records show him questioning and wriggling in private, but ultimately sticking with the policy in public. In the end, Germany had to be fought to almost complete destruction, while it took two atomic bombs to bring Japan to her knees. In the case of the former, external fear of the Soviets and internal fear of the Gestapo played their role in keeping the German populace fighting, while the British and Americans remained committed to the Russian alliance and were thus unable to consider a separate peace. Unconditional surrender helped guarantee that commitment, and undoubtedly complicated life for Churchill, but it is difficult to see how in itself it significantly prolonged the war. It was a manifestation of the uneasy alliance between the Anglo-American allies and the Soviet Union.

Yet there is a piece of evidence that suggests that in the end, with the benefit of hindsight and faced with the post-war Soviet domination of Eastern Germany, that Churchill recognised this as a mistake and not a masterstroke. In 1948, he wrote a short essay called *The Dream* about a conversation with the ghost of his father, Lord Randolph Churchill. It is a very personal and introspective piece, and was, almost uniquely, written for private family consumption rather than publication. When his father's apparition materialises in his painting studio, Winston dutifully answers the spectre's questions about events since Lord Randolph's passing in 1895. The discussion inevitably turns to the two great world wars, and Churchill explains that:

> 'They were the wars of nations, caused by demagogues and tyrants'.
> 'Did we win?'
> 'Yes, we won all our wars. All our enemies were beaten down. We even made them surrender unconditionally'.
> 'No one should be made to do that. Great people forget sufferings, but not humiliations'.[75]

---

[75] Churchill, W., *The Dream*, (International Churchill Society, 1994), p.26.

Things had come full circle. Unconditional surrender had, at least in part, been justified as necessary in demonstrating to the Germans that they had been comprehensively defeated, thereby preventing the myth of betrayal that had contributed to the rise of the Nazi Party. But now Churchill feared that the very scale of German humiliation at the hands of the Allies, and especially the Soviets, might have the same result.

In this respect, the debate linked to the issue that dominated Churchill's thinking after Casablanca and which had already been identified by Soviet Ambassador Maisky, namely the timing and nature of the Anglo-American intervention in Europe. The Allied intervention had to be judged very carefully, so as to come 'not too early and not too late' to prevent Moscow's domination of Europe.

Chapter 8

Mind or Body?

How did Churchill cope with the build-up to D-Day

It is the early hours of 12 December 1943. The setting Tunisia, in a villa not far from the ruins of the ancient city of Carthage.

'Hullo, Hullo, Hullo!' A plaintive cry breaks the silence. Suddenly, General Sir Alan Brooke is awake. He grabs his torch and points it toward the end of his bed. The moaning apparition that greets his still-adjusting eyes is clothed in a brightly coloured gown decorated with Chinese dragons, its face partially obscured by a large brown bandage. What goes through the half-waking mind of the Chief of the Imperial General Staff? Perhaps he wonders whether this is some ghostly visitation from the age of Hannibal, or steels himself to face a strange and colourful oriental assassin. Within a few seconds, he must have realised that it was his boss, Winston Churchill, and that all was not well with the Prime Minister.[1]

This night time wandering marked the beginning of a serious bout of pneumonia. Over the course of the next few days, Churchill's temperature, pulse and respiration all rose to worrying levels. His lungs were congested, and his heartbeat was sometimes dangerously irregular. The Cabinet were informed, public bulletins were issued, experts were summoned, new-fangled antibiotics were administered, and Clementine Churchill flew from London to be at her husband's bedside.[2]

The popular perception and image of Winston Churchill is that of a bulldog with an iron constitution: the war leader with the omnipresent

---

[1] Danchev & Todman, *Alanbrooke Diaries*, p.497.
[2] Moran, *Struggle for Survival*, pp.148-154.

cigar who had 'taken more out of alcohol than alcohol has taken out of me', and whose relentless drive and energy shamed much younger men.[3] When Montgomery announced that he did not smoke, he did not drink, and was 100% fit; Churchill replied in a flash, that he did drink, that he did smoke, and that he was 200% fit.[4] Such stories have become part and parcel of the Churchill canon. Yet, even while Churchill may have said such things, it does not mean they were always true. We would not expect him as wartime leader to admit to spells of exhaustion or ill-health, and yet the reality of his workload and the pressures upon him surely made them inevitable.

In December 1943, he had just undertaken a particularly gruelling month of travel and diplomacy: meeting first with Roosevelt and Chiang Kai-Shek of China in Cairo, and then with the American President and Marshal Stalin for the first wartime 'Big Three' meeting in Tehran. While previous trips had often acted as a welcome tonic and a break from the London routine, this time he seems to have been in poor health from the beginning. Though already suffering with a heavy cold, compounded by a slight fever brought on by injections against typhoid, he had sailed from Plymouth on 12 November.[5] On HMS *Renown*, he took to his cabin and was nursed by his daughter Sarah.[6] In Malta, he met with the Chiefs of Staff from bed where Brooke thought him far from his best, and his doctor's verdict was that he was 'still mouldy'.[7] Upon arrival in Egypt he cabled to Clementine admitting that he had only just mastered a bad cold on his chest. Five days later he still had a 'nasty cough' in the mornings, and arrived in Tehran with no voice, leading to the cancellation of the opening dinner and to his eating alone in bed 'like a sulky little boy'.[8] Prime Minister Smuts of South Africa 'was not at all happy about the condition of the PM. He considered he worked far too hard, exhausted himself, and then had to rely on drink to stimulate him again'.[9] The final blow came when Churchill's aircraft was diverted en route to Tunis, and he had to spend the best part of an hour sitting 'chilled to the bone' on an upturned packing case in a remote airfield.[10]

---

[3] Eade, C., *Churchill by his Contemporaries*, (Hutchinson & Co, 1953), p.364.
[4] Montgomery, B., *Memoirs*, (Collins, 1958), p.69.
[5] Moran, *Struggle for Survival*, pp.125-129.
[6] Churchill, *The Second World War*, Vol. V, p.287.
[7] Danchev & Todman, *Alanbrooke Diaries*, p.472; Moran, *Struggle for Survival*, p.129.
[8] Soames, *Speaking For Themselves*, pp.485-489; Dilks (ed), *Cadogan Diaries*, p.578; CAC, Sarah Churchill Papers, SCHL 1/1/7.
[9] Danchev & Todman, *Alanbrooke Diaries*, p.493.
[10] Pawle, *The War & Colonel Warden*, p.273.

It was probably will power and adrenalin alone that had sustained him through his high-powered meetings with Roosevelt and Stalin, but by the time of his collapse in Carthage it was clear that Churchill was running on empty. He later wrote that he no longer even had the energy to dry himself after a bath, 'but lay on the bed wrapped in my towel till I dried naturally'.[11] Nor was it to be a quick recovery. He remained in Tunisia over Christmas, and was 'still feeble' when he moved to Marrakesh to convalesce on 27 December.[12] He did not return to London until 18 January, by which time he had been away for nearly two months.[13] Attlee, as Deputy Prime Minister, had been chairing the War Cabinet. The latest investigation by medical historians has confirmed that Churchill's North African illness was both potentially life threatening and concluded that it must have temporarily interfered with his ability to operate at the highest level.[14]

Churchill had celebrated his sixty-ninth birthday on 30 November 1943 at Tehran, and was now entering on his seventh decade. He had served as Prime Minister for forty-two months. According to calculations by Captain Pim of the map room, made while en route to that first 'Big Three' conference, he had already travelled 111,000 miles by sea and air since September 1939, spending some 792 hours at sea and 339 hours in the air, the latter in very basic conditions in crudely converted military aircraft.[15] The press of business had been unrelenting, and the stakes had been consistently high and often mortal.

Physically, Churchill's poor health in 1944 can be attributed to his slow recovery from pneumonia. But the pneumonia itself was also surely a symptom? It was in part a manifestation of the particular set of problems he now found himself facing.

Churchill was aware that his ability to set the agenda and to influence the flow of events had declined. His illness in Carthage seems to have been induced as much by mental frustration as physical exhaustion. The conferences at the end of 1943 saw increasing pressure from both the Americans and the Soviets. They wanted to prioritise the Second Front in France, thereby curtailing the British-led operations in Italy

---

[11] Churchill, *The Second World War*, Vol. V, p.372.
[12] Moran, *Struggle for Survival*, p.156.
[13] Gilbert, *Winston S. Churchill*, Vol. VII, p.655.
[14] Vale, J. & Scadding J., 'In Carthage ruins: the illness of Sir Winston Churchill at Carthage, December 1943', *Journal of the Royal College of Physicians Edinburgh*, Vol. 47, 2017.
[15] Gilbert, *Winston S. Churchill*, Vol. VII, p.552; Pawle, *The War & Colonel Warden*, pp.261-262.

and the Mediterranean; transferring men and materials to Britain in preparation for the assault on Normandy, now codenamed *Overlord*. This was vigorously opposed by both Churchill and the British Chiefs of Staff, especially Brooke, who saw advantages in continuing to push up the spine of Italy, either as an alternative to operations in France, if successful, or as means of pinning down as many German divisions as possible in order to prevent them reinforcing France. Churchill argued strongly for the symbolic importance of capturing Rome, and the tactical advantage of being able to bomb southern Germany from the north Italian airfields. He still felt that there was potential to build on Italian success by bringing in Turkey, reinforcing Greece, and taking the fight to the enemy in Albania, Yugoslavia, Romania and Bulgaria, before turning from Italy towards Austria. He had been especially incensed by General Eisenhower's refusal to countenance a diversion of troops to garrison some of the Greek Dodecanese islands.[16] At Malta, he gave a 'long tirade on evils of Americans' and felt inclined to say, 'all right if you won't play with us in the Mediterranean we won't play with you in the English Channel'.[17] In the event, at Cairo, he seems to have restricted himself to warning about the dangers of the tyranny of *Overlord*.[18] He apparently echoed these sentiments while flying to Tehran, telling his doctor that, 'Because the Americans want to invade France in six months' time, that is no reason why we should throw away these shining, gleaming opportunities in the Mediterranean'.[19] And when he complained to Clementine about how terrible it was 'fighting with both hands tied behind one's back', she was wise enough to caution 'patience and magnanimity', reminding him of his saying 'that the only worse thing than Allies is not having Allies'.[20]

The conferences themselves would not have improved his mood. The discussions in Cairo were dominated by the presence of Chiang Kai-Shek and focused almost exclusively on the Pacific.[21] When Europe was discussed, the British found themselves fighting hard to block an American plan for a single Supreme Commander for all operations against Germany; a proposal which would have allowed the United States to subordinate all operations in the Italian theatre to the build-up

---

[16] Churchill, *The Second World War*, Vol. V, pp.291-294 & pp.304-305; Eisenhower, *Crusade in Europe*, pp.210-211.

[17] Danchev & Todman (eds), *Alanbrooke Diaries*, p.472.

[18] Danchev & Todman (eds), *Alanbrooke Diaries*, p.480.

[19] Moran, *Struggle for Survival*, p.133.

[20] Soames, *Speaking for Themselves*, pp.485-486.

[21] Churchill, *The Second World War*, Vol. V, p.290; Danchev & Todman (eds), *Alanbrooke Diaries*, p.480.

for the invasion of France. In his note of rebuttal, Churchill argued strongly for the principle that 'command in any theatre should go to the ally who has the largest forces deployed or about to be deployed there'. By this logic, he was adamant that the Mediterranean was to remain a British theatre.[22] It seems that Churchill's only agreeable memory from Cairo may have been watching Roosevelt carve the Thanksgiving turkey and then dancing with General 'Pa' Watson to a gramophone recording.[23]

At Tehran, Roosevelt carefully resisted Churchill's entreaties for a private lunch.[24] Cadogan felt that the President was 'promising everything that Stalin wants in the way of an attack in the West' with the result that Churchill was 'becoming an object of suspicion to Stalin'. The primacy, Churchill would have said tyranny, of *Overlord* was confirmed, and Churchill was left feeling that his 'subsidiary but gleaming opportunities were cast aside unused'.[25] When the Soviet leader and the American President joined forces in teasing the British Prime Minister over dinner, it must have served to reinforce the impression of exclusion and of a new US-Soviet alignment.[26] Brooke felt that, 'We were reaching a very dangerous point where Stalin's shrewdness, assisted by American short-sightedness, might lead us anywhere'.[27] In fact, it was agreed that they would lead to an assault against Normandy in May 1944, with an accompanying operation against the south of France. Churchill took consolation from the fact that he was authorised to make new advances to Turkey, and that the operation in southern France, coming from Italy, would temporarily leave him with some landing craft for other operations in the Mediterranean. Yet it was clear to all that the main focus of Anglo-American strategy had switched to France. There were still moments of pomp and circumstance to savour, like Churchill's presentation to Stalin of the Sword of Stalingrad, or his inspection in the desert of his old regiment, the Fourth Hussars, but his influence on the international stage was ebbing.[28] According to Brooke, there still lay 'in the back of his mind the desire to form a purely British theatre where the laurels would be all ours'.[29] But it was becoming harder to achieve.

---

22 Churchill, *The Second World War*, Vol. V, pp.296-300.
23 Churchill, *The Second World War*, Vol. V, p.301.
24 Moran, *Struggle for Survival*, p.136.
25 Churchill, *The Second World War*, Vol. V, p.306.
26 Dilks (ed), *Cadogan Diaries*, p.580; Churchill, *The Second World War*, Vol. V, p.330.
27 Danchev & Todman (eds), *Alanbrooke Diaries*, p.484.
28 CAC, Sarah Churchill Papers, SCHL 1/1/7.
29 Danchev & Todman, *Alanbrooke Diaries*, p.473.

Indeed, the whole nature of Churchill's war was now very different from that of 1940-42. What had begun as a very intense but narrowly focused battle for survival in France and Britain, had now widened out into a global conflict of tremendous military, political and logistical complexity. The immediate needs of many and often competing theatres of war now sat side by side with an increasingly tangled web of diplomatic alliances and growing questions of post-war reconstruction, strategy and security. Preliminary discussions had begun at Tehran on the hugely difficult issues of the post-war composition of Germany and the borders of Poland. These would soon come to dominate the last year of the war in Europe. It is at this time that Colville captures Churchill as saying that, 'this world, "this dusty and lamentable ball" is now too beastly to live in'.[30]

In April 1944 the issues coming before the War Cabinet for discussion included: the applicability of the Atlantic Charter to Germany; the question of whether to bomb French railway centres and accept large civilian casualties; how to respond to industrial unrest in the British mining industry; negotiations with the United States over control of oil supplies; the shortage of trained medical personnel; the future of the civil aviation industry; the response to the deteriorating political and military situation in Greece; the status of the French Committee of National Liberation; the backing of Tito's communist partisans in Yugoslavia; Russian demands in Romania, Finland and Poland; special measures to preserve the secrecy of the invasion of France; the decision to expand the Heathrow runway; manpower requirements for the ongoing war against Japan; the need to target German secret weapon sites; the famine in India; the meeting of the Dominion Prime Ministers; and the proposed nature of the post-war World organisation.[31] Even allowing for the assistance of a highly efficient secretariat, the number of papers crossing the desks of War Cabinet members, and that of the Prime Minister in particular, was now enormous and clearly taking a toll.

The diaries of Brooke and Cadogan for the first half of 1944 record their personal frustrations with the Prime Minister, and do so in terms that often reflect on his declining physical and mental health. To Cadogan, Churchill was complaining of his legs, and could no longer walk or even stand for very long; he was 'flushed' and 'very woolly; he was 'not the man he was 12 months ago' and was rambling 'without a pause'.[32] At times, the Under Secretary of State longed for the more

---

[30] Colville, *The Fringes of Power*, p.478.

[31] TNA, CAB 65/42.

[32] Dilks (ed), *Cadogan Diaries*, pp.597-598, p.611 & p.621.

organised and dispassionate chairmanship of Chamberlain.[33] While Brooke speculated that the Prime Minister might not last three months. He was 'failing fast'; was 'dull, lifeless and missing the main points'; while at other times it seemed as if Churchill had 'lost all balance' so that Brooke felt as though he were 'chained to the chariot of a lunatic'.[34]

Perhaps these observations tell us as much about the pressures on Brooke and Cadogan as they do about those on Churchill. When reflecting on this period, General Brooke later admitted that 'I cannot have been very far off from nervous breakdown at that time'.[35] While Cadogan vented his frustrations in his journal entry for 29 January: 'When is this bloody war going to end? I'm tired of it, and getting rather stale altogether – getting myopic from constant close-up view of the grindstone'.[36] The cumulative effect of bearing such burdens for so long was inevitably beginning to show on all those at the centre of affairs, not just the Prime Minister.

Yet, for Churchill, who often had to act as the final arbiter for both Brooke's military questions and Cadogan's diplomatic issues, while simultaneously wrestling with so much more, the pressures must have been immense. It is noticeable that in early 1944 both Brooke and Cadogan record uncharacteristic admissions of weakness. On Tuesday, 21 March, Churchill confessed to the War Cabinet that he was tired and Cadogan noted 'he's almost done in' and 'everyone's exhausted'.[37] While, on 7 May, Brooke recorded watching a film after dinner at Chequers, after which:

> Winston took me down to the little study where the secretaries work. There he sat by the fire and drank his soup. He looked very old and very tired. He said Roosevelt was not well and that he was no longer the man that he had been, this he said also applied to himself (Winston). He said he could still always sleep well, eat well and especially drink well! but that he no longer jumped out of bed the way he used to, and felt as if he would be quite content to spend the whole day in bed. I have never yet heard him admit that he was beginning to fail.[38]

Exhaustion and overwork now sat alongside a real concern about strategy. It is wrong to say that Churchill opposed *Overlord per se*. He

---

[33] Dilks (ed), *Cadogan Diaries*, p.621 & p.630.
[34] Danchev & Todman (eds), *Alanbrooke Diaries*, p.528, p.534, & p.542.
[35] Danchev & Todman, *Alanbrooke Diaries*, p.466.
[36] Dilks (ed), *Cadogan Diaries*, p.601.
[37] Dilks (ed), *Cadogan Diaries*, pp.611-612.
[38] Danchev & Todman, *Alanbrooke Diaries*, p.544.

certainly did not wish to see it undertaken until the criteria for success had been fulfilled, by which he meant mastery of the seas and skies, and the ability to bring superior forces against a greatly weakened enemy. From the Casablanca Conference onwards, he had backed plans for an operation in France, and by the end of 1943 he could see that the huge American build-up of men and materials and the Russian successes on the Eastern Front made an operation inevitable. It was the weight to be given to that operation at the expense of all other theatres, especially the Mediterranean, that concerned him. Strip away the layers of hindsight and look at the events of 1944 from Churchill's perspective, and it is possible to see why he was reluctant to place all his eggs in one basket.

Churchill ended the fifth volume of his war memoirs with the confident assertion that:

> The immense cross-Channel enterprise for the liberation of France had begun. All the ships were at sea. We had the mastery of the oceans and of the air. The Hitler tyranny was doomed.[39]

He wrote those words between 1949 and 1951, and published them in 1952.[40] It seems to me that this quote sums up the problem we have when talking about the D-Day landings, namely that same benefit of hindsight and the luxury of knowing that the Allies succeeded. The American casualties on Omaha beach not-withstanding, the operation was a triumph of planning, preparation and execution. The vast naval operation got the troops safely across the Channel, Allied aircraft obtained complete mastery of the skies, deception plans largely achieved the element of surprise, and within a week the beach heads had been secured and the initial mission objective of gaining a lodgement on the enemy occupied shore had been fulfilled. When the break-out came, it was faster and more sweeping than most would have dared to predict. Paris was liberated on the 25 August, Strasbourg in November, and by the end of the year Allied forces were preparing for the crossing of the Rhine and the final assault on Nazi Germany.

The scale of the operation was certainly well beyond anything the Allies had attempted prior to that date. The logistics for *Overlord* were simply staggering: The initial naval operation was supported by seven battleships, twenty-three cruisers, more than 100 destroyers, over

---

[39] Churchill, *The Second World War*, Vol. V (1952), p.558.
[40] Reynolds, *In Command of History*, pp.361-364.

1,000 other fighting ships, and over 4,000 landing craft.[41] The assault on the beaches may have been by five army divisions, but that was just the start of a much longer campaign to liberate France and push into Germany. By the end of August 1944 there were twenty American, twelve British, three Canadian, one French and one Polish division, on the continent. These were being protected by 4,035 heavy bombers, 1,720 light, medium and torpedo bombers, 5,000 fighters and 2,000 transport planes. The allied armies were consuming 600-700 tons of supplies per day, requiring the delivery from the ports to the front line of some 20,000 tons per day.[42] This was a huge operation, but success could not be guaranteed. The return to France brought with it the possibility of huge military and civilian casualties, and real fears about the consequences of failure.

Churchill's caution derived in part from his own experience. He later wrote: 'the fearful price we had had to pay in human life and blood for the great offensives of the First World War was graven in my mind. Memories of the Somme and Passchendaele and many lesser frontal attacks upon the Germans were not to be blotted out by time or reflection'.[43] He chose not to reference Gallipoli and the Dardanelles campaign, but the costly failure of that amphibious, inter-allied operation, and its cost to his earlier career, must surely have preyed upon him. This was certainly the view of General Eisenhower, the Allied Supreme Commander for the campaign, who remembered the Prime Minister expressing his fear that the tides might 'run red with the blood of American and British youth, or the beaches be choked with their bodies'.[44] Surveying the more recent past, Churchill must have brooded on the failure of the British to hold the Norwegian coastline and the ease with which they had been thrown out of France in 1940. The failure of the raid in force against the beaches of Dieppe in August 1942 had certainly illustrated the perils of landing on a well defended enemy shoreline.

He also knew that the return to the continent was likely to trigger a resumption of the German bombing of Britain. The Luftwaffe no longer had the capability to inflict the same level of damage as in the days of the Blitz, but Churchill was aware that the Germans were developing launch sites on the other side of the Channel for new flying bombs and rockets, named V-1 and V-2. The exact nature and strength of these

---

[41] Kennedy, P., *The Engineers of Victory*, (Allen Lane, 2013), p.253.

[42] Eisenhower, *Crusade in Europe*, (1948), pp.317-319.

[43] Winston S Churchill "The Closing of the Ring", *The Second World War*, Vol. V (1952), p.514.

[44] Eisenhower, *Crusade in Europe*, pp.213-214.

weapons remained unknown. Churchill's son-in-law, Duncan Sandys, was tasked with heading the relevant committee, working alongside scientists Lord Cherwell and R.V. Jones.[45] By January the Chiefs of Staff were reviewing the evidence on a weekly basis and attempts were being made to identify and destroy possible launch sites.[46] The first V-1 jet propelled flying bombs were launched shortly after D-Day on 13 June, and attacks continued until all the firing sites were overrun by the Allies in the autumn. By this time, the Germans had also begun V-2 ballistic missile rocket attacks, which could be fired from much further away. While inflicting some damage on London, and introducing a new element of terror for the civilian population, these new weapons could not be made in sufficient numbers or fired with enough accuracy to deliver the wholesale destruction promised by Hitler. Yet Churchill did not know this prior to the Normandy invasion, and so could not ignore the possibility of an effective German retaliation from the skies.

What he did know was that preliminary bombardments by the Allies were likely to result in huge numbers of French civilian casualties, and he initially refused to sanction the wholesale bombing of French railway centres, depots and marshalling yards. The issue was raised by Portal, the Chief of the Air Staff, at the War Cabinet on 3 April. He asked for the lifting of the existing operational restrictions, which limited bombing to thirteen out of seventy-four railway centres in France and Belgium. Churchill first queried whether it might be better to bomb other targets, such as arms dumps and military camps, before backing Eden, who argued that the proposed operations might damage both the reputation of the RAF in France and risk turning French and Belgian public opinion away from Britain and towards Russia, whose reputation already stood very high in those countries. The issue clearly divided the military leaders, who were entirely focused on the coming battle, from the politicians who were already having to think about the wider repercussions and the political aftermath of the invasion.[47]

The matter was referred to the Defence Committee, which Churchill chaired, and was endlessly debated in a series of late night meetings in the Map Room throughout April.[48] In his opening remarks for the first meeting on 5 April, the Prime Minister made his views clear: 'It was one thing to launch attacks which would result in heavy loss of civilian life during the hot blood of battle; it was quite another to begin, when

---

45   Churchill, *The Second World War*, Vol. V, pp.201-213.
46   Danchev & Todman (eds), *Alanbrooke Diaries*, p.511.
47   TNA, CAB 65/46, WM (44) 43.
48   TNA, CAB 69/6, DO (44) 5, DO (44) 6, DO (44) 7 & DO (44) 8.

no fighting was going on, a policy which was bound to result in the butchering of large numbers of helpless French people'.[49] Three weeks later, on 26 April, he was still concerned that the bombing would 'build up a volume of dull hatred in France which would effect our relations with that country for many years to come'. He was fearful that British public opinion would react against it, and he was concerned that the Americans were not involved as equal participants and that the odium would therefore fall on Britain alone.[50] Such was his uneasiness about the bombings, that he seems to have been unwilling and unable to bring the matter to a successful resolution. At each meeting Churchill led some of his political colleagues in expressing reservations and in trying to limit or halt the policy, and each week it was agreed that the bombings could be continued on a limited basis and would be reviewed. All the while his military colleagues were becoming more and more frustrated with the lack of clarity. In the end, Eisenhower was forced to intervene. He later recalled Churchill being 'genuinely shaken by the fearful picture' and arguing that 'Post-war France must be our friend. It is not alone a question of humanitarianism. It is also a question of high state policy'. Yet the Supreme Commander stood firm on the bombing as a 'critical feature of the battle plan'.[51] Churchill summarised Eisenhower's view to the War Cabinet on 2 May, which put starkly was that, 'If air operations were to be limited, the perils of an already hazardous undertaking would be greatly enhanced'. Yet Churchill still stated that he 'had not fully realised that our use of air power before OVERLORD would assume so cruel and remorseless a form'. He felt that the War Cabinet should draw up 'laws of war' to govern such operations, and advocated immense leaflet dropping to warn the inhabitants of the threatened areas.[52] The matter was back in the Defence Committee the following day, where Churchill was still arguing that acceptable civilian casualties might be capped at 10,000. He also wanted 'a definite assurance' from the Americans that they agreed with the policy and wrote to President Roosevelt in order to obtain this on 7 May.[53]

These discussions clearly consumed an awful lot of time and energy in the immediate run up to the Normandy assault. It is interesting to contrast Churchill's attitude with his decision to sink the French fleet at Oran in the summer of 1940. Then he had been unflinching in his

---

[49] TNA CAB 69/6, DO (44) 5.
[50] TNA CAB 69/6, DO (44) 8.
[51] Eisenhower, *Crusade in Europe*, pp.253-255.
[52] TNA, CAB 65/46, WM (44) 61.
[53] TNA, CAB 69/6, DO (44) 9; Churchill, *The Second World War*, Vol. V, pp.466-467.

resolve and quick in taking the crucial decision, even though it was also a calculated act taking place outside the 'hot blood of battle'. It suggests that context was everything. In 1940, British defeat was a real possibility, and the message that Churchill's actions needed to send was one of defiance and determination to fight on, if necessary, alone. In the spring of 1944, victory was a possibility, and it was important, for audiences at home and abroad, now and in the future, that Britain be seen to be returning to the continent as a liberator not a warmonger. For Churchill, as indeed for Attlee and Eden, it was vital to win the hearts and minds of the French: to maximise their help against the Germans, but also to help strengthen post-war ties, countering Soviet and American influence.

On the night before D-Day Churchill dined alone with Clementine and told her that, 'Do you realise that by the time you wake up in the morning twenty thousand men may have been killed?'[54] She was aware of his mood and had already written him a touching letter expressing her feelings for him 'at this agonising moment – so full of suspense, which prevents me from rejoicing over Rome'. [Rome had finally fallen to the Allies on 5 June].[55] Interestingly, Brooke felt he had the opposite problem, and that Churchill was too optimistic about the prospects of success on 5 June.[56] Perhaps the Prime Minister was putting on a brave face for his Chiefs of Staff, or perhaps his mood was alternating in the excitement and uncertainty of the moment.

In any event, it would be wrong to think that any streak of pessimism was a lonely manifestation of Churchill's black dog. It was not. Strip away the layers of hindsight and you see that it was shared by almost all the senior Allied commanders. Admiral Ramsay, the oft-forgotten architect of the naval planning for *Overlord*, aptly named Operation *Neptune*, wrote in his diary for 5 June 1944, 'I am under no delusions as to the risks involved in this most difficult of all operations & the critical period around H-Hour when, if initial flights are held up, success will be in the balance'.[57] Field Marshal Sir Alan Brooke, the Chief of the Imperial General Staff, went even further in his private journal of the same day, writing: 'It is very hard to believe that in a few hours the cross Channel invasion starts! I am very uneasy about the whole operation.

---

[54] Mary Soames, *Clementine Churchill*, (revised edn, 2002), p.392 (cited from Pawle, *The War and Colonel Warden*).

[55] CAC, Baroness Spencer-Churchill Papers, CSCT 1/28; Soames, *Speaking for Themselves*, p.496.

[56] Danchev & Todman, *Alanbrooke Diaries*, pp.553-554.

[57] Love, R., & Major, J. (eds), *The Year of D-day: The 1944 Diary of Admiral Sir Bertram Ramsay*, (Hull Academic Press, 1994), p.83.

At best it will fall so very very far short of the expectation of the bulk of the people, namely all those who know nothing of its difficulties. At the worst it may well be the most ghastly disaster of the whole war. I wish to God it were safely over'.[58]

Even the Supreme Commander, General Eisenhower, after giving the momentous order to go, retired to write and seal a letter to be opened in the event of failure that night accepting personal responsibility upon withdrawing the troops from the beach heads. Later in his book *Crusade in Europe* he concluded: 'The two countries [Britain and the United States] were definitely placing all their hopes, expectations, and assets in one great effort to establish a theatre of operations in Western Europe. Failure would carry with it consequences that would be almost fatal'. He argued that such a catastrophe would mean the withdrawal of all United States forces from the United Kingdom and their redeployment to other theatres, presumably including the Pacific. Allied morale would be damaged 'beyond calculation' and defeat would 'react violently' on the Russian situation, where the Soviets might give up on their Allies and consider a separate peace.[59] Churchill was far from alone in worrying about failure.

Britain, in the run up to D-Day, was a huge armed camp. Unprecedented measures were required to try and ensure the secrecy of such a huge operation. Churchill had quipped to Stalin at Tehran that in wartime, 'truth is so precious that she should always be attended by a bodyguard of lies'.[60] The lies now included the creation of a fictional First United States Army Group, under the command of General George Patton. False radio signals, fake documents, and a host of other measures were used to create the impression that Patton was planning to come ashore in the area of Pas de Calais; thereby pinning German troops to the defence of that shoreline, when they might otherwise have been diverted to the Normandy beaches.[61]

The fear that *Overlord* might be anticipated led to the introduction of draconian measures. From midnight on the 17 April uncensored communications by Allied and neutral diplomats (other than those of the United States and Soviet Union) were banned.[62] Travel to coastal areas or to Eire was restricted. Delays were introduced to mail, overseas telegrams and even shipping to non-Allied ports. Immigration was

---

[58] Danchev & Todman (eds), *Alanbrooke Diaries*, p.554.
[59] Eisenhower, *Crusade in Europe*, p.244.
[60] Churchill, *The Second World War*, Vol. V, p 338; see also TNA, CAB 99/25.
[61] van Ee, D., 'D-Day and the Bodyguard of Lies', in *Churchill and the Great Republic*, (Library of Congress, 2004), p.87.
[62] TNA, CAB 65/42, WM (44) 51.

severely curtailed and controlled.[63] On 30 May, the editor of the *Chicago Tribune*, whose newspaper had previously incurred the wrath of President Roosevelt and the Prime Minister for announcing that the United States had broken the Japanese codes, was barred from leaving Britain and returning home. The War Cabinet ruled that permission to travel could be withheld to any person unless the Government were satisfied that the journey was in the 'interests of the prosecution of the war'.[64]

Such measures were both unpopular and difficult to implement. In January 1944, Churchill had warned Ismay that, 'we must beware of handing out irksome for irksome's sake'.[65] On 15 April, Churchill informed President Roosevelt of the imminent ban on uncensored diplomatic communications, whether sent by cypher or special bag. Because this did not apply to American diplomats, he asked for the help of the American State Department in sending secret messages from any country where the government retaliated in kind by banning uncensored British communications.[66] By the end of May, on the eve of the operations, he was prepared to tell General Eisenhower that the ban could only be extended to D+7 and to refer to 'the enormous inconvenience and friction which this system has caused'.[67] Nerves must have been frayed and worries compounded as the anticipation built.

Churchill insisted on personally chairing the *Overlord* Preparations Committee which met eight times in February and March 1944.[68] This was a major affair, as large as most Cabinet meetings, and attended by the relevant ministers from within and outside of the Cabinet, as well as the Chiefs of Staff, the head of the Secret Intelligence Service and senior public servants. It looked at security measures and logistical issues, and clearly involved the Prime Minister in a certain amount of internal arbitration. For example, when the ban on uncensored diplomatic communications was first recommended in March, the Cabinet Secretary Edward Bridges had to set up a pre-meeting for the Prime Minister with the security services who opposed its early imposition on the grounds that it would both 'leave us in the dark as to what information was leaking out of the country' and hamper British ability to disseminate false cover plan material through diplomatic channels. Bridges noted that the extent of our knowledge of what leaks through diplomatic

---

[63] TNA, PREM 3/345/7.
[64] TNA, CAB 65/42, WM (44) 69.
[65] CAC, Churchill Papers, CHAR 20/179/34.
[66] CAC, Churchill Papers, CHAR 20/162/35.
[67] CAC, Churchill Papers, CHAR 20/137C/260-262.
[68] TNA, PREM 3/345/7.

channels would have to be explained orally. He clearly did not want to put in writing our methods of spying on foreign diplomats![69]

A further pressure was provided by General de Gaulle, who felt that the campaign in France should be accompanied by a recognition of his Committee of National Liberation as the new civil authority. Churchill found himself caught between the need to involve the Free French forces in the freeing of their homeland, and the American fears that to do so might compromise security and involve them in recognising de Gaulle's committee as the legitimate government of France. In the end if fell to Churchill to summon de Gaulle, who arrived 'bristling' from his headquarters in French Algiers on 4 June. There then followed an uneasy meeting at which Churchill told the general that if there was a split between his committee and the United States, 'we should almost certainly side with the Americans'.[70] In words that have often been quoted since, de Gaulle recalled Churchill as saying, 'each time we have to choose between Europe and the open sea, we shall always choose the open sea'.[71] Thereafter, de Gaulle refused to broadcast immediately after Eisenhower, unless it was acknowledged that it was his French authorities rather than the Allies who would re-establish civil government. He also prevented French liaison officers from accompanying the Allied troops and subsequently declined to approve the new special French currency notes that the Allies were proposing to use to buy food and supplies.[72] Valentine Lawford, a private secretary to Eden at the Foreign Office, acted as interpreter for Churchill and de Gaulle at their meeting on the 4 June and captured the deteriorating atmosphere:

> Luncheon was long and not genial…. De Gaulle has no small talk…and declined to respond to W[inston]'s badinage. At one moment W[inston] leant slightly forward in his seat, turned his face round and up towards the General, and gave an entirely childish grin. De Gaulle (whose head is badly shaped & whose museau [muzzle] has something of the mule) smiled a faded smile and looked as if someone had made him an improper proposal. Those two will never be happy together.[73]

---

[69] TNA, PREM 3/345/7.

[70] Churchill, *The Second World War*, Vol. V, pp.554-556.

[71] Harwood, R. (trans), de Gaulle, C., *War Memoirs*, Vol II, 'Unity', (Weidenfeld & Nicolson, 1959), p.227.

[72] TNA, CAB 65/46, WM (44) 72 & WM (44) 73; de Gaulle, *War Memoirs*, Vol II, 'Unity', pp.226-230.

[73] CAC, Lawford Papers, LWFD 1.

By the time of the War Cabinet on the evening of 5 June, with all hanging in the balance before the initial assault, Churchill could no longer contain his frustration and argued that it, 'would not be possible for us to have any further discussions with General de Gaulle on civil or military matters. It might even be necessary to indicate that an aeroplane would be ready to take him back to Algiers forthwith'.[74] Cadogan described this as 'the usual passionate anti-de G[aulle] harangue from PM' and felt that Churchill, Roosevelt and de Gaulle were all behaving 'like girls approaching the age of puberty'.[75] By 7 June, he was complaining that about forty of the last seventy-two hours had been wasted in 'wrangling about purely imaginary and manufactured grievances against de Gaulle'.[76] Yet these were surely further manifestations of the enormous tension of the time. Both Churchill and de Gaulle had everything to lose if the invasion were to go wrong, but neither had any real power to influence the outcome of the military events.

The effects of poor health and declining influence, combined with worry about the huge operation that was about to be launched, with its additional restrictions on everyday British life and its risks to relations with France, placed a huge burden on Churchill. For a man who liked action and being in control, it was clearly frustrating to be made to wait upon events. It was a strain that manifested itself in his uncharacteristic admissions of weakness, and in his ability to resolve the debate on the bombing of France, torn between his conflicting desires to support the military and to prevent French bloodshed and future hostility.

Despite the mounting pressures and his own misgivings about strategy and worries about success, Churchill had no real choice but to fall in line behind the plan for the D-Day assault. In the end, he did not obstruct the bombing of the French railway system, nor did he send de Gaulle back to Algiers. He twice visited Montgomery's Headquarters at St Paul's School in London to hear presentations on the coming operation, on 7 April and 15 May, and on both occasions, he addressed the commanders. Brooke thought that he was in a 'very weepy condition' on the 7th and lacking his 'usual vitality'[77], but Churchill wrote to Roosevelt describing how:

---

[74] TNA, CAB 65/46, WM (44) 72.
[75] Dilks (ed), *Cadogan Diaries*, p.635.
[76] Dilks (ed), *Cadogan Diaries*, p.635.
[77] Danchev & Todman (eds), *Alanbrooke Diaries*, p.538.

On Good Friday I gave a talk to all generals, British and American, who were gathered at General Montgomery's HQ expressing my strong confidence in the result of this extraordinary but magnificent operation. ... I do not agree with the loose talk which has been going on on both sides of the Atlantic about unduly heavy casualties which we shall sustain. In my view it is the Germans who will suffer very heavy casualties when our band of brothers get among them.

He prefaced these remarks with the observation that he was 'becoming very hard set upon *Overlord*'.[78] He had already used similar language in a telegram to General Marshall in March, in which he had stated that he was 'hardening very much on this operation as the time approaches'[79]; a phrase which he repeated in his second address at St Paul's to the Anglo-American leadership on 15 May.[80] According to Eisenhower, he made 'one of his typical fighting speeches' and used the expression, 'Gentlemen, I am hardening towards this enterprise'. For the Americans this was proof that the British Prime Minister had been lukewarm in his support prior to that date, something that Churchill was at pains to rebut in his post-war history.[81] However, his repeated use of this type of language when writing or speaking to the American leadership surely suggests that he was aware of the need to demonstrate and articulate his support to his ally. In his diary for 27 May, Brooke spoke of the terrible responsibility of high command at such a time when, 'once decisions are taken the time for doubts is gone, and what is required is to breathe the confidence of success into all those around'.[82] He felt his task was made more difficult by prima donna politicians. Churchill would no doubt have had similar feelings about the military commanders, his political colleagues, American allies, and de Gaulle.

His coping strategy was to keep busy and throw himself into the preparations. While he could no longer influence the strategy, he could scrutinise and improve the detailed plans. We have already seen how he chose to chair the *Overlord* Preparations Committee and immerse himself in the complexities of the security operations. Another particular area of personal interest was the development of new equipment to facilitate the landing on the beaches. Working through his own scientific adviser, Lord Cherwell, who was now in the Cabinet as

---

[78] CAC, Churchill Papers, CHAR 20/161/113-114.
[79] Churchill, *The Second World War*, Vol. V, p.521.
[80] . Churchill, *The Second World War*, Vol. V, p.543.
[81] Eisenhower, *Crusade in Europe*, p.269; Churchill, *The Second World War*, p.543.
[82] Danchev & Todman (eds), *Alanbrooke Diaries*, p.551.

Paymaster General, Churchill had consistently supported the work of specialist teams. He acted as a patron to Major General Sir Percy Hobart whose 79th Armoured Division was charged with developing specially adapted tanks and armoured vehicles that could swim ashore, lay roads, bridges and ramps, carry spotlights, flamethrowers or mortars, or use flails to traverse minefields.[83] Twice he had intervened to save Hobart's career against the military authorities who had wanted to dismiss him, in 1940 and again in 1942. Churchill was adamant that the 'High Commands of the Army are not a club', and his investment paid dividends on D-Day.[84] It was a similar story with Colonel Jeffries, whom Churchill set up with his own experimental unit in Buckinghamshire to develop an impressive array of new bombs, mines and fuses.[85]

The Prime Minister's concern about the difficulties of the invasion operation prompted him to take a leadership role in the development of the synthetic harbours which would enable the Allies to keep the beachheads supplied even though they did not possess a port. He versed himself in the details of 'Mulberries', large concrete caissons that could be towed into position and then sunk to form artificial harbours, and 'Gooseberries', which were artificial breakwaters created by sunken ships. Not all ideas reached fruition. Plans were explored but rejected for artificial aircraft carriers made from Pykrete, a remarkably strong composite of ice and wood pulp, and for temporary floating runways made from steel pontoons. Attempts to bypass the beaches altogether by using cliff bridging devices that could be extended from the front of landing ships were also deemed 'technically feasible' but 'not tactically applicable' to the Normandy beaches.[86] Churchill kept a watching brief over it all. On 19 January 1944, he demanded a conference to look at the 'continual failures on the Synthetic Harbour buisness'.[87] The 'provision of synthetic ports and preparations for them and on methods of dealing with underwater obstacles' was the subject of a meeting on 4 May which Brooke found unnecessarily long and meandering.[88] While Churchill may not have been able to supply the technical answers himself, he was clearly playing a key convening role in sponsoring and bringing together the different departments that could, and in prioritising the solution of problems that undoubtedly aided the invasion.

---

[83] http://www.iwm.org.uk/history/the-funny-tanks-of-d-day.
[84] CAC, Churchill Papers, CHAR 20/13/7; CHAR 1/355/45; CHAR 20/67/7.
[85] See Macrae, *Winston Churchill's Toyshop*.
[86] Nuffield College, Cherwell Papers, file G310/36.
[87] Nuffield College, Cherwell Papers, G310/36.
[88] Danchev & Todman (eds), *Alanbrooke Diaries*, p.543.

Churchill's interest in the detail sometimes seemed excessive to those around him. During the conference at St. Paul's School on 15 May, he became highly concerned on hearing presentations about the 'staggering' quantities of non-fighting support staff, equipment and vehicles that would need to accompany any invasion. In his own later account, he downplayed any disagreement about this with Montgomery, but it is quite clear that he raised it with Brooke two days later, complaining from his bed in a morning meeting about 'the 1000 clerks of the 3rd echelon and the fact that invasion catered for one lorry for every five men'.[89] It marked a return to one of his favourite obsessions, and one that was calculated to enrage his generals. The fact that he chose to raise it again at this juncture can be seen as further proof of his concern for the operation, which he feared might become bogged down on the beaches, especially if they were choked by non-essential supplies. It is an illustration of his role as a 'prod'. Yet, it is also indicative of his tendency, which we have already seen, to concentrate on the fighting and offensive capability of his troops, and to ignore or belittle the wealth of support services that were needed to sustain a modern army in a protracted campaign.

The conference at St. Paul's on 15 May was also the moment that the British Prime Minister seems to have been taken with the idea of accompanying the invasion force himself, asking Admiral Ramsay, the Naval Commander-in-Chief of the Allied Expeditionary Force, to come up with a plan. Ramsay duly obliged and, in a letter of the following day, outlined arrangements that would have seen Churchill board HMS *Belfast* on D-1, originally scheduled for 4 June, before participating in the initial naval bombardment and then transferring to a destroyer for a short tour of the beaches. The request clearly placed Ramsay in an awkward position, as he knew that the last thing any of the military commanders wanted was the added burden of ensuring the Prime Minister's security. Churchill had asked Ramsay not to tell the First Sea Lord, knowing that Admiral Cunningham would object, but the Admiral felt compelled to follow his own chain of command for *Overlord* and inform General Eisenhower, who was naturally very averse to Churchill's going.[90]

Churchill recounted what happened next in his own history.[91] He stuck to his guns, and, perhaps realising that constitutionally the only

---

[89] Churchill, *The Second World War*, Vol V, p.544; Danchev & Todman (eds), *Alanbrooke Diaries*, p.547.
[90] CAC, Churchill Papers, CHAR 20/136/11.
[91] Churchill, *The Second World War*, Vol V, pp.546-551.

person who could stop him was the King, he used a Royal audience on 30 May to try and enlist the support of the Sovereign, by suggesting that the two of them might go. While this clearly appealed to George VI as a former sailor who had seen active service in the First World War, it was an anathema to the Royal Household and had the potential to cause a major political incident, as it would have been opposed by both Eisenhower and the Cabinet. Sir Alan Lascelles, the King's Private Secretary, quickly talked George VI out of the idea, and then set about using the monarch to persuade Churchill to stand down. But Churchill was not so easily moved. It took a further audience and two very personal and hand-written appeals from the King, the second sent on the 2 June, before Churchill finally relented. When he did so, it was done with reservations and at the last moment. The Prime Minister was in his private train on the south coast, making a final tour of the military preparations for the assault, and sent a letter by despatch rider in the early hours of the 3 June, in which he grudgingly deferred to His Majesty's 'wishes and indeed commands'. Even then, he protested that, 'I ought to be allowed to go where I consider it necessary to the discharge of my duty', and asserted that, 'I rely on my own judgment, invoked in many serious matters, as to what are the proper limits of risk which a person who discharges my duties is entitled to run'.[92] The King had voiced many sound arguments why the Prime Minister should not run such a risk, including his inaccessibility 'at a critical time when vital decisions might have to be taken'[93], but to Churchill this was outweighed, as he later reflected, by his view that:

A man who has to play an effective part in taking, with the highest responsibility, grave and terrible decisions of war may need the refreshment of adventure. He may need also the comfort that when sending so many others to their death he may share in a small way their risks. His field of personal interest, and consequently his forces of action, are stimulated by direct contact with the event.[94]

The King's Private Secretary, Sir Alan Lascelles, was scathing in his response, noting privately for the King that, 'Nothing will persuade me that the Minister of Defence is going to do his job any better by having sat for some hours (mostly in pitch darkness) on the bridge of a bombarding cruiser'.[95] Yet, after six months of waiting, worry and

---

92 CAC, Churchill Papers, CHAR 20/136/4, 6-7, & 10.
93 CHAR 20/136/4.
94 Churchill, *The Second World War*, Vol. V, p.551.
95 Royal Archives, PS/PSO/GVI/C/069/46.

frustration, Churchill needed the release of action. He was finally able to cross over to the beaches on D-Day plus 6, the 12 June. He observed the synthetic harbours in action, stepped ashore from a landing craft, drove to Montgomery's headquarters, toured the Allied bridgehead and finished 'a most interesting and enjoyable day' in the British destroyer HMS *Kelvin* firing on the enemy.[96] Thereafter, it was difficult to keep him away from the action. He was back in Normandy from 20-23 July, and there again on 7 August.[97]

On 17 August, Winston wrote to Clementine from Naples, where he had gone to confer with Alexander and the generals in the theatre. The letter talks of a 'busy but delightful time', with 'lovely' tourist expeditions to the isles of Ischia and Capri. He describes sailing out in a destroyer to watch the naval bombardment accompanying the Allied landings in southern France, and expresses his regret at not being able to get closer to the action on the beaches. The whole tone is one of enjoyment, and yet he is also critical of 'this well-conducted but irrelevant' operation. To his mind, Operation *Dragoon*, the seizure of the French Mediterranean coast, was taking place too late and too far from northern France to help the Allied armies there, and he did not like that it was diverting resources away from his Mediterranean theatre.

The letter captures Churchill's mood in that moment. He was delighted at the progress of the *Overlord* operations, gleefully noting that they 'appear to be the greatest battle of the war and may result in the destruction of the German power in France', and that such a victory may lead to 'more mutual respect between the Russians and the Anglo-American democracies'. But he was also worried that 'our forces are being mis-employed for American convenience', with the British army in Italy 'relegated to a secondary and frustrated situation'.[98] Here is a wonderful juxtaposition: joy at the Allied military success, tempered by frustration at an inability to exploit this by adopting a strategy that will bring the laurels to Britain and allow him to see through his strategy in the Mediterranean. It was a view he confirmed in a letter to the King two days later, repeating his fear that Alexander's army will 'be so mauled and milked that it cannot have a theme or plan of campaign', while also admitting that, 'The change and movement and the warm weather have greatly restored my vigour'.[99]

---

96 Churchill, *The Second World War*, Vol. VI, pp.10-12.
97 Churchill, *The Second World War*, Vol. VI, pp.22-24 & pp.27-28.
98 CAC, Baroness Spencer-Churchill Papers, CSCT 2/33; Soames, *Speaking for Themselves*, pp.500-502.
99 Royal Archives, PS/PSO/GVI/C/069/50a.

Churchill's own international profile could not have been higher, and victory now seemed assured, a matter of when not if. All worries about the success of the cross-Channel invasion were lifted, but real concerns remained about Britain's declining status within the Grand Alliance and her ability to influence the outcome of the conflict and the post-war settlement. The campaign in the Mediterranean was now a sideshow. The Allied Expeditionary Force in north-west Europe was commanded by an American, answerable to the Combined Chiefs of Staff in Washington, and increasingly dominated by American troops and material. The war in the Pacific was also being led from the United States, while Russia was emerging as the dominant force in Eastern Europe. Churchill also knew that the clock was ticking. His coalition had been forged in war and would end with victory. The increasing importance of post-war issues was likely to hasten party political divisions. His own health was not what it had been, even if temporarily re-energised by success. His will had triumphed over his body and brought him to the 'beginning of the end', but he was now entering the final phase of the war with only limited room to manoeuvre, and would need to choose his remaining battles carefully.

What kept Churchill going was willpower and his determination to see things through to victory. He may have been tired, but he still believed that he did have something to contribute, and he was not prepared to see all that he had worked for side-lined. It is a spirit that he perhaps best articulated by his oft-quoted reflection on the Tehran Conference:

> There I sat with the great Russian bear on one side of me with paws outstretched, and, on the other side, the great American buffalo, and between the two sat the poor little English donkey, who was the only one, the only one of the three, who knew the right way home.[100]

---

[100] Wheeler-Bennett, *Action This Day*, p.96, quoting TV interview with Lady Violet Bonham Carter.

Chapter 9

Impotence or Independence?

What did Churchill hope to achieve in Poland and Greece?

Greece and Poland. Two very different countries at opposite ends of Eastern Europe, but united in tragedy during the Second World War. Britain had issued military guarantees to both in 1939, but in each case, this had failed to prevent German invasion and occupation. Hitler's attack on Poland in September 1939 had acted as the *causus belli* for Britain and France that had started the war in Europe. Unfortunately for Warsaw, the Allied guarantees had been designed primarily to deter German aggression, not to confront it. The distance and the lack of their forces in Poland had ruled out any meaningful assistance. The country had been quickly overrun and then partitioned by Germany and the Soviet Union. By contrast, Churchill's government had sent military forces to Greece when she was threatened in the spring of 1941; though only after much debate, and not in sufficient strength to prevent their subsequent defeat and evacuation. Both Warsaw and Athens had fallen; their leaders, and in the case of Greece, their King, joining the swollen ranks of the European governments in exile in London, and pledging themselves to the Atlantic Charter and the cause of the United Nations. Thereafter, both had supplied armed forces that had fought for the British Imperial and Allied armies, while London had fostered resistance movements against their occupation.

Yet it was only when the German retreat began in earnest in 1944 that the two countries found themselves once again at the centre of British foreign policy. Churchill later wrote:

The fate of Poland and Greece struck us keenly. For Poland we had entered the war; for Greece we had made painful efforts. Both their Governments had taken refuge in London, and we considered ourselves

205

responsible for their restoration to their own country, if that was what their peoples really wished. In the main these feelings were shared by the United States, but they were very slow in realising the upsurge of Communist influence, which slid on before, as well as followed, the onward march of the mighty armies directed from the Kremlin. I hoped to take advantage of the better relations with the Soviets to reach satisfactory solutions of these new problems opening between East and West.[1]

He seized his chance in the Kremlin at 22.00 hours on the night of 9 October 1944. There were just seven people in the room. The British party comprised Churchill and Eden, newly arrived that afternoon, their Ambassador to Moscow, Sir Archibald Clark Kerr, and their interpreter, Major Birse. For the Russians, it was just Stalin, Molotov, and their interpreter, Pavlov. No American representatives were present. Churchill opened the proceedings by expressing the hope that by talking to each other they might 'avoid innumerable telegrams and letters' and 'give the Ambassador a holiday'. Stalin replied that he 'was ready to discuss anything'. What then followed provides a vivid insight into the verbal jousting at such encounters, as the two leaders manoeuvred around one another, setting out their stalls for the days of detailed discussion that would follow.[2]

Churchill wanted to prioritise Poland and to use the meeting to bring together representatives of the Polish government in exile in London, which he was supporting, with members of the communist-controlled Lublin Committee, backed by Stalin. He broke the ice with a joke, remarking that 'the difficulty about the Poles' is 'that they had unwise political leaders. Where there were two Poles there was one quarrel'. To which Stalin added, 'where there was one Pole he would begin to quarrel with himself through sheer boredom'. But Churchill got his way, and it was agreed to summon the London Poles to Moscow in an attempt to force the two sides to resolve their differences.[3]

Churchill then raised the question of Greece, but chose to do so in the context of the future of Romania, which he regarded as 'very much a Russian affair. ... But in Greece it was different. Britain must be the leading Mediterranean power' and he hoped Stalin would give him 'the first say about Greece' in exchange for the Soviet Union having the same on Romania.[4] It was around this point that the British Prime

---

[1] Churchill, *The Second World War*, Vol. VI, p.181.
[2] TNA, PREM 3/434/7.
[3] TNA, PREM 3/434/7.
[4] TNA, PREM 3/434/7.

Minister took up a small piece of paper and wrote out by hand the names of various Balkan countries – Romania, Greece, Yugoslavia, Hungary and Bulgaria – assigning to them possible percentages of British and Soviet influence. Romania was to be 90 per cent Russian, 10 per cent other; Greece 90 per cent British and 10 per cent Russian; Yugoslavia and Hungary 50/50; and Bulgaria 75 per cent Russian. He then pushed the document across the table to Stalin, who ticked it and passed it back. In the contemporary British record, Churchill is recorded as saying that 'it was better to express these things in diplomatic terms and not to use the phrase "dividing into spheres" because the Americans might be shocked'.[5] Writing about the moment later, he recalled: 'At length I said, "Might it not be thought rather cynical if it seemed we had disposed of these issues, so fateful to millions of people, in such an offhand manner? Let us burn the paper." "No, you keep it," said Stalin'.[6]

Thereafter, Stalin pointed out that if Britain was interested in the Mediterranean, then Russia was equally interested in the Black Sea, and angled for Churchill's support in wresting sole control of the Dardanelles Straits from Turkey at any future peace conference. Churchill replied that it was 'no part of British policy to grudge Soviet Russia access to warm water ports'. Shortly afterwards, he raised the political future of Italy and how helpful it would be for the Soviet Union to 'soft pedal' the communists there and not to stir them up.[7]

This was horse trading at the highest level. Churchill was later at pains to explain that they 'were only dealing with immediate war-time arrangements', and that 'all larger questions' were reserved for the peace conference at the end of the conflict.[8] Yet he knew that any future conference was likely to be influenced, if not constrained, by the political and military realities established on the ground during the final phase of the war. He also knew that this was how Stalin sought to do business. Molotov had first raised such issues during the Anglo-Soviet Treaty negotiations in the first half of 1942, when he had sought to obtain British recognition of Soviet domination of the Baltic States, parts of Finland and eastern Poland. Then, Russia was weak and Churchill was able to resist. But now, Russia was dominant, with the Red Army set to sweep across Eastern Europe and the Balkans. Churchill clearly felt that he would have to make concessions to get what he wanted. But what did he want?

---

[5] Churchill, *The Second World War*, Vol. VI, p.198; TNA, PREM 3/434/7.
[6] Churchill, *The Second World War*, Vol. VI, p.198.
[7] TNA, PREM 3/434/7.
[8] Churchill, *The Second World War*, Vol. VI, p.198.

One aim was simply to affirm and strengthen bilateral relations with Moscow and with Stalin. Churchill had confided to Colville before departure that the visit was necessary because he wanted 'to discourage any idea that the U.K. and U.S.A. are very close...to the exclusion of Russia. His visit will make it quite clear that our counsels with Russia are close too, and that there is no tendency to leave her in the cold'.[9] At Tehran, it was Churchill who had felt squeezed out; frustrated by Roosevelt's decision to reject attempts to plan a co-ordinated British and American position, and by the President's efforts to cultivate his own relationship with the Russian leader. This time, in the President's absence, the White House had sent Averell Harriman as its representative to attend the talks in Moscow, but Churchill was clear in his opening meeting with Stalin that, while 'he would welcome Mr. Harriman to a good number of their talks, ...he did not want this to prevent intimate talk between Marshal Stalin and himself'.[10]

Thus, on one level, this meeting was about Churchill reasserting himself on the world stage and defining a role for Britain in the post-*Overlord* world. Much of the 'intimate talk' he had in mind was going to focus on the Mediterranean theatre, which he regarded as a solely British sphere. Ever since Eisenhower's departure to command the Normandy invasion, the whole area had been under a British Commander-in-Chief, General Wilson. The Allied army in Italy had a preponderance of British and Imperial forces. It was the Royal Navy that was controlling the sea lanes, Britain that was garrisoning Egypt and Palestine, and London that was sustaining the resistance movements in Albania, Greece and Yugoslavia. Economically, the Mediterranean and the Suez Canal remained vital to Britain's communications with India and the Far East. Politically, the British had fought hard to maintain their strong position in Egypt and the Middle East, and Churchill had famously 'not become the King's First Minister in order to preside over the liquidation of the British Empire'.[11] Indeed, as he had just admitted to Stalin, it was his view that, 'Britain must be the leading Mediterranean power'.

Churchill saw one of the main threats to British dominance coming from the growth of communism and its challenge to the established order. In many of the Mediterranean countries there were strong communist resistance movements, formed in reaction to fascism, which were now seeking political power. To the British Prime Minister, these

9   Colville, *The Fringes of Power*, p.523.
10   TNA, PREM 3/434/7.
11   Rhodes James, *Complete Speeches*, Vol. VI, p.6695.

were destabilising forces. In the short term, they would undermine the Anglo-American armies still fighting in the theatre; in the longer term, they would expand Soviet influence in the Mediterranean at the expense of the British. His own preference at this time tended to be for constitutional monarchies, where the presence of an existing Royal House brought historical continuity and a conservative stability. When, after dinner on 11 October, Stalin described the young King Peter of Yugoslavia as ineffective, Churchill tried to defend him by saying 'he was very young'. To which Stalin responded by pointing out that Peter the Great had been Tsar of all Russia at the age of seventeen.[12] When Eden lunched alone with Churchill at his Moscow town house on 12 October, he found the Prime Minister holding forth about kings, and complaining about the dropping of King Zog in Albania. The Foreign Secretary could only argue that, 'it was impossible to regard Kings in most of these Balkan lands as other than coming and going like a Labour Government at home'.[13] Yet, it is unlikely that Churchill would have agreed. Over the course of his long political life, he had grown to know many of these Royal families, and he was no republican. In 1934, he had written an article lamenting the 'veritable holocaust of Crowns' that had resulted from the First World War, explaining that in his own lifetime he had:

> seen the destruction and the overthrow of the Imperial Houses of Brazil, China, Turkey and in Europe of the Romanovs, the Hohenzollerns and the Hapsburgs, and the abolition of the monarchies of Greece, Spain and all the German States.

To his mind it was a tragedy that, 'the silly idea that republics are more free or better governed than monarchies dominated the treaty makers at Paris' and 'one could speak also of Portugal and Spain, who have sunk into such troubles and eclipse since they drove out their sovereigns'.[14]

As a policy, it had the potential to bring him into conflict not just with Stalin's communist regime, but also with a United States administration that was republican, suspicious of British imperialism, and committed by the Atlantic Charter to allowing people to choose their own form of government. Roosevelt had been stung by popular criticism of Eisenhower's support for Darlan in French North Africa in 1942, and was

---

[12] TNA, PREM 3/434/7.
[13] Eden, A., *The Eden Memoirs*, 'The Reckoning', (Cassell & Company Ltd, 1965), p.485.
[14] CAC, Churchill Papers, CHAR 8/498A/43.

determined to avoid accusations, especially during his 1944 Presidential re-election campaign, that he was keeping fascists in power.

This is why the White House had opposed Churchill's attempts to prop up the armistice government of the King and Marshal Badoglio in Rome; favouring the establishment of a more representative government over the continued influence of two men who had been involved in Mussolini's regime.[15] By October 1944, the King's only son was acting as Regent in his stead and a new government was in place, but there was still friction. Churchill remained almost irrationally suspicious of the leading Italian anti-fascist Count Sforza, whom the Americans had encouraged to return, and who Churchill accused of reneging on his promises to work with the King and Badoglio. He implied to Stalin that the real reason for the American interest in Italy was the 'good many [Italian] votes in New York State'.[16]

It was a similar story in Greece, where, since 1941, Churchill had been supporting the 'status quo' of the exiled government of George II, King of the Hellenes, first in London and then in Cairo. By 1944, the success of the strong left-leaning, communist-backed, republican resistance movement called EAM, with its own armed force called ELAS, was threatening to completely destabilise the political situation. Though supplied by the British, EAM had already incurred Churchill's wrath in April by sparking a short-lived mutiny in the Greek armed forces fighting with the Allies in Egypt. By August an uneasy compromise had been reached, which brought EAM representatives into a new and enlarged Greek government formed by George Papandreou. At the same time, Churchill believed he had obtained Roosevelt's blessing to send a British force into Athens in order to prevent a political vacuum as the Germans withdrew, and to avoid 'the prospect either of chaos and street fighting or of a tyrannical Communist government being set up'.[17]

A small British force under General Scobie was despatched in late September. Papandreou's government was established in Athens by mid-October. The situation on the ground remained highly volatile, and it was not yet clear whether the King would be able to return without destroying the fragile political consensus. The British view was that some form of regency was needed as an interim measure, while the Greeks decided on their future form of government.[18] For Churchill, the percentages agreement was part of the prerequisite for

---

[15] See Barker, *Churchill and Eden at War*, chapters 13, pp.162-181.

[16] TNA, PREM 3/434/7.

[17] Barker, *Churchill and Eden at War*, p.193.

[18] Barker, *Churchill and Eden at War*, Chapter 14, pp.182-198.

that British intervention and temporary occupation. Believing that he had Roosevelt's blessing, he needed to make sure that Stalin would not intervene. His Mediterranean policy was to side-line the Americans while securing a free hand from the Soviets.

But in Poland there could be no free hand to intervene. The Red Army was already advancing across the east of the country and the nearest Anglo-American armies were still in northern Italy or fighting in France and the Low Countries. Churchill was certainly driven by a sense of obligation to his Polish ally, whose forces had been fighting the enemy since September 1939. Britain had gone to war to guarantee Polish independence, and the British government was therefore clearly susceptible to criticism if Poland did not emerge as an independent entity. She had also agreed by treaty with Poland not to recognise any changes to her August 1939 borders.[19] But it was more than that. An independent Poland would provide a buffer between the Soviet Union and the heart of Western Europe, just as she had done after the First World War, when Churchill as Secretary of State for War had spoken out in support of the Poles in the Russo-Polish War of 1919-21.[20] She was also the most high-profile test case for judging future Soviet intentions and the possibility of post-war collaboration.

The issue had been festering for months before the Moscow meeting. Churchill had already anticipated that a compromise would be necessary. Towards the end of the Tehran Conference on 1 December 1943, he had suggested, and seemed to have won, provisional Russian and American acceptance for a settlement of Poland's eastern borders based on the Curzon Line. This boundary, running through Brest-Litovsk, had originally been proposed by Lord Curzon, the British Foreign Secretary, during the Russo-Polish War in 1920, before being rendered obsolete by Polish success. The border had then been established much further east, incorporating parts of what the Russians regarded as Belarus, Lithuania and the Ukraine. Here it had remained until September 1939 and Poland's partition by Hitler and Stalin. It was this pre-1939 boundary that the Polish government in exile refused to relinquish. Yet, in spite of their opposition, Churchill held to the view that the Poles could be compensated by being offered German territory on their western border.

By January 1944, it had become a real rather than a hypothetical problem as the Soviets crossed the Polish 1939 frontier. The problem

---

[19] TNA, CAB 66/23, WP (42) 144.
[20] Churchill, *The Aftermath*, p.262; see also Corbett, H., *Churchill the Defender of Polish Independence: The War of 1919-21 and its Repercussions*, unpublished MPhil dissertation, (University of Cambridge, 2017).

of how Poland was going to be governed and by whom now had the potential to sow real dissension between London and Moscow. Eden's Private Secretary, Valentine Lawford, vented in his diary in March that:

> If there was even a chance of our influencing the Russians in a more tolerant & civilised direction, it was before – not after – Russian troops crossed the Polish border. And a long time before. Our foreign policy is non-existent because we try to make 'deals' with honesty. I believe you've either got to be scrupulously honest or wholly unscrupulous. Of the two courses the former is, I believe (& force myself to believe) the better. I can't prove it yet; but I wouldn't be surprised if, five years after the war, Russia is the best-hated country in the world. For with the Russians there are absolutely no scruples.[21]

By October 1944, the auguries were not good. Churchill had seen enough evidence to know that the 10,000 Polish officers whose remains had been unearthed by the Germans at Katyn had almost certainly been murdered by the Russians, and not the Germans as the Allies were saying publicly. At the end of January 1944, he asked the British Ambassador to the Polish government in exile, Sir Owen O'Malley, to conduct a second investigation into the affair, while noting to Eden that, 'All this, merely to ascertain the facts, because we should none of us ever speak a word about it'.[22] This confirms that his doubts were already high. There was no need for secrecy if it was a German atrocity. Eden sent him O'Malley's new report at the end of February noting 'that the cumulative effect of the evidence is to throw serious doubts on the Russian disclaimers of responsibility'. Churchill minuted back that, 'This is not one of those matters where absolute certainty is either urgent or indispensable'. With the Normandy invasion and an accompanying Soviet offensive in the east imminent, he knew that he could take no public action without undermining the alliance at a crucial moment, but, after reading the report, he ordered that it be circulated 'in a box from hand to hand' to the ministers of the War Cabinet.[23]

In late summer, he had become infuriated at the Red Army's intransigence in the face of the popular uprising in Warsaw against the Germans. When Stalin refused to send help to the beleaguered Polish resistance in the city, or even to allow American or British aircraft to land to refuel on Soviet airfields, Churchill told Mikolajczyk, the Polish Prime Minister in London, that Stalin's attitude 'was pure folly, which

---

21 CAC, Lawford Papers, LWFD 1.
22 TNA, PREM 3/353.
23 TNA, PREM 3/353.

would strike a chill on all those who hoped for future cooperation with Russia'.[24] A few days later, with the uprising about to be suppressed, he got the British government to send a message to Molotov, copied to President Roosevelt, stating that, 'Our people cannot understand why no material help has been sent from outside to the Poles in Warsaw', and that prevention of this help being sent by the Soviet Union, 'seems to us at variance with the spirit of Allied cooperation to which you and we attach so much importance both for the present and the future'.[25] Yet he still could not risk a public breach with Moscow. He knew that large elements of the British press, public and parliament were supportive of the Russians, was anxious to prevent any split on the issue with the Americans, and realised that to walk away would leave the Soviets in possession of the field. He saw the Moscow Conference as an opportunity to bring the two sides together so that he and Stalin could broker a settlement.

On both Greece and Poland, Churchill knew that he had to tread carefully, both at home and abroad. As a co-founder and signatory of the Atlantic Charter he was already being accused of breaching the clauses on imposing territorial changes against the free wishes of the people, and respecting their rights to choose their own form of government. Hence his wariness about how the percentages agreement might be perceived. Yet there was no real alternative to engagement with Moscow. He gave voice to his underlying frustrations in a minute to Eden on 31 March, asking:

What are we to say to our Parliaments and nations about modifications in the Atlantic Charter? We are being blamed today for departing from idealistic principles. Actually all this is done for the sake of Russia, which is resolved to seize the Baltic States and take what she wishes from Poland and Rumania. Nor do we know that a second series of demands may not follow her further military victories.[26]

But how much influence could Britain still exert? Could a defence of her interests be reconciled with the idealism of the Atlantic Charter and the reality of Russian domination?

The first, and perhaps ultimately decisive, campaign for the future of Poland was fought out almost immediately in Moscow. On 13 October, there were two consecutive meetings in the Spiridonovka House. At 17.00 hours, the British and Russian principals met with Mikolajczyk

---

[24] TNA, PREM 3/352/12.
[25] TNA, PREM 3/352/12.
[26] TNA, PREM 3/485/8.

and representatives of the Polish government in London. Five hours later, with the Americans in attendance, they met with Berut and other leaders of the rival Lublin Poles. The official British records captured a court house atmosphere, with the two Polish delegations in the dock and facing cross-examination.

Mikolajczyk began the first session by presenting an existing memorandum as his basis for a settlement. Once Warsaw had been liberated, which was yet to happen, the Polish government should be reconstructed from five existing political groupings: the peasants, the national democratic socialists, the Christian democrats and the workers. The fascists should be excluded. The aim of this government would be to hold elections as soon as possible, so that a Polish parliament could then make a new constitution and elect a president. Touching on the boundary issue, he expressed the hope that Poland 'would come out of this war undiminished'. When Churchill said that there were points in the memorandum which he liked, Stalin shot back that he had not noticed them. The Soviet leader then proceeded to set out his objections. The plan ignored the existence of the Lublin Committee, but 'How could it be ignored? One could not shut one's eyes to the facts'. In the second place, it made no mention of the Curzon Line, without which 'there could be no good relations'. On the boundary question, Churchill backed Stalin. 'Russia had suffered severely from the German invasion and the Russian armies were the only means by which the Polish liberation could be achieved'. It followed that, 'The British government supported the proposed frontier [the Curzon Line] because they felt it their duty. Not because Russia was strong but because Russia was right in this matter'. He then attempted to heap further moral pressure on Mikolajczyk by reminding him of Britain's support for Poland in 1939 and by warning him that, 'At this stage it was unwise for the Polish government to separate themselves from Britain'. The London Poles were urged to meet with their Lublin counterparts.

At the second meeting with the Lublin Poles, Churchill began with an appeal for unity and compromise:

> British aims were well known. They were to unite all Poles in the fight against the Nazis and to create a decent country for them to live in. ...He had been upset by the differences between the Poles. All Poles seemed to be against each other. It was painful to see such bitter divergences among men who had lost nearly everything. ...The world would get tired of it, of these Polish quarrels.

He explained that Britain had recognised the Polish government that had come to England five years ago, as he believed had the United States, and, 'They could not desert the people with whom they had worked. Britain tried to make loyalties endure to the end of the struggle'.

Unfortunately, this heartfelt plea did have the desired effect on its listener. Berut replied with a detailed argument explaining that the 'Polish emigré Government' was based on an unacceptable 1935 constitution, and unlike his Lublin Committee was not pledged to land reform or favourable relations with the Soviet Union. His colleague Morawski denounced General Bor, who had led the Warsaw uprising as a criminal. It was all too predictable that when Churchill tried to argue that, 'he [Bor] had won the admiration of millions not by his wisdom but by his courage', Stalin said he disagreed.[27] Churchill's verdict on the whole occasion was damning. For the King he described it as 'all Poles day', commenting that, 'Our lot from London are, as your Majesty knows, a decent but feeble lot of fools but the delegates from Lublin seem to be the greatest villains imaginable'.[28] His later reflection was that 'the Lublin Poles were mere pawns of Russia' and that the achievements of this six-hour conference were small.[29] Eden agreed, noting, 'We made no progress, Stalin calling for public acceptance of the Curzon Line and Mik[olajczyk] being unable at that moment to give it'. He found the Lublin Poles 'creepy' and remembered describing Berut and Morawski in a whispered comment to Churchill as, 'The rat and the weasel'.[30] There was a general atmosphere of disappointment in the British camp, summed up by Churchill's secretary, Elizabeth Layton. 'I do not think much was gained at this meeting. The chief subject was Poland, and we went home with no agreement signed', though she did note 'the heart-warming feeling of comradeliness', which was perhaps stimulated by the lavish Russian hospitality.[31]

Moscow was certainly not the end of Churchill's attempts to get a settlement on Poland. The issue would go on to dominate the plenary sessions of the next meeting of the 'Big Three' at Yalta in February 1945. But it was perhaps the best opportunity, conducted at a time before the Red Army had taken Warsaw or western Poland, and at a moment when Stalin seemed inclined to deal with Churchill. Eden later acknowledged that, 'Our best chance was to protest the damage

---

[27] TNA, PREM 3/434/7.
[28] Royal Archives, PS/PSO/GVI/C/069/52.
[29] Churchill, *The Second World War*, Vol. VI, p.205.
[30] Eden, *The Reckoning*, p.486.
[31] Elizabeth Nel, *Mr Churchill's Secretary*, p.152.

to Anglo-Soviet relations which must result from failure to agree a fair settlement for the Poles, but that was an uncertain weapon'.[32] This was particularly so, while Churchill was actively seeking Soviet cooperation, or at least non-interference in Italy and Greece.

Failure was protracted rather than immediate. On 30 October, the War Cabinet was faced with a demand from the Soviet Embassy that the Lublin Committee be allowed to represent Poland at the forthcoming conference on the European Inland Transportation Organisation, which came with the threat that if such invitations were not issued, the Russians would not attend. Churchill was adamant that 'we could not be manoeuvred in this way into recognising the Lublin government' and he advocated a holding reply while hoping that Mikolajczyk would return and continue negotiations in Moscow.[33] He continued to believe that the London Poles would have to accept a compromise, but it was clear that they were dragging their feet over any further negotiations.

Mikolajczyk and his colleagues now submitted a number of questions to the British government. In response to these, the War Cabinet, guided by Churchill, confirmed that they would back territorial compensation for Poland in Germany 'up to the line of the [River] Oder'. They were non-committal on the precise composition for any future Polish government, though Churchill said he had told Stalin that the Lublin Committee's demands for 75 per cent of any new government was 'wholly excessive' and would not be seen by world opinion as a 'free agent'. More worryingly for the London Poles, the Prime Minister felt that the boundary issue must be settled first, and that 'out of these discussions must come either agreement or disagreement'. Finally, Attlee spoke against the possibility of guaranteeing the independence and integrity of the new Poland, citing 'the lesson of 1939' and the need to avoid guarantees 'which we could not implement'. Churchill's War Cabinet was only prepared to offer a joint guarantee with Russia, with which the United States might then be asked to associate, pending the creation of the new World Organisation. Such a limited promise, from which the British could disassociate themselves in the event of a breach by Moscow, was not what the Poles were looking for.[34]

Behind the scenes, Mikolajczyk had been working for some form of compromise. Yet, in the end, he could not carry the majority of his colleagues, who no longer believed in 'Russian good faith or that, in these circumstances, negotiations with Russia would be of any value'.

---

[32] Eden, *The Reckoning*, p.481.
[33] TNA, CAB 65/48, WM (44) 142.
[34] TNA, CAB 65/48, WM (44) 143.

His resignation at the end of November was recognised as a huge blow. Having expended so much effort on trying to get an agreement, Churchill was clearly sore. He acknowledged that there could be no question of breaking off relations with the Polish government in London, 'but we should adopt an attitude of complete detachment and of frigidity and leave them to look after their own affairs'.[35] The year ended with the British Polish policy in tatters. Against the stated wishes of both Churchill and Roosevelt, Stalin recognised the Lublin Committee as the provisional government of Poland.

Looking further ahead, the Yalta conference would confirm the Curzon Line and feature intense debate about the mechanisms for creating a more representative national government, to which the Russians would pay lip service. Roosevelt would describe Poland as a distant problem, whereas to Churchill it would remain a matter of honour, and crucially to Stalin a matter of security.[36] This was the harsh reality. Russia had suffered repeated invasions through Poland. Stalin was not going to let that happen again, and that meant securing a 'friendly' Poland and excluding those who might assert an independent, and in the case of the London Poles, probably hostile policy. Indeed, information smuggled out with the former KGB archivist Vasili Mitrokhin indicates that the Russians were aware of suggestions by the London Poles for a post-war federation of eastern European countries to keep the Red Army from entering Germany.[37] With hindsight, it is difficult to see how the outcome could have been different. Even if all the Poles had been united and prepared to submit to the Russian dictation of borders, it seems most unlikely that Stalin would have allowed them true independence of action. On 27 February, after defending his Polish policy against some Conservative opposition in parliament, Churchill told MP Harold Nicolson, 'Not only are they [the Russians] very powerful, but they are on the spot; even the massed majesty of the British Empire would not avail to turn them off that spot'.[38]

To make matters worse, while Churchill was still wrestling with Poland, the situation in Greece suddenly exploded. EAM objected violently to plans to disarm large parts of their military wing ELAS, especially while internal security forces, whom they regarded as fascist collaborators,

---

[35] TNA, CAB 65/48, WM (44), 157.

[36] CAC, Churchill Papers, CHAR 23/15.

[37] CAC, Mitrokhin Papers, MITN 1/7, translation provided for author by Barbara Laughlin.

[38] Olson, S. (ed), *Harold Nicolson, Diaries and Letters 1930-1964*, (Penguin, 1984), p.281.

and army regiments loyal to the King were being allowed to keep their weapons. They responded by demanding increased representation within the government. Initially, it looked as though Papandreou was giving way. *The Times* for 27 November reported that another EAM general had been appointed to the Cabinet, thereby increasing their representation to seven out of twenty-four members. On the same day, Churchill circulated to the War Cabinet a note from General Scobie to General Wilson. It was scathing about EAM's domination of the Greek provinces claiming that there was 'widespread intimidation and victimisation' and 'no freedom of speech; no freedom of press'. Scobie was convinced that the 'overwhelming majority of population is praying for a lead from us', and that 'any utterance by [the] British Prime Minister will be accepted with utmost relief by Greek population'.[39] This both confirmed all the Prime Minister's existing fears and pressed all the right buttons in encouraging him to take executive action. In a cable to Eden the next day he was scathing about Papandreou, asking, 'Are we getting any good out of this old fool at all' (Papandreou was younger than Churchill), and opining that, 'we must make up our minds whether we will assert our will by armed force, or clear out altogether'. He proposed sending a message to the Greek Prime Minister urging Papandreou to arouse himself, 'before we have to say goodbye and your country slithers into ruin for another decade'. Eden persuaded him not to send it.[40]

On Friday, 1 December, the EAM Ministers resigned and a General Strike was proclaimed. General Scobie issued a proclamation stressing the need for unity and emphasising British support for the present Greek government. The fact that this no longer contained EAM, opened the British to the accusation of taking sides. This did not faze Churchill who backed Scobie on the Saturday with an unequivocal endorsement from 10 Downing Street, 'made with the knowledge and entire approval of H.M. government'.[41] Then, on the Sunday morning, EAM supporters took part in a banned demonstration. The British Ambassador, Reginald Leeper, sent an urgent cable just before midnight summarising the result:

> When demonstrators were about 100 yards from the police station an incident occurred for which it is impossible to fix responsibility. Exchange of fire grenades between the demonstrators and the city police resulted

---

[39] TNA, PREM 3/212/10.
[40] TNA, PREM 3/212/10.
[41] Churchill, *The Second World War*, Vol. VI, p.251; *The Times*, Issue 50007, 4 December 1944, *The Times* Digital Archive 1785-2011 (Gale), accessed June 2017.

according to the latest checked reports in the following casualties. Police – one killed 3 wounded, demonstrators – 10 killed 60 wounded.

By 14.30 hours, demonstrators were protesting outside the British Embassy with banners dipped in the blood of the casualties. Papandreou moved from his flat into the comparative safety of the Hotel Grande Bretagne.[42] In a second telegram, sent at 00.31 on Monday, 4 December, Leeper confirmed that ELAS forces had moved to encircle Athens and warned that, 'If this is not stopped in time the Greek forces will be unable to stem the tide. Infiltration is already under-way and is expected to continue tonight'.[43] The civil war had begun, and the small British forces of General Scobie were now firmly in the firing line.

On Monday morning, British readers of *The Times* woke up to a vivid description of the previous day's bloodshed from the paper's special correspondent in Athens. It would have made uncomfortable reading for Churchill, for while it made clear that, 'No British soldier played any part in the events', it asserted that 'the presence of our units served only to associate Britain with what is everywhere condemned as "Fascist action" and stopped neither the police shooting nor the crowd demonstrating'. It also carried an update from EAM headquarters claiming that fifteen persons had been killed and 148 wounded.[44]

Yet Churchill's response was characteristically bullish. He did not hesitate, he did not attempt to gather the Cabinet, and he did not contemplate the withdrawal of British forces. Instead he took personal responsibility for the late-night drafting of a telegram to General Scobie ordering him to maintain order in Athens and to destroy or neutralise all EAM or ELAS forces approaching the city. His message included the very Churchillian line, 'Do not however hesitate to act as if you were in a conquered city where a local rebellion is in progress'.[45] Unfortunately, the lateness of the hour meant that the duty private secretary, Jock Colville, was too tired to remember to despatch the telegram to the combined Anglo-American headquarters at Caserta with the code word 'Guard'. Its presence would have restricted distribution to the British staff. Instead this potentially inflammatory text was now seen by the Americans and by 12 December had been leaked to the *Washington Post*.[46] Churchill's position was that a restoration of order and security

---

[42] TNA, PREM 3/212/10.

[43] TNA, PREM 3/212/10.

[44] *The Times*, Issue 50007, 4 December 1944, *The Times* Digital Archive 1785-2011 (Gale), accessed June 2017.

[45] CAC, Churchill Papers, CHAR 20/176/80; Churchill, *The Second World War*, Vol. VI, p.252.

[46] Colville, *Fringes of Power*, pp.532-535.

must precede any political settlement. In a further telegram to Leeper, that would also be used against him, he instructed the Ambassador:

> This is no time to dabble in Greek politics or to imagine that Greek politicians of varying shades can affect the situation. You should not worry about Greek Government compositions. This matter is one of life and death.[47]

Churchill's blood was up, and he was clearly enjoying issuing orders once again to those in the field. He despatched Macmillan to be his man on the spot and wrested control from Eden, presumably on the grounds that this was now a military rather than a diplomatic crisis, and so more fitting to the jurisdiction of the Minister of Defence. But his policy of all-out backing for Papandreou was not without risk. After being subjected to a morning tirade on the subject of the cowardice of the communists, Clementine Churchill was anxious and felt compelled to write one of her warning letters to her husband, advising him to tone down such rhetoric in public.[48]

While the British troops dug in, political opposition to their role was mounting. Churchill took strong exception to the BBC coverage of the events in Athens, 'which left him with the impression that the rioting was simply a dispute between E.A.M. and the Royalists', when it was, in fact, 'between E.A.M. on the one hand and the legally constituted Greek government on the other'.[49] By 6 December, *The Times* was running the story that he had blocked attempts to allow Papandreou to resign in favour of the veteran Liberal politician Sofoulis, informing the Ambassador that 'any change at present in the head of the Greek Government was impossible'. The source was clearly Sofoulis, who was probably manoeuvring for the Greek premiership, but it was based on a conversation with Leeper who must have reported to him the contents of Churchill's telegram.[50] As if this was all not bad enough, it was at this moment that the new American Secretary of State, Stettinius, chose to issue a most unhelpful intervention. Ostensibly about Italy, and opposing Churchill's opposition to Sforza, the statement read, 'we expect the Italians to work out their problems of government along democratic lines *without influence from the outside* [my italics]'.

---

[47] Churchill, *The Second World War*, Vol.VI, p.253.
[48] CAC, Baroness Spencer-Churchill Papers, CSCT 1/28; Soames, *Speaking For Themselves*, p.507.
[49] TNA, PREM 3/212/10.
[50] *The Times*, Issue 50009, 6 December 1944, *The Times* Digital Archive 1785-2011 (Gale), accessed June 2017.

But it concluded by adding that such a policy would apply even more 'with regard to governments of the United Nations in their liberated territories'. Here was a clear reference to Greece.[51] It coincided with twenty members of the Labour Party tabling an amendment for discussion in parliament that, 'His Majesty's Forces will not be used to disarm the friends of democracy in Greece and other parts of Europe, or to suppress those popular movements which have valorously assisted in the defeat of the enemy and upon whose success we must rely for future friendly cooperation in Europe'.[52] Colville's diary confirms that Greece was dominating the political agenda at this point. He noted the 'clamorous demands' from those on the Left wing, like Aneurin Bevan, who saw a 'heaven-sent opportunity for saying that we are supporting by our arms the forces of reaction in Italy and Greece'.[53]

Churchill's frustrations were evident. In an unusually strongly worded telegram to the President, he complained about the 'acerbity of the State Department's communique', and made it clear that he regarded this as 'a public rebuke to His Majesty's Government' which stood in marked contrast to his previous loyalty to Roosevelt's administration.[54] At the War Cabinet meeting on the evening of 7 December, he complained that the American announcement had created the impression that Britain's policy was anti-democratic, for which 'there was no shadow of foundation'. He rehearsed the arguments that he would use the next day in parliament: 'Fair play, a fair trial, the untrammelled vote of the people, the will of the people freely expressed without fear or favour, no leaning to one or other political party was, and would be, our policy'. His colleagues backed this line, but the sanitised official minutes hint at cracks emerging at the highest level, with the Labour Ministers aware of the scale of the feeling about Greece in their own rank and file. Concern was expressed that, 'There was a feeling in certain quarters that 'we', – meaning perhaps particularly the Prime Minister, – 'had a preference for the restoration of dynasties', sometimes against the will of the people 'and it would be well to dissipate this'. The Labour Home Secretary, Herbert Morrison, raised the allegation that Greek nationalist forces were not being disarmed, but rather merged into the regular Greek army 'on a basis which would give it a tendency to favour the right'.[55]

---

51 ibid.
52 ibid; TNA, CAB 65/48, WM (44) 162.
53 Colville, *Fringes of Power*, p.533.
54 CAC, Churchill Papers, CHAR 20/176/91-92.
55 TNA, CAB 65/48, WM (44) 162.

The next day Churchill defended his policy in the House of Commons, making it clear that he saw it as a confidence vote. With Greece in mind, but speaking in generalities, he drew a distinction between true democracy and 'a swindle democracy, a democracy which calls itself democracy because it is Left Wing'. He argued that democracy was neither 'mob law' nor a 'harlot to be picked up in the street by a man with a tommy gun'. He admitted that during the war it had been necessary to 'arm anyone who could shoot a Hun', but this did not mean that the recipients should be able to:

> engross to themselves by violence and murder and bloodshed... all those powers and traditions and continuity which many countries have slowly developed and to which quite a large proportion of their people, I believe the great majority, are firmly attached.

On Greece specifically, he said Britain had a right to express a point of view, in order to redeem her pledged word, and in recognition of the casualties she had sustained in Greece's defence. But he was keen to stress that she did so with American and Russian consent and at the invitation of a Greek government of all parties. The Greeks had 'an absolute right to determine their own future as soon as conditions of normal tranquillity were regained'.[56]

Macmillan thought it a 'superb Parliamentary performance' of magnificent courage, but felt that it was not profound and 'oversimplified the problem'.[57] Harold Nicolson, who also spoke in the debate, was more critical. Churchill was interrupted and heckled and responded, 'like a spaniel who is diverted by the smell of a rabbit and dashes off wildly into the bracken. He keeps on being "drawn" by the Opposition'.[58] The Prime Minister comfortably won his vote by a margin of 279 to 30, but once again the figures were not the whole story. Many in the Labour Party had chosen to abstain, and there were public demonstrators outside the Palace of Westminster, of whom fifty had been admitted into the Central Lobby.[59] The press was still largely critical, and it was not clear that the Prime Minister had done enough to silence mounting opposition on the issue. That evening Macmillan was summoned to the Downing Street Annexe and found Churchill exhausted and rambling 'in rather a sad and depressed way. ... He

---

56 *Hansard*, House of Commons, 8 December 1944, Vol. 406, cc908-1013.
57 Macmillan, *War Diaries*, p.599.
58 Olson (ed), *Harold Nicolson, Diaries and Letters*, (Penguin, 1984), p.275.
59 *The Times*, Issue 50011, 8 December 1944, *The Times* Digital Archive 1785-2011 (Gale), accessed June 2017.

has won the debate but not the battle of Athens'.[60] Macmillan, as the Resident Minister for the Mediterranean, was now despatched to Greece to help bring victory.

The related military question was whether the British forces could hold Athens against the EAM insurgency. If they were overwhelmed or had to be withdrawn, then British influence and prestige in the country would be at an end. Reinforcements were promised and despatched but there was a short period in early December when defeat seemed possible. Macmillan arrived in the Greek capital to find, 'it could hardly be worse. We have really been taken by surprise and seem to have hoped, up to the last, that things would be settled'. He found the British forces 'besieged and beleaguered in the small central area of Athens', holding the Embassy, but without regular power or water, and at risk from sniper fire. It was also immediately clear to him, as it was to Scobie and Leeper, that while a quick military victory was needed to give Britain back the ascendancy, it would not in itself solve the underlying crisis. The British could no more hold Greece than the Germans against a determined and organised guerrilla resistance movement; the longer the troops stayed, the more they would be viewed as occupiers rather than liberators by the ordinary Greek population caught up in the bloodshed. It was the unanimous view of the British authorities on the spot that a neutral head of state was needed to restore order and form a credible national government. The King was unacceptable to EAM and to others who might back them, and his return would only inflame the situation. They therefore revived the idea of the regency and promoted the Archbishop of Athens, Damaskinos, as a non-party figure with the authority and ability to reach out to all the warring factions.[61]

The regency was now discussed repeatedly in the War Cabinet. The Greek King was opposed, and only prepared to consider the Archbishop as Prime Minister in succession to Papandreou. On 12 December, Churchill and Eden adjourned a War Cabinet session and unsuccessfully tried to convince the monarch of the merits of a regency 'divorced from party strife'.[62] Colville recorded an afternoon of Cabinet discussions interspersed with visits from the King of Greece, who 'proved very obstinate to the Cabinet's wish'.[63] The next day, Macmillan confirmed by telegram that, 'Nothing else was likely to meet the case'

[60]   Macmillan, *War Diaries*, pp.599-600.
[61]   Macmillan, *War Diaries*, pp.602-603.
[62]   TNA, CAB 65/48, WM (44) 165 & 166.
[63]   Colville, *Fringes of Power*, p.534.

and that, 'The regency should remain until by plebiscite or free election the people were themselves able to express their will'.[64] This was an acceptance that the regency might end in a republic. The War Cabinet agreed that the King should be pressed again, though it must have been clear why he might have reservations.

He was not the only one. Churchill had the ability to impose the regency. He could withdraw his support from the King and instruct his team in Greece to recognise the Archbishop. This contingency was discussed by the War Cabinet on 12 December. Yet Churchill was clearly reluctant to do this. One reason was fear of further criticism about interfering in the internal politics of another country, but there were other factors at play. On 16 December, he read out two documents to his War Cabinet colleagues. The first was a message from his close friend, Field Marshal Smuts, the Prime Minister of South Africa, which argued that once the EAM revolt had been suppressed, the Greek King should return to 'discharge his proper constitutional functions'. The other was a letter from the King of Greece making 'a strong and reasoned plea against the immediate establishment of a Regency'. Churchill then questioned the degree of support for the Archbishop as Regent. In the general discussion that followed it seems highly probable that it was Churchill who noted that Damaskinos 'was said to be a worldly and ambitious Prelate'.[65] No progress was made. The only consensus was that Leeper and Macmillan should be consulted further and that the King be pressed once again.

It was an almost identical story when the War Cabinet met on 18 December. Churchill reported that he and Eden had seen the King again, and that, 'It was plain that His Majesty was under great stress'. The monarch remained opposed to the creation of the regency, and Churchill remained wary of replacing a constitutional monarch with a dictator.[66] Writing later, Churchill claimed that on the Greek issue, 'the War Cabinet stood like a rock against which all the waves and winds might beat in vain', yet the contemporary records show that cracks were starting to appear.[67] On the 21st, Churchill's continued intransigence over the regency led to uncomfortable exchanges. According to Cadogan, 'the P.M. rambled on till 7, stating with vehemence opinions based on no ascertained facts'. His assertion that he would not install a 'Dictator of the Left', caused Attlee to challenge him to produce

---

[64] TNA, CAB 65/48, WM (44) 168.
[65] TNA, CAB 65/48, WM (44) 169.
[66] TNA, CAB 65/48, WM (44) 171.
[67] Churchill, *The Second World War*, Vol. VI, p.255.

a 'scintilla of evidence' for his thesis.[68] Eden noted in his diary that Churchill was convinced that the Archbishop was both 'a quisling and a Communist', who had taken de Gaulle's place as the Prime Minister's *bête noire*. When Eden spoke in support of the regency, Churchill rounded on him and accused him of having the support but not the confidence of the Cabinet.[69] The Prime Minister seems to have been isolated and angry. According to the official minutes, he refused to put any further pressure on the King or even meet with him again.

Yet, according to Eden, a further interview with the King did take place the next day, though he doubted whether it 'did much more than confirm King in W[inston]'s support of him, last sentence being to remind King that Charles I had lost his head by fighting but had perpetuated Crown and Church'.[70] The reservations revealed by Churchill's words and actions were an unwillingness to force the Greek King to act against his will, and an uncertainty about the political intentions and ambitions of the Archbishop. The very fact that Damaskinos was acceptable to EAM as regent must have made him suspect in Churchill's eyes. The Prime Minister was also loyal to the ruler he had supported since 1941, and wary of an unknown quantity who had the power to wreck his plans. The result was a temporary paralysis.

Churchill must have felt that he was being assailed on all sides; attacked by his American ally, the press, parliament and now by his Cabinet colleagues. The Greek crisis was unfolding alongside the failure of the Polish negotiations, and Churchill was frustrated by both. As late as 17 December, the Prime Minister was cabling Macmillan that, 'At the moment Greek question is somewhat obscured by Poland in which far graver issues are concerned'. Yet, two days later, he sent a 'a very angry telegram' criticising Macmillan for using arguments about British public opinion and Anglo-American relations to press for the regency, which Macmillan interpreted as revealing that he was 'anxious and beginning to realise what a troublesome affair this is going to be'.[71]

The issue certainly showed no signs of being contained or going away, and continued to sow dissension. The Canadian Prime Minister, Mackenzie King, expressed his uneasiness and gave 'a public assurance that Canadian troops would not serve in Greece without the consent of the Canadian government'.[72] Ernest Bevin worked hard to prevent hostile motions at the Trades Union Congress, but there remained

---

[68] Dilks (ed), *The Cadogan Diaries*, p.689.
[69] Eden, *The Reckoning*, p.499.
[70] Eden, *The Reckoning*, p.500.
[71] Macmillan, *War Diaries*, p.609 & p.612.
[72] TNA, CAB 65/48, WM (44) 169.

a huge level of interest within the Labour Party.[73] On 13 December, their Conference passed a motion by the overwhelming majority of 2,455,000 votes to 137,000; regretting the tragic situation in Greece and calling upon the British government to facilitate an armistice and 'to secure resumption of conversations between all sections of the people who have resisted the Fascist and Nazi invaders with a view to the establishment of a provisional government'.[74] Such strength of feeling, albeit contained for the moment by the Labour leadership, illustrated that Greece had the potential to become a threat to Churchill's coalition, and that was something he could not risk ahead of the defeat of Germany. It also had the potential to damage his relations with the United States and some Commonwealth allies, and to weaken his authority. There would have to be a British general election at some point in 1945, and he did not want to see that complicated by opposition to his policy in Greece. Poland may have involved 'far graver issues' surrounding the long-term relationship with the Soviet Union, but those could not be easily resolved. In Greece, there was still scope for unilateral action; and so, after two weeks of delay, Churchill roused himself.

'Hell. I was looking forward to a quiet family Christmas'. That was Anthony Eden's understandable reaction to the Prime Ministerial summons.[75] On Christmas Eve, Churchill decided that he and his Foreign Secretary would fly to Greece, to see the situation for themselves and to try and break the political impasse. The Prime Minister's new Douglas C-54 Skymaster plane touched down at Kalamaki airfield on the afternoon of 25 December. Here it was met by Field Marshal Alexander, the Commander-in-Chief in the Mediterranean, who had sailed in specially from Italy, and by the local team of Macmillan and Leeper. There then followed a two-hour conference in the plane on the tarmac. Macmillan found Churchill in a 'most mellow, not to say chastened mood'.[76] That may have been the result of the long journey, or possibly of the extreme cold. Elizabeth Layton, who was there as one of the Prime Minister's two secretaries, recalled him 'wrapped up in overcoat and scarf, looking flushed and uneasy'. Churchill's doctor, Lord Moran, was present, but she 'wondered what on earth we should do in this witheringly cold place under the fire of rebel forces, if he were again to contract a feverish cold'.[77] The Prime Minister was now

---

[73] Churchill, *The Second World War*, Vol. VI, p.261.
[74] TNA, PREM 4/81/4.
[75] Eden, *The Reckoning*, p.500.
[76] Macmillan, *War Diaries*, p.616.
[77] Nel, *Mr Churchill's Secretary*, p.158.

seventy years old, and had decided to abandon a family Christmas party to travel two thousand miles into a war zone.

Against the backdrop of distant gunfire, a plan of action was hatched. Alexander reported that while the immediate danger to the British troops was past, he feared that behind the ELAS units 'there was a strong corps of resistance, this corps was Communist, stronger than we thought and would be very difficult to eradicate'. This prompted Churchill to confirm that the British government 'had no intention of becoming indefinitely involved in Greek civil strife, but they could not on the other hand leave Greece except with honour and with due protection for those Greeks who had helped us'. Macmillan then reported that he, Leeper and Alexander had already been planning a conference of all the political leaders, including EAM, with the Archbishop as chairman. Churchill and Eden agreed that it should proceed, and the Prime Minister then worked on the amended press communique convening the conference for the following day.[78] Thereafter the party decamped into armoured cars and was driven to its temporary headquarters on the British cruiser HMS *Ajax;* the British Embassy being considered too unsafe.

That evening Archbishop Damaskinos came aboard, and Churchill seems to have undergone his own immediate Damascene conversion. The next day he wrote to Attlee in the most glowing terms about this 'magnificent figure' who 'impressed me with a good deal of confidence'. What had impressed most was clearly the Archbishop's anti-communism, as, 'When he came to see us [on board the Ajax] he spoke with great bitterness against the atrocities of E.L.A.S. and the dark sinister hand behind E.A.M.'.[79] Here then was someone that Churchill could work with. Interestingly, Eden appears to have had some reservations, causing Colville to note with wry amusement that they were now in 'the curious topsy-turvy position of the Prime Minister feeling strongly pro-Damskinos (he even thinks he would make a good Regent) while the S.[Secretary] of S.[State] is inclined the other way'.[80]

The next two days were full of the sort of drama and high excitement that Churchill relished. When Captain Cuthbert told him that HMS *Ajax* might have to fire, the Prime Minister was delighted, replying: 'Pray remember, Captain, that I come here as a cooing dove of peace, bearing a sprig of mistletoe in my beak – but far be it from me to stand in the way of military necessity'.[81] The 26th began on the quarter

78   TNA, PREM 3/213/12.
79   Churchill, *The Second World War*, p.272.
80   Colville, *Fringes of Power*, p.540.
81   Pawle, *The War & Colonel Warden*, pp.338-339.

deck, watching British Beaufighters attacking ELAs strongholds, while occasional shells landed in the water nearby. Then it was into the armoured cars, the Prime Minister complete with pistol, while his private secretary borrowed a tommy gun from their driver.[82] Across town large quantities of dynamite were discovered under the Hotel Grande Bretagne where Papandreou and the Greek politicians were assembling.[83] At the British Embassy Churchill was photographed with the Archbishop in a garden that was considered 'exposed' to sniper fire, before giving 'a stirring speech' to the diplomatic staff who had endured so much.[84] Plans were then co-ordinated with Damaskinos, from whom Churchill secured the commitment that 'collaboration with the Communists in any form would be fatal to the welfare of the country and would alienate the majority of the Greek population'.[85] Yet all of this was preliminary to the main event, which then took place at the Greek Ministry of Foreign Affairs.

In a large unheated room, emptied of all furniture except a large table and chairs, and dimly lit by the glow of hurricane lamps, the cast of the Greek drama assembled. The Archbishop in his black robes and headdress sat in the middle on the right-hand side of the door, with Churchill and Eden on his right, Alexander and Macmillan on his left. Opposite them were the representatives of the mainstream Greek political parties. Churchill was facing Papandreou. Next to the Greek Prime Minister, resplendent in uniform and waxed moustache, sat the imposing figure of the republican General Plastiras. Soufalis and others were also there. The American Ambassador, the French Minister and the Soviet military representative were all in attendance. The only people who were not present were the EAM representatives, and it looked as though they were not going to show. Then, after the Archbishop had given his welcome address, and just as Churchill was starting to speak, there was a disturbance at the door and the three EAM leaders entered in khaki battledress.[86] Churchill began again, with an opening address that bore many similarities to his speech to the Lublin Poles in Moscow. After stating that, 'if all our efforts fail', the British would have a duty of rescuing the city of Athens from anarchy, he explained that Britain did not desire 'any material advantage from Greece':

---

[82] Colville, *Fringes of Power*, pp.540-541; Churchill, *The Second World War*, Vol VI, pp.273-274.

[83] Macmillan, *War Diaries*, p.617.

[84] Colville, *Fringes of Power*, p.541; Moran, *Struggle for Survival*, pp.210-211.

[85] TNA, PREM 3/213/12.

[86] Churchill, *The Second World War*, Vol. VI, p.274; Colville, *Fringes of Power*, pp.542-545; Moran, *Struggle for Survival*, pp.211-213; Macmillan, *War Diaries*, pp.617-618.

We do not want an inch of your territory; we seek no commercial advantages save those which are offered by Greece to all the nations of the world. We have not the slightest intention of interfering with the way in which a normal and tranquil Greece carries on its affairs. Whether Greece is Monarchy or a Republic is a matter for Greeks and Greeks alone to decide.[87]

Macmillan thought it 'very good – clear, firm and persuasive. He [Churchill] left no doubt in the minds of the ELAS on the one hand of our military power. On the other hand, he made it clear to the politicians that he did not mean us to be used for a reactionary policy'.[88] Having convened the meeting and brought the parties together under the Archbishop's chairmanship, Churchill and the British then left the Greeks to their discussions. The Prime Minister shook hands with the EAM delegates on leaving, and subsequently had to be restrained from accepting their invitation for a private meeting. This might have satisfied his own curiosity, but it would have interfered with the Archbishop's attempts at mediation.[89]

The next day, the Prime Minister came close to being hit when a burst of machine gun fire struck a house above him, killing a woman in the street.[90] This does not seem to have dampened his enjoyment at inspecting the military positions. He also gave a press conference at the Hotel Grande Bretagne, where dynamite had been uncovered just the day before. Here, he defended his decision to order the British troops to intervene, reported on the conference, and addressed criticism of British policy:

A tale has been telegraphed all over the world that we were supporting a Fascist to impose a particular rule on this country, endeavouring to bring back the King, endeavouring to get some advantage or influence for ourselves out of it. All these stories are absolutely without the slightest foundation. We seek nothing from Greece.[91]

The result of the Greek conference was the acceptance of the principle for a regency under Damaskinos. Churchill returned to London re-energised and with a new-found willingness to tackle the Greek King. On Saturday 30 December, he reported to the War Cabinet

---

[87] TNA, PREM 3/213/12.
[88] Macmillan, *War Diaries*, p.618.
[89] Churchill, *The Second World War*, Vol. VI, pp.276-277.
[90] Colville, *Fringes of Power*, p.545.
[91] TNA, PREM 3/213/12.

that after discussions starting at 22.00 hours on Friday evening and only finishing at 04.30 that morning, 'the King had agreed to issue a declaration appointing the Archbishop to be Regent during the period of emergency'. The news was to be broadcast by the BBC that night.[92] Cadogan's final diary entry for 1944 juxtaposed Churchill's Greek success with his Polish failure:

> Well, that's the end of *that* year... By the way, broadcast last night showed King of Greece had capitulated. Lublin Committee also proclaimed themselves Provisional Government![93]

The immediate legacy in Greece was positive for Churchill. The British forces cleared EAM from the area around Athens. Damaskinos formed a government with General Plastiras as Prime Minister. An uneasy truce was reached with EAM, and after a post-war plebiscite King George returned to Greece. Churchill was made an Honorary Citizen of Athens. Stadium Street was renamed for him, and on 14 February 1945, on his way back from the Yalta conference, he returned in triumph to make an impromptu speech to fifty thousand people in Constitution Square.[94] Greek success contrasted with Polish stalemate. He felt vindicated in his negotiations with Stalin. The Russian leader had been true to his word and done nothing to interfere as Churchill prevented a communist takeover. Honour had been preserved and British policy reasserted in the Mediterranean. On a personal level, he had enjoyed the freedom of action, but the flashes of resolve and decisiveness had been accompanied by a period of uncertainty that was perhaps revealing of a greater underlying national and personal weakness.

In the longer term, Churchill would continue to be criticised for his handling of the Greek crisis and particularly his bellicose response to the EAM demonstrations on 3 December. British troops did not fire on the crowd, but they stood by and allowed others to do so. The episode also damaged his relations with the Labour Party and contributed to the inevitable return of divisive partisan politics.

Churchill responded to the new realities in eastern Europe by trying to deal directly with Stalin. With regard to Poland he was ultimately impotent, thwarted by Stalin's refusal to do a deal that would

---

[92] TNA, CAB 65/48, WM (44) 176.
[93] Dilks (ed), *Cadogan Diaries*, p.692.
[94] CAC, Churchill Papers, CHUR 2/301/120-121; Churchill, *The Second World War*, Vol. VI, pp.346-347.

compromise Russian security, and by an understandable refusal on the part of the London Poles to engage. With regard to Greece, where the Soviet Union had no forces or immediate aims, he was able to carve out a unilateral policy. Yet, even here, he had to accept real constraints on his power and independence. The British were not strong enough to impose their will militarily on Greece, and to do so risked the wrath of both the United States and the Labour Party, on whom Churchill's coalition government depended. He had to expend a considerable amount of his own political capital and personal energy in order to drive through a solution, and there was undoubtedly a cost to both. But while Poland disappeared behind the iron curtain, Greece would ultimately emerge from years of civil war to take her place in NATO, and so remain a source of personal pride and consolation.

Poland and Greece illustrate Churchill's belief in face to face diplomacy. But they also show the constraints he was working under. In practice, he could only achieve what he wanted when he was negotiating from a position of strength. If it was difficult enough to impose British will on communist rebels in Athens, it was almost impossible to try and convince Stalin that he should not impose his will on Poland. The percentages agreement allowed Churchill to convince himself that Stalin was acting in good faith, and this may have led him to overestimate his wider influence. His preoccupation with Greece was born partly out of a debt of honour, and he clearly wrestled with his own conscience before accepting a solution that side-lined King George. That he did so, shows that it was also about power politics and securing an ongoing British presence and influence in the area. His initial vacillation was followed by resolute action, demonstrating considerable personal bravery, though his Christmas flight was prompted by rising criticism at home and abroad. The grand alliance of the United Nations and the wartime coalition had been held together by a common enemy. Now, they were starting to be pulled apart by very different visions of the post-war world. The iron curtain was beginning to descend, and the war was entering its final act.

Churchill met with a deputation from the Parliamentary Labour Party on 15 January 1945. They had come to discuss Greece. The presence of one of his most vocal critics, Anuerin Bevan, was particularly galling and Churchill insisted that Colville have the entire group seated before he arrived, so that he could avoid shaking hands.[95] In the subsequent conversation, he admitted to them that American criticism had been 'a great grief to me'. It is very unusual to find Churchill venting

---

[95] Colville, *Fringes of Power*, p.552.

frustrations about the United States, but he obviously felt very let down by Roosevelt's administration over Greece, and accused his ally of taking 'no responsibility in these matters' and noted that, 'instead of wishing to come and share the burden of the difficulties', they 'find it much easier to stand on the bank on the other side if the thing goes right; if it goes wrong they come in and criticise'.[96] Here was a rare moment of agreement between Churchill and Bevan. But, as the rest of the conversation made clear, there was far more they disagreed on.

Churchill used the occasion to defend his foreign policy actions in the Mediterranean against charges of self-interest:

> Let them vote; let them, men and women, vote, all of them... Let there be no intimidation. Let there be the secrecy of the ballot... We want nothing else for any of these countries, Yugo-Slavia, Italy. We stand on that foundation and it is a very hard one for people to knock you off. There is no other idea at all.[97]

That was not quite true. The other idea was to create a British sphere of influence in the Mediterranean: one that relied on preventing communism and trying to create the political environment for stable regimes with whom the British could work. Ideally, these should be democracies, for as Churchill now told the deputation:

> I do not believe in Governments that do no rest on popular election. The Government in Italy does not rest on popular election, a good many Governments do not. You may say our Government does not rest on popular election. Very well, I am willing that it should as soon as it can be done.

The thoughts of both Churchill and the Labour deputation were already turning towards the prospect of that British general election.

---

96 TNA, PREM 4/81/4.
97 TNA, PREM 4/81/4.

Chapter 10

Victory or Defeat?

Why did Churchill fight the 1945
election so aggressively?

The Deputy Prime Minister and Labour Party leader was furious. Clement Attlee sat down at his typewriter and hammered out an angry six-page letter to the Prime Minister. It began:

> I have for some time had it in mind to write to you on the method or rather lack of method of dealing with matters requiring Cabinet decisions. The proceedings last night (Wednesday) at the Cabinet have brought matters to a head. I consider the present position inimical to the successful performance of the tasks imposed upon us as a Government and injurious to the war effort.

Thereafter, it continued in the same vein, systematically setting out Attlee's objections to the way that Churchill was running the meetings at the heart of his government. Here is a taste of it, commenting on what happened when ministers submitted papers on civil affairs:

> Frequently a long delay before they can be considered. When they do come before the Cabinet it is very exceptional for you to have read them. More and more often you have not read even the note prepared for your guidance. Often half an hour and more is wasted in explaining what could have been grasped by two or three minutes reading of the minute or document. Not infrequently a phrase catches your eye which gives rise to a disquisition on an interesting point only slightly connected with the subject matter. The result is long delays and unnecessarily long Cabinets imposed on Ministers who have already done a full day's work and who will have more to deal with before they get to bed.

Even worse, was the accusation that Churchill was then undermining his colleagues by seeking alternative views from two Conservative ministers outside the War Cabinet; the Lord Privy Seal, Lord Beaverbrook, and the Minister of Information, Brendan Bracken. The allegation was that this was being done for party political reasons, and was unconstitutional, as it was the War Cabinet that must take responsibility for making such decisions. Attlee concluded by calling on Churchill to put himself in the position of his colleagues and reminded him that he might not have been so patient when he was a minister.[1]

This angry draft survives in a small collection of Clement Attlee's papers, given by him to the Churchill Archives Centre. It is not dated, but the reference to the Cabinet on a Wednesday would suggest that it was written in response to either the meeting of Wednesday 13 December, to which Beaverbrook and Bracken submitted a paper criticising proposals for the future distribution of industry, or to that of Wednesday 20 December, at which the two ministers were present for a debate on the future of local government.[2] It captures Attlee's frustration, but he did not send it straight away or in quite this form. Instead, he sat on it until 19 January, when a modified and slightly toned-down version was delivered to the Prime Minister's office. The direct reference to Churchill's 'lack of method' had been diplomatically removed, but the inference and the allegations were all still there.[3]

The response was predictable. Jock Colville recorded how Churchill 'exploded over Attlee's letter, drafted and redrafted a sarcastic reply, said it was a socialist conspiracy … and worst of all, finally read Atlee's very personal letter – poorly typed by his own hand so that none of his staff should see it – to Beaverbrook on the telephone, having first of all discussed it with Mrs Churchill'.[4] The heavily annotated draft responses survive in Churchill's own papers and, like Attlee's first attempt, are revealing of the Prime Minister's true frustrations and feelings. In passages that Colville probably regarded as particularly sarcastic, he admitted his own shortcomings 'in the matter of civil affairs', cited the 'great mass of war and foreign business' as well as the 'heavy parliamentary work' falling upon him, noted what Attlee had said about his 'laxity in these matters' and promised to try and become 'better acquainted with these subjects in the future, so as not to

---

[1] CAC, Attlee Papers, ATLE 2/2/16-21.
[2] TNA, CAB 65/44, WM (44) 168 & WM (44) 172.
[3] CAC, Churchill Papers, CHUR 2/4/86-88.
[4] Colville, *Fringes of Power*, p.554.

take up your valuable time in explaining them to me in the Cabinet'.[5] His red pen was much in evidence, adding to one draft the sentence, 'I need scarcely say I am deeply conscious of my own failings & that I will certainly try to live up to the standards you require'.[6]

Yet the main body of his intended reply was devoted to a detailed defence of his actions; arguing that it was his duty to counterbalance the 'dominating force' of the Labour politicians on the Home Affairs Committee and to ensure that a Conservative viewpoint was heard in his coalition Cabinet before any final decision was reached. In an interesting passage which he then crossed through, Churchill admitted, 'I am by no means a typical Conservative myself'. He stated that he was weak in the War Cabinet 'on Party grounds', where there were three Socialist leaders (Attlee, Bevin, Morrison), two Ministers with no political affiliation (Woolton and Anderson), and only two Conservatives (Eden and Lyttelton).[7]

But just like Attlee, Churchill now thought twice before sending his full response. Colville admitted to his diary that 'there is much in what Attlee says, and I rather admire his courage in saying it'. He was not alone. On this occasion that view was shared by both Clementine Churchill and Lord Beaverbrook.[8] Consequently, deserted by his friends and even by his wife, Churchill abandoned his detailed drafts to the archive, told his private secretary that they should 'think no more of Hittlee or Attler'[9], and fired off a wonderful two-line riposte to his Deputy Prime Minister. The final reply as received by Attlee, simply read:

> I have to thank you for your Private and Personal letter of January 19.
> You may be sure I shall always to endeavour to profit by your counsels.[10]

The exchange ended on a humorous note, but it had been a serious one for both Churchill and Attlee and is illustrative of the tensions that were starting to weaken the coalition government. On a personal level, all of the principal actors were exhausted. By May, Churchill was, by his own admission, 'very tired and physically so feeble' that he had to be carried upstairs in a chair by Marines from the underground

---

5   CAC, Churchill Papers, CHUR 2/4/78 & 82.
6   CAC, Churchill Papers, CHUR 2/4/82.
7   CAC, Churchill Papers, CHUR 2/4/85.
8   Colville, *Fringes of Power*, p.554.
9   Wheeler Bennett (ed), *Action This Day*, p.117.
10 CAC, Attlee Papers, ATLE 2/2/22.

Cabinet War Rooms.[11] Meeting the same people in the same smoke-filled rooms day after day, to wrestle with the same complex issues, must have taken a mental toll on all of the inner circle of the War Cabinet and their leading advisors. The relentless and claustrophobic atmosphere of wartime Whitehall is surely one of the reasons why Churchill loved the escape afforded by international conferences and his visits to the frontline. It is also why his loquacious and discursive style of chairmanship sometimes grated with his colleagues. These human frailties were now being exacerbated by the re-emergence of political divisions.

Since the end of the first phase of his premiership, and the fall of France, Churchill had kept the military policy of the war firmly in his own hands. He had run it through his personal contact with the Chiefs of Staff, his domination of the Defence Committee, and his ability to convene and chair ad-hoc conferences and sub-committees. Foreign policy had been undertaken largely in partnership with Eden, with the Prime Minister taking the lead in Anglo-American relations and in personal diplomacy with Roosevelt and Stalin. Meanwhile, the running of civil affairs and the Home Front had been delegated to the relevant ministers on the Lord President's Committee. As its name suggests, this was chaired by the Lord President of the Council, and so had initially been run by Neville Chamberlain. According to James Stuart, the Conservative Chief Whip, when Chamberlain died in 1940, Churchill had said, 'What shall I do without poor Neville? I was relying on him to look after the Home Front for me'.[12] He was prepared to take on Chamberlain's role as Leader of the Conservative Party, thereby making him less dependent on the support of his Labour and Liberal coalition partners, but he did not have the time or the inclination to assume additional administrative burdens.

So, the Lord Presidency and its Committee had passed to former civil servant John Anderson, before being vested, in September 1943, in Clement Attlee. The Committee included two other big Labour beasts in the persons of Ernest Bevin, Minister of Labour, and Herbert Morrison, the Home Secretary; both of whom had jobs grounded in the Home Front as befitted their respective pre-war roles running the unions and the local government of London. This was a division of labour that played to the strengths and experience of the individual team members and benefitted the coalition as a whole while there was a common enemy. But as victory loomed, and thoughts began to turn

---

11   Churchill, *The Second World War*, Vol. VI, pp.512-513.
12   Stuart, *Within The Fringe*, p.87.

to a return to Party politics, it led to mutual suspicions. Labour feared that military and foreign policy was in the hands of the Conservative Party; while the Conservatives were worried that Labour had too much influence over domestic policy and civil affairs. Thus, there were those in the Labour Party who spoke out against Conservative support for the forces of reaction in Greece and Italy, and who criticised Churchill for an anti-Russian policy; while some in the Conservative Party began to express the fear that Labour ministers were planning to prolong wartime controls and regulations on the Home Front. The Churchill-Attlee correspondence was a manifestation of this division. Both men had chosen to pull their punches because they still rated their national roles above their responsibilities as Party leader. Neither wanted to break up the coalition ahead of Germany's defeat.

At the end of January 1945, the war in Europe still had just over four months to run, but its course was clear. With the American and British armies advancing across Germany from the west, and the Soviets from the east, the fate of the Axis powers was sealed. Mussolini was captured by Italian partisans and executed on 28 April. Two days later, with the Russians in Berlin and about to storm his final underground stronghold, Hitler committed suicide.

On 8 May 1945, Churchill fulfilled the pledge that he had made in parliament five years earlier and announced victory over Nazi Germany. The celebrations on that historic day have been well documented. Churchill broadcast to the nation and then spoke to the House of Commons. He attended a service of thanksgiving at St Margaret's church in Westminster, appeared on the balcony of Buckingham Palace beside the King and Queen, and twice addressed the crowds from the Ministry of Health in Whitehall. At the end of his short BBC broadcast he turned from the celebration of victory to 'the toils and efforts that lie ahead' and reminded his listeners that 'Japan with all her treachery and greed, remains unsubdued'. His annotated notes reveal that he had originally wanted to say 'unpunished'. His conclusion was that, 'We must now devote all our strength and resources to the completion of our tasks', after which added in his own pen 'both at home and abroad'.[13] It was a theme that he took up again in the longer broadcast that he made on 13 May, five years to the day after his 'blood, toil, tears and sweat' speech:

---

[13]   CAC, Churchill Papers, CHAR 9/169/99.

I wish I could tell you tonight that all our toils and troubles were over, then indeed I could end my five year's service happily, and if you thought you had had enough of me and that I ought to be put out to grass, I assure you I would take it with the best of grace.

But on the contrary, I must warn you, as I did when I began this five year's task, and no-one knew then that it would last so long – that there is still a lot to do and that you must be prepared for further efforts of mind and body and further sacrifices to great causes if you are not to fall back into the rut of inertia, the confusion of aim and the craven fear of being great.[14]

His message was simple and public; he regarded the role as unfinished, and had no intention of standing down. There were two overriding objectives going forward. Firstly, Britain had to make sure that in continental Europe the 'simple and honourable purposes' for which she had entered the war were not brushed aside. No specific country was named, but his assertion that there would be 'little use in punishing the Hitlerites for their crimes… if totalitarian police governments were to take the place of the German invaders', was clearly consistent with his thinking on both Greece and Poland. Secondly, Britain had to fulfil her pledge to the United States and the Dominions, particularly Australia and New Zealand, in defeating Japan.[15]

Yet, even as he made these pronouncements, Churchill was aware that his coalition government might only last a few days. His own administration had been forged in the extraordinary circumstances of wartime, and had been a voluntary alliance of the major political parties, entered into for the duration of the emergency. He had become Prime Minister because the Conservatives were the biggest party in the House of Commons, and he was the only leading Conservative felt to be willing and able to form a national coalition. His rising stock with the general public had clearly been a factor in this decision, but his government had received no popular mandate at the polls. In fact, the country had not had a general election since 1935. Under normal conditions a parliament was not allowed to sit for more than five years, and such a vote should have taken place in 1940. Instead, special legislation had been enacted in each year of Churchill's premiership to allow the existing parliament to prolong its life without an appeal to the people, but the rationale for this had just been removed by victory in Europe. Speaking in the Commons on 31 October 1944, the last time prolongation had been sought, Churchill had indicated that,

---

14 CAC, Churchill Papers, CHAR 9/169/114.
15 CAC, Churchill Papers, CHAR 9/169/115-116.

'unless all political parties resolve to maintain the present Coalition until the Japanese are defeated we must look to the termination of the war against Nazism as a pointer which will fix the date of the General Election', and '... I have myself a clear view that it would be wrong to continue this parliament beyond the period of the German war'.[16] By the new year, as the Attlee-Churchill correspondence shows, the matter was to the fore in the minds of the senior politicians. Indeed, on 17 January, just before he sent his letter of complaint to Churchill, Attlee was reporting to parliament for the government on the practical arrangements for any vote. The 'exceptional circumstances' of trying to conduct a general election in wartime conditions, meant that special permission had been granted by the King for the date of any election to be announced three weeks before the formal proclamation, which would then be seventeen days before the poll. This would make for a longer period of campaigning, and MPs of all political persuasion were now wondering when Churchill would fire the starting gun.[17] His speech for the Conservative Party conference on 15 March only served to increase the tension. He spoke directly about the possibility of the impending break-up and told the party faithful to prepare themselves 'for the clash of party principles and party interests inseparable from an appeal to the judgment of the people'.[18]

The first question facing Churchill at this time was the one that has perhaps been least asked, both at the time and since. Namely, why did he decide to contest the election at all? VE Day was his moment of personal triumph. When he told the crowd gathered in Whitehall, 'This is your victory', they replied, 'No – it is yours'.[19] His place in history was secure, and, after five years of war and hardship, no one was going to begrudge him a retirement of painting and writing, or the status of an honoured and much-loved international statesman well above the party fray. According to the Churchills' youngest daughter, Mary Soames, this was very much Clementine's view: 'she felt very strongly that, having led a coalition Government and a united nation, he should retire rather than become the leader of one-half of the nation against the other'. Churchill's response to this, as told to Mary

---

[16] *Hansard*, 31 October 1944, House of Commons, Vol. 404, CC662-712: Churchill, *The Second World War*, Vol. VI, p.510.

[17] *Hansard*, 17 January 1945, House of Commons, Vol. 407, CC166-168; also in TNA, PREM 4/65/2.

[18] CAC, Churchill Papers, CHAR 9/207A/12.

[19] Gilbert, *Winston S. Churchill*, Vol. VII, p.1346.

by Duncan Sandys, was to say that he was not ready 'to be put on a pedestal'.[20]

At least one author has suggested that Churchill made Wavell not Eden Viceroy of India in 1943 because he had made up his mind to retire, and wanted Anthony to be available to succeed him.[21] Interestingly, correspondence in the Royal Archives suggests just the opposite. For, in April 1943, Churchill wrote to the King that his mind was 'turning very decidedly towards Mr. Eden' for the post, prompting the King's private secretary, Alan Lascelles, to encourage the monarch to object on the grounds that Eden was the only person who could talk to the Prime Minister as an equal, and that if this role were to be played by another, 'one dreads to think that it might be Beaverbrook'.[22] All of which implies that Churchill was not so wedded to keeping his Foreign Secretary close-by as heir apparent. However, the memoirs of James Stuart, the Conservative Chief Whip, who worked closely with Churchill on the plans for the 1945 election, refer to a personal minute of 18 March 1945. In it, the Prime Minister asked him to look up an old parliamentary bill of about 1888 in which the politicians Curzon, Brodrick and Wolmer petitioned for relief from automatically going to the House of Lords on the deaths of their titled fathers. Churchill noted that, 'It is a terrible thing for a father to doom his son to political extinction'. Stuart recorded this as an example of Churchill's far sightedness, and felt he was anticipating later attempts by politicians like Alec Douglas Home and Tony Benn to relinquish their aristocratic titles so as to be able to stay in the House of Commons and run for high office. Yet, Churchill's thoughts may have been closer to home. Perhaps he was thinking of the potential repercussions for his son, Randolph, should he (Winston) decide to accept a peerage or even a dukedom from the King.[23] If so, it was an isolated moment of doubt and quickly forgotten, for the rest of his words and actions, such as his speech for the Conservative Party conference just three days earlier, made it clear that he intended to carry on.

One reason for staying may have been loyalty to the Conservative Party, or at least a sense of duty. Having become their Leader in 1940, it would have been odd, and potentially hugely damaging for the party, for him to abandon them at the moment of triumph in 1945. In the aftermath of victory, Churchill appeared to be a huge electoral asset.

---

[20] Soames, *Clementine Churchill*, p.420.
[21] Pawle, *The War & Colonel Warden*, p.380.
[22] Royal Archives, PS/PSO/GVI/C/069/30-31.
[23] Stuart, *Within the Fringe*, p.98.

Dated 12 June 1945, an early survey result from the Daily Express Centre of Public Opinion, posed the question, 'Whom would you like to see as Prime Minister following the General Election?' Churchill topped the poll with 48 per cent of the responses, his fellow Conservative Eden came second with 18 per cent and Attlee was relegated to third place with just 13 per cent. With only 37 per cent of the respondents describing themselves as Conservative, it suggested that Churchill had an appeal that transcended Party lines, which ought therefore to have been an advantage, especially with non-decided voters. Churchill certainly saw this and presumably liked what he saw, sending it on to Clementine.[24]

The questionnaire may well have been sent to Churchill by Lord Beaverbrook. According to Chief Whip, James Stuart, 'It was easy to argue that the great war leader, Churchill, was an obvious odds-on favourite, and this Beaverbrook never failed to do, pointing to the rest of us as a collection of gutless oafs with perpetual cold feet'.[25] A.J.P. Taylor confirmed that Beaverbrook's electoral strategy 'was to base everything on Churchill's name' and in his biography of his former friend he published a letter from another senior Conservative, Lord Woolton, stating that, 'The mixture we want is Churchill the war-winner, Churchill the British bull-dog breed in international conference, and Churchill the war leader of a government with a programme of social reform'.[26] But, as we have seen, even in 1945 Churchill did not regard himself as a typical Conservative, and had spent much of his long career as a Liberal or as a backbench Tory rebel. Yet, having spent so long in the wilderness, it is unlikely that he wanted to give up his new-found popularity. The Conservative Party needed him, and he needed the Conservative Party, or so they both thought.

Since his first election to the House of Commons in 1900, at the age of just twenty-five, Churchill's life had been dominated by politics. The only political office that he had ever voluntarily relinquished was that of Chancellor of Duchy of Lancaster in November 1915; a position with no real power or portfolio, which he had been given after his sacking as First Lord of the Admiralty over the Dardanelles crisis. By resigning to take up a commission as an officer in the trenches of the Western Front, he had been able to restore his personal honour and facilitate his subsequent return to front-rank politics. By way of contrast, he knew

[24] CAC, Churchill Papers, CHAR 2/548B/218-219.
[25] Stuart, *Within the Fringe*, p.136.
[26] Taylor, A., *Beaverbrook*, (Hamish Hamilton, 1972), p.565.

241

that there would be no way back from his retirement as Prime Minister in 1945 and he does not appear to have seriously contemplated such a course. Struck down with pneumonia in Carthage in December 1943, he did tell his daughter Sarah that, 'it doesn't matter if I die now, the plans of victory have been laid'.[27] But one suspects that for Churchill there was a world of difference between dying in harness at the height of his powers like Nelson, or fading away impotently like Napoleon. It was not in his nature to give up.

Even though his health was now often poor, and there were days when he could not get through the paperwork in his boxes, he relished, and perhaps even needed, the excitement of life at the centre of critical affairs. According to Lord Moran, by 22 June, he was already lamenting that he felt 'very lonely without a war'.[28] Linked to this was his continuing self-belief and confidence in his own abilities. He had negotiated the percentages agreement with Stalin, and had led the intervention in Greece.

Churchill felt an obligation to finish what he had started and believed that he was best placed to deliver. If he was to continue in office, he had two options. He could ask the other parties to extend the coalition for a defined period, or he could lead the Conservative Party in a general election and attempt to win a majority of seats. In his memoirs, he was keen to emphasise his desire that 'national comradeship and unity should be preserved till the Japanese war was ended'.[29] There was no doubt a lot of truth in this, but it was not a straightforward proposition, as no-one knew when the Japanese war would end, and thus it was not clear how long a programme the parties would be signing up for. In the end, the atomic bomb would bring victory in the Far East far more quickly than any dared anticipate; but Churchill's best guess in May 1945 was that the war would continue well into 1946 or perhaps even into 1947. The alternatives were to hold a snap election in the summer or to delay till the autumn. The political parties began to make contingency plans for a break-up and to consider the options. By April, it is clear that a process of consultation was well under way within the Conservative Party, but the signals were conflicting. Backbench Conservative MPs on the Conservative Members Committee 'favoured an early appeal to the country', while some of the local Association Chairmen expressed the 'gravest apprehension' at the prospect of a summer election.[30] Yet

---

[27] Churchill, S., *A Thread in the Tapestry*, (Sphere, 1968), p.77.
[28] Moran, *Struggle for Survival*, p.254.
[29] Churchill, *The Second World War*, Vol. VI, p.512.
[30] CAC, Churchill Papers, CHAR 2/549/16-17; CHAR 2/549/21-23.

Churchill was aware that the 'Conservative Managers', his election inner circle including Beaverbrook, inclined to June.[31]

Once the VE Day celebrations had ended, Churchill was open to accusations of governing without a popular mandate and being in breach of his previous promises to parliament. He had no choice but to address the issue. Cross party discussions began in earnest on Friday, 11 May. At 12.30 hours, Churchill and the Conservative Chief Whip, James Stuart, met with Herbert Morrison and Ernest Bevin of the Labour Party, who confirmed Labour's preference for an October election.[32] This was not surprising. The Labour Party feared that a quick June election would favour the Conservatives, who, with VE Day fresh in the public mind, would be able to present Churchill as the architect of victory. A delay till the autumn would allow the euphoria to dissipate, and would also give time for the introduction of a new electoral register, which it was felt might favour Labour.

At 15.30 hours, Churchill held a conclave of Conservative Ministers and asked them for their views in writing.[33] He would later write that, 'All but two were for June'.[34] Yet the returned slips survive in his archive, and they reveal a more nuanced situation. Most of the Conservative politicians thought that an offer should be made to continue the coalition until the end of the war with Japan, or for a specified period. They favoured a June election but only after such an offer had been refused, and though they saw the advantages of an early poll, they also saw the risks of being attacked for capitalising on victory. This was spelt out by the two members who advised against an early poll. 'Rab' Butler, the Under Secretary of State for Foreign Affairs, argued that it was 'essential that the Prime Minister should stand before the British public as a believer in a National/broadbased Govt' and should not appear to go for a quick election 'in the interests of his party just after his great success in defeating Germany', as Lloyd George had tried to do in 1918.[35] While Harry Crookshank, the Postmaster General, advised against, 'Anything which looks like either cashing in on the victory, or kicking out Labour'.[36]

This line was supported by Clementine Churchill, who was also asked to submit her views on this 'vexed question'. She replied on 12 May that, 'I feel that the interests of the country would be best served

31 Churchill, *The Second World War*, Vol. VI, p.511.
32 CAC, Churchill Papers, CHAR 2/550/60-62.
33 CAC, Churchill Papers, CHAR 2/550/60-62; Churchill, *The Second World War*, p.511.
34 Churchill, *The Second World War*, p.511.
35 CAC, Churchill Papers, CHAR 2/549/2.
36 CAC, Churchill Papers, CHAR 2/549/3.

if the present Government could continue until the end of the war with Japan. ... If, however, they [Labour] persist in their refusal, I think if I were you I would then hold the Election when it suits you best'.[37] On the same day Churchill received a note from Beaverbrook, attaching the results of another questionnaire from the Daily Express Centre of Public Opinion. It reported on the responses of 5,200 people to the question, 'Do you want a General Election as soon as Germany is defeated, or do you think it should be postponed until the Autumn?' Seventy-four per cent were in favour of postponement, while the accompanying analysis showed that this included 83 per cent of the Conservative respondents. Beaverbrook's note observed that, 'In the past the answers given to questions asked by the Centre of Public Opinion have proved a reliable indication of the views of the electorate'. Churchill was clearly worried enough to annotate, 'Please talk to me about this'.[38] The upshot of these deliberations was his offer to prolong the life of the coalition until after the defeat of Japan.

Attlee's trip to the United States meant that the two main party leaders did not meet till the evening of Wednesday 16 May. The Labour leader appeared open to the possibility of continuation and wanted a letter to take to his party conference, which was about to meet in Blackpool. The following evening saw a further meeting with Attlee, sandwiched between meetings of the Conservative ministers, to debate and refine the draft. On 18 May, the letter was sent to Attlee and to the two other coalition party leaders, Archibald Sinclair of the Liberals and Ernest Brown of the National Liberals.[39] In it, Churchill expressed the view that, 'It would give me great relief if you and your friends were found resolved to carry on with us until a decisive victory has been gained over Japan'. He suggested finding some means 'of taking the nation's opinion, for example a referendum, on the issue whether in these conditions the life of this Parliament should be further prolonged'.[40] That afternoon Attlee suggested a further amendment confirming that the coalition government would work 'to implement the proposals for Social Security and full employment' contained in the existing White Papers. The Labour leader's price was a continued commitment to social reform, and the implementation of aspects of the 1942 Beveridge Report (which had advocated universal social security and insurance). This was accepted by Churchill and confirmed in writing.[41]

---

37 CAC, Churchill Papers, CHAR 2/549/12.
38 CAC, Churchill Papers, CHAR 2/549/27-30.
39 CAC, Churchill Papers, CHAR 2/550/60-62.
40 CAC, Attlee Papers, ATLE 2/2/24-26; Churchill Papers, CHAR 20/194A/23-25.
41 CAC, Attlee Papers, ATLE 2/2/29.

The complexity of these negotiations is revealing. Churchill may have instinctively preferred some form of continuation, but his overriding aim was to find a way of staying in office. His offer to Attlee was based on the political calculation that the Conservatives would have the best chance of winning a general election in the immediate aftermath of victory, whether against Germany or Japan. He did not want to let the Labour Party set the election timetable, but nor did he want to be seen as breaking up the coalition. His strategy put the onus firmly on the Labour Party. It had been a Labour Party conference in Bournemouth that had helped bring Chamberlain down and Churchill to office in May 1940. Ironically, it was now the Party conference in Blackpool that would bring things full circle and end his wartime coalition. Attlee and some of Labour coalition ministers were hesitant, worried about a snap election and in favour of carrying on in coalition until the defeat of Japan, but the National Executive Committee and the Parliamentary Labour Party were firmly for dissolution.[42] On 21 May, Churchill received Attlee's reply refusing the offer, as 'too uncertain'. The Labour leader felt a referendum would be 'alien to all our traditions', and accused Churchill of rejecting an autumn election for 'considerations of party expediency', stating, 'It appears to me that you are departing from the position of a national leader by yielding to the pressure of the Conservative Party which is anxious to exploit your own great services to the nation in its own interest'.[43]

Churchill was with his son, Randolph, and Harold Macmillan when the reply was received. Colville noted how, 'At once all was swept aside and electioneering became the only topic'. He also confirmed that the Conservatives felt they had outmanoeuvred Labour, putting on them 'the onus of refusing to continue and of preferring faction to unity at a time when great dangers still remain'. To Colville 'the most assiduous intriguer and hard-working electioneer' was Lord Beaverbrook, while Churchill seemed less happy.[44] But that said, Churchill and his son now threw themselves enthusiastically into drafting and redrafting a reply to Attlee's letter. The expectation was that this correspondence would be made public and form part of the argument before the electorate. Churchill loved nothing better than a war of words and did not hold back. He rejected Attlee's demand to prolong the coalition until October on the grounds that, 'we should be continually preparing

[42] Brooke, S., 'The Labour Party and the 1945 General Election', *Contemporary Record*, Volume 9, 1995, p.16.
[43] CAC, Churchill Papers, CHAR 2/550/16-18.
[44] Colville, *The Fringes of Power*, p.601.

for an Election', and had 'already suffered several months of this electioneering atmosphere'. While, on the allegation of pandering to party expediency, he accused Attlee of darkening the correspondence with aspersions, and argued:

> I have concerned myself solely with trying to create tolerable conditions under which we could work together. It is clear from the tone of your letter and the feelings of your Party that these no longer exist and it is odd that you should accompany so many unjust allegations with an earnest request that we should go on bickering together till the Autumn.[45]

This set the combative tone for Churchill's election campaign. The next day he submitted his resignation to the King and was called upon to form a 'caretaker' government during the period until the poll could be conducted. This he did, drawing largely from the ranks of the Conservative Party, but including some non-party ministers. The wartime Coalition was over; the starting gun for the election had been fired. The poll would take place on 5 July. Due to the extra difficulty of counting the overseas Service votes, the result would not be announced until 26 July.

Having decided to stand, and forced an early show-down with Labour, Churchill had to decide how he was going to campaign. With the benefit of hindsight, we know that the election would be a disaster for him, culminating in a Labour landslide and overall majority in the House of Commons of 146. Many reasons have been given for the defeat: a lack of trust in a Conservative Party that had presided over the descent into war; a belief that the Labour Party was more likely to facilitate the quick return of the troops from overseas and provide them with houses, schools, jobs and hospitals; a new generation voting for the first time, which had been shaped by the egalitarianism of the war years; and a belief that Churchill was more a man of war than peace.[46] All these surely played their role, and it seems that unseen, and untested since 1935, the political tide had shifted. Churchill's government had lost a number of by-elections to left wing independent or Common Wealth Party candidates, and polls by the British Institute of Public Opinion conducted between 1943 and 1945 had consistently indicated

---

[45] CAC, Churchill papers, CHAR 20/194A/35-38 & ATLE 2/2/27-28.
[46] Best, G., *Churchill: A Study in Greatness*, (Hambledon & London, 2001), p.269; Brendon, P., *Winston Churchill: A Brief Life*, (Pimlico, 2001), p.198; Addison, P., *Winston Churchill*, (Oxford University Press, 2007), pp.104-105; Stuart, *Within the Fringe*, pp.136-137.

a Labour lead of between eight and eighteen percentage points.[47] When it came to the campaign itself, the Labour Party appeared unusually united behind a strong manifesto, while the Conservative organisation was suffering from years of benign neglect and an over reliance on Churchill as a winning asset.[48] Though all of this must also be set against a near universal view that Churchill played the hand he had been dealt very badly.

The Conservative case for putting Churchill at the heart of their campaign was that he was the national leader who had brought them safely to victory in Europe, and who could – in the words of their election literature – be trusted to 'Finish the Job'. The electorate was being asked to put their confidence in his judgment and in his strong and stable leadership. Indeed, Churchill announced that his was to be a national government that would draw from outside the Conservative Party. Yet, from the outset, such a policy was undermined by the approach that he took to the campaign. Rather than remain statesmanlike and concentrate on his programme at home and abroad, he chose to launch a full-bodied attack on the doctrine of socialism. His first election broadcast of 4 June set the tone. The socialist policy was 'abhorrent to the British ideas of freedom'. There was 'no doubt that Socialism was inseparably interwoven with totalitarianism and the abject worship of the State'. A Socialist State would not suffer opposition, tolerate a free parliament, and most controversially would 'fall back on some form of Gestapo, no doubt very humanely directed in the first instance'.[49]

Listening to the first broadcast, Churchill's Conservative colleague Leo Amery was dismayed as:

> Winston jumped straight off his pedestal as world statesman to deliver a fantastical exaggerated onslaught on Socialism which, while cheering a good many of our supporters, will put off a lot of those who might otherwise have voted on the main international issue.[50]

Churchill had relied on the Labour Party to sustain his coalition, and given their leaders a prominent role in running civil affairs. Yet now he had compared them to the very Nazis they had been fighting. The left-wing press was up in arms, and even the more right-wing publications seemed stunned. The *Daily Mail* newspaper acknowledged that, 'Even

---

[47] Brooke, 'The Labour Party and the 1945 General Election', p.8.
[48] See Kandiah, M., 'The Conservative Party and the 1945 General Election', *Contemporary Record*, Vol. 9, 1995, pp.22-47.
[49] CAC, Churchill Papers, CHAR 9/170/7-9.
[50] CAC, Amery Papers, AMEL 7/39.

the most cautious political observers regarded it as an indication of the fierceness of the campaign which is to be fought'.[51] While the *Spectator* warned that, 'constructive campaigning is much to be preferred to destructive. In war attack may be the best form of defence, but an election is not precisely a war'.[52] Thereafter, Churchill did not let up. In his second broadcast of 13 June he asserted that a socialist system would mean an end to 'healthy opposition and the natural change of Parties', and repeated that it would require a political police.[53] On 21 June, he warned that a centralised Labour government would 'plan for all our lives and tell us exactly where we are to go and what we are to do, and any resistance to their commands will be punished'.[54]

Such statements, especially the 'Gestapo' speech, played directly into the hands of the Labour politicians. Attlee broadcast a response in which he thanked the Prime Minister for helping the electors to understand the 'difference between Winston Churchill, the great leader in war of a united nation, and Mr. Churchill, the party Leader of the Conservatives' and mouthpiece of Lord Beaverbrook.[55] Ernest Bevin used a speech in Wandsworth to develop the analogy still further, describing the Prime Minister 'as a Jekyll and Hyde personality', and it was as Mr. Hyde that 'he was now appearing as the Party hack of the Tories'.[56] After years of working together in the Cabinet, the Labour Ministers knew exactly which buttons to press to goad Churchill, and their interventions led him to publish further angry statements in the press which only served to reinforce this partisan image. His last two radio broadcasts included long sections on the attempts by the Labour Party Chairman, Professor Harold Laski, to limit the role of Clement Attlee at the Potsdam Conference, and the extent to which this proved that the Labour Party was really controlled by its National Executive Committee and so was unaccountable to parliament. It was an issue that was unlikely to resonate with all but the most well-informed and politically obsessed of voters.

In one sense, the Labour Ministers were right, Churchill was exhibiting a dual personality towards them in this period. When the coalition dissolved and Bevin tendered his letter of resignation, Churchill replied with, 'You know what it means to me not to have your aid in these terrible times', before personally annotating his first draft, 'We must hope for re-union when Party passions are less

---

[51] CAC, Churchill Press Cuttings, CHPC 22.
[52] CAC, Churchill Press Cuttings, CHPC 22.
[53] CAC, Churchill Papers, CHAR 9/170/55.
[54] CAC, Churchill Papers, CHAR 9/170/93.
[55] Jenkins, R., *Churchill*, (Macmillan, 2001), p.793.
[56] TNA, PREM 4/65/2.

strong'.[57] At the end of the month, he offered Attlee, and through him Bevin, special facilities at the Cabinet Office to see papers on foreign affairs and strategy, and on 2 June, he invited the Labour leader to accompany him to the final 'Big Three' Conference in Potsdam so that, 'however the Election may go, the voice of Britain is united'.[58] Later, he even suggested that Attlee have a government servant to look after his luggage and personal requirements while staying in Germany.[59] This was partly about doing the right thing under the constitution, but it also reflected Churchill's ability to compartmentalise, and to separate personal and professional relations.

His gestures to Attlee and Bevin raise the question of his confidence about the election result. Did he suspect that he might be defeated? If he did, it was not something that he could show as a leader. There were certainly some reservations in his family circle. After his 'Gestapo' broadcast, Sarah Churchill sent her father a letter gently warning him that his violent attack on socialism might backfire:

> You see the people I know who are labour, don't vote labour for ideals or belief, but simply because life has been hard for them, often, an unequal struggle and they think that only by voting labour will their daily struggle become easier.

She also pointed out that 'Socialism as practised in the war, did no one any harm, and quite a lot of people good'.[60] His younger daughter, Mary, wrote to her mother in a similar vein complaining of feeling 'gloomy and uncertain'. On active service with the Auxiliary Territorial Service in Europe, she noted that, 'Papa's first election address was not received very well' and felt that the 'Army votes will largely go to Labour'.[61] Lady Violet Bonham Carter, one of Churchill's oldest friends and a lifetime Liberal now standing for election as an MP, was clear that, 'You should have remained a National Leader – above the battle, and then we could all have followed you into the peace'.[62]

Of course, there were those, like Conservative Party Chairman Ralph Assheton and Lord Beaverbrook, who continued to predict a Conservative majority right up until the results were declared.[63] While

---

57 CAC, Churchill Papers, CHAR 20/207/17.
58 CAC, Churchill Papers, CHAR 20/194A/67-69; Churchill Papers, CHAR 20/194A/88.
59 CAC, Churchill Papers, CHAR 20/194B/177.
60 CAC, Churchill Papers, CHAR 1/387/23.
61 Soames, *A Daughter's Tale*, p.342.
62 CAC, Churchill Papers, CHAR 20/196/61.
63 CAC, Churchill Papers, CHAR 2/548/157 & 189-190.

Churchill would undoubtedly have taken much encouragement from the huge and generally enthusiastic crowds that received him on his four-day election tour of the country at the end of June. In Manchester alone, it was reported that 100,000 people had gathered to see him.[64] *The Times* reported his passage through the Midlands on 25 June in triumphal terms:

> If there ever existed any doubt about the continuing popularity of the Prime Minister among all classes in the country it was completely dissipated to-day. Throughout the whole length of his first day's tour – and it was a long one – from Chequers through the heart of the industrial Midlands his reception was so tumultuous and overwhelming that his programme was seriously delayed.[65]

Yet under the telling headline, 'Churchill in the Midlands. Cheers for him, but not for the Tories', the *News Chronicle* presented a more nuanced picture:

> Amid cheers, amid catcalls, amid the singing of 'For He's A Jolly Good Fellow' and the boisterous roaring of the 'Red Flag', Mr. Winston Churchill made his first day's electioneering journey through the Midlands today.[66]

When Churchill suggested that the size of the cheering crowds encountered put the election beyond doubt, Jock Colville reminded him that it was not a Presidential election.[67] Further indications of dissent were encountered during the final days of campaigning in London, when he faced a hostile crowd in Walthamstow and had a squib thrown at him from the crowd in Tooting Bec.[68]

The evidence is that Churchill was aware that this was an increasingly bitter and divisive fight, indeed he had helped to set that tone. His last election broadcast complained that, 'a flood of violent altercations and extreme bitterness has broken loose'. Yet he remained confident in his own popularity and his abilities. He used this final radio address to reassert his conviction that only he could help the country 'through the dangers and difficulties of the next few years with more advantages than would fall to others' and to deny 'stories now being put about that you can vote for

---

[64] Churchill, W.S., *His Father's Son*, (Weidenfeld & Nicolson, 1996), p.271.
[65] CAC, Churchill Press Cuttings, CHPC 22.
[66] CAC, Churchill Press Cuttings, CHPC 22.
[67] Colville, *Fringes of Power*, p.609.
[68] Soames, *Clementine Churchill*, p.421.

my political opponents at this Election… without at the same time voting for my dismissal from power'. He may have taken such stories as further proof of his popularity, whereas perhaps they were a warning that there were many who admired him but were not going to vote for him.[69]

What caused Churchill to fight the campaign in the way he did? In the final volume of his history, *The Second World War*, he chose not to discuss the election in detail. Instead he placed the narrative focus firmly on the international scene; the preparations for the Potsdam Conference and the ongoing war in Japan. In the one paragraph that he did devote to the campaign he described June as being 'hard to live through', with 'strenuous motor tours' and 'laboriously prepared broadcasts' that consumed his 'time and strength'. He emphasised that the election was not something that he had sought or wished to prioritise above the 'sombre background' of world affairs.[70] It is easy for us to forget that he was struggling with two roles throughout this period, and that in his role as Prime Minister he was carrying the accumulated tiredness of five years of high office. Clementine wrote to Mary on 21 June, the date of Churchill's third election broadcast, reporting that, 'He is very low, poor Darling. He thinks he has lost his "touch" & he grieves about it'.[71]

The crowds must have had a rejuvenating effect on his spirits, but the four-day tour, when accompanied by the ever-present demands of the prime ministerial boxes, must have been gruelling, and he admitted in a letter to Lord Long that they were 'wonderful experiences but very tiring'.[72] Tiredness may well have affected his performance and possibly his judgment, but he did not let it prevent him from taking centre stage. He wrote and made his four broadcasts and he threw himself into campaigning.

It has been argued that Lord Beaverbrook had an excessive and ultimately unhealthy influence on the campaign. As early as 6 December 1944, Macmillan came away from a meeting with him convinced 'that his power was greater than last year. He seems to be getting his hands on the Conservative machine in some mysterious way'.[73] In January, Attlee complained about the way the Prime Minister was using Beaverbrook to undermine Cabinet government, and in June dismissed Churchill's first broadcast as being the 'mind of Lord Beaverbrook'.[74]

---

[69] CAC, Churchill Papers, CHAR 9/170/104, & 109-110.
[70] Churchill, *The Second World War*, Vol. VI, p.528.
[71] Soames, *Clementine Churchill*, p.420.
[72] CAC, Churchill Papers, CHAR 20/194B/69.
[73] Macmillan, *War Diaries*, p.598.
[74] CAC, Attlee Papers, ATLE 2/2/16-21; Jenkins, *Churchill*, p.793.

According to Mary Soames, Clementine Churchill objected to much of his counsel, and that of Brendan Bracken, as 'ill-judged' and 'rashly optimistic'.[75] There is no doubt that Churchill was in very regular contact with Beaverbrook at this time and was relying both on his advice and media contacts. His input into the strategy for the election was clearly large, but the key letters, statements and broadcasts were still dictated and corrected by Churchill himself. He was not just the voice of the virulent anti-socialist campaign, he was also its architect. Churchill had shown during the war that he was perfectly capable of ignoring or even dismissing Beaverbrook. He was using him now, because as he admitted to Attlee, he regarded him as a voice of the Conservative Party, and a voice that he agreed with. Churchill did not listen to the warnings of his friends and family because he did not want to hear them, and because he had fixed views on how the campaign should be fought.

In part, this was a return to his political roots. Churchill had been a passionate opponent of socialism throughout his political career. Even in his most radical phase, as a young Liberal politician in 1908, he had castigated it as a barren philosophy that sought to pull down wealth, destroy private interests, kill enterprise, assail the pre-eminence of the individual, exalt the rule rather than the man, and attack capital.[76] As a Conservative Chancellor of the Exchequer in the 1920s, he had led the government opposition to the General Strike. Now, Leo Amery felt that there was 'no getting round the fact that he is essentially a Mid-Victorian Whig and means to fight the election on the purely negative tack of the Socialist bogey'.[77] It was a conviction that must have been strengthened by Churchill's view of the international scene, where he saw communist forces seeking to install themselves in Albania, Greece, Italy, Poland and Yugoslavia, and where he feared a consequent loss of democratic freedoms. The rhetoric and language he had used to condemn the aspirations and actions of EAM in Greece was still fresh in his mind and on his tongue.

Churchill was also finally free from the constraints of coalition and able to respond to some of his most vociferous critics on the left, people like Aneurin Bevan and Harold Laski whom he felt had been undermining his foreign policy and his premiership. It may have been a big leap to argue that the British Parliamentary Labour Party would lead inexorably to Soviet-style communism, but Churchill was seeking

---

[75] Soames, *Clementine Churchill*, p.420.
[76] CAC, Churchill Papers, CHAR 9/22/128.
[77] CAC, Amery Papers, AMEL 7/39.

to present two alternative visions for the future of Britain. This went to the heart of why he had become Prime Minister, and why he had waged war for five long years. In his speech to the Conservative Party Conference in March 1945 he had acknowledged the need for State regulation and control in wartime, as a means to a specific end, but once that end was reached, 'control for control's sake is senseless':

> Controls under the pretext of war or its aftermath which are in fact designed to favour the accomplishment of totalitarian systems however innocently designed, whatever guise they take, whatever liveries they wear, whatever slogans they mouth, are a fraud which should be mercilessly exposed to the British public.[78]

He had been fighting to preserve British independence and Empire but also British liberties. Rather than break with the past, he was looking for continuity. Thus, in his final election broadcast, he looked back to the Britain of September 1939, arguing that it was already peopled by 'a far stronger, healthier, better-bred, better-led, better-housed and better educated race' than had been the case before the First World War. Britain did not need a brave new world, she needed to be able to return and pick up where she had been forced to leave off. When Lord Moran told Churchill that there were 'two opposing ideas in the country', and that universal gratitude to him was tempered by the notion that he was not keen on 'this brave-new-world business', Churchill replied, 'The desire for a new world is nothing like universal; the gratitude is'.[79]

In his third election broadcast, Churchill equated British democracy to 'hearth and home in the land of Hope and Glory'.[80] It was archaic language of the type that had permeated his oratory throughout the war. Yet whereas this had struck the right chord with many when hearth and home were under attack, it seemed less relevant to the realities of post-war reconstruction. Churchill did emphasise his credentials as a pioneer of social insurance, and talk about his commitment to new housing, but the headlines were grabbed by his violent attacks on the Labour Party, and these too struck the wrong note. His attacking style had not changed, but as the *Spectator* had pointed out, an election was not a war, and as Bevin subsequently told Eden, 'the people nowadays like dignity. They don't even like you to mention your opponent'.[81]

---

78 CAC, Churchill Papers, CHAR 9/207A/24.
79 Moran, *Struggle for Survival*, p.251.
80 CAC, Churchill Papers, CHAR 9/170/101.
81 Eden, *The Reckoning*, p.553.

Ultimately, Churchill fought and lost the campaign on the principles he believed in, using the only methods he knew. He did not have the patience, time or the energy to adapt his tactics. He fought aggressively because he was a fighter. He kept going because he was not ready to become an icon, believing in his own abilities to do the job, and disliking the alternatives. His conviction and self-belief blinkered him to the changed political reality. By 1945, Anthony Eden had spent five years working alongside Churchill. Of the election campaign, and Churchill's failure to see beyond the cheers of the crowds, he wrote: 'He could not be expected to sense that there was also something valedictory in their message. He would not have been Winston Churchill if he had'.[82] To Clementine Churchill, who feared for her husband's health if he remained in office, it was 'a blessing in disguise'.[83]

---

[82] Eden, *The Reckoning*, p.550.
[83] Soames, *Clementine Churchill*, p.424.

Conclusion

How Did Winston Wage War?

'This is the first time for very many years that I have been completely out of the world'.[1] So wrote Winston Churchill from the shores of Lake Como in the first week of September 1945. He had exchanged the 'windy, rainy, misty skies' of an exhausted and bomb-scarred Britain for a marble palace in the sunshine of northern Italy.[2] This abandoned home of a former Italian business magnate was now the official residence of Field Marshal Alexander, who had been only too pleased to place it at the disposal of his former boss. In a wonderfully considerate gesture, a detachment of the Fourth Hussars, Winston's old cavalry regiment, was transferred from Austria to guard and protect him, complete with two young officers to serve as his personal aides. The presence of these brave, young men, fresh from the battlefield, along with that of his daughter Sarah, was designed to reinvigorate. Here was the ideal retreat from the aftermath of the election defeat; a place where Churchill could seek solace and recuperation in painting, bathing, reading and dining. His own letters home, and the accounts of his daughter Sarah and doctor, Lord Moran, confirm that this rest cure quickly worked its magic. So much so, that Churchill was even prepared to admit to Clementine that, 'It may all indeed be "a blessing in disguise"'.[3] This was confirmed by Sarah, who wrote to her mother:

> I really think he is over it, it is hard to tell, but he said last night: 'Every day I stay here without news, without worry I realize more and more that it may well be what your mother said, a blessing in disguise. The war is over, it is won and they have lifted the hideous aftermath from

---

[1] CAC, Baroness Spencer-Churchill Papers, CSSCT 2/34; Soames, *Speaking for Themselves*, p.535.

[2] CAC, Churchill Papers, CHUR 1/41/20; Soames, *Speaking for Themselves*, pp.533-534.

[3] CAC, Baroness Spencer-Churchill Papers, CSCT 2/34; Soames, *Speaking for Themselves*, p.535.

my shoulders. I am what I never thought I would be until I reached my grave "sans soucis et sans regrets" [without troubles and without regrets]'.[4]

It was over dinner with his young protectors that Churchill apparently said that the most important advice he could give them was to learn how to 'command the moment to remain'. The importance of living in the moment was a sentiment that he had expressed nearly half a century earlier, when he was young and in uniform like them. Writing to his mother from Atbara Fort, in the 113 degrees Fahrenheit heat of the Sudanese desert, on 16 August 1898, his twenty-three-year-old self, had reflected, 'I like this sort of life – there is very little trouble or worry but that of the moment – and my philosophy works best in such scenes as these'.[5]

Churchill had spent his formative years in the Victorian army, fighting for Queen and Empire, but also striving to emerge from his dead father's shadow and his own lack-lustre school years. Between 1895 and 1900, he had seen action in Cuba, the Indian North-West Frontier, the Sudan and South Africa. A few days before the battle of Omdurman, where he had charged with the 21st Lancers and killed men in battle, he had told his mother:

> Nothing – not even the certain knowledge of approaching destruction would make me turn back now – even if I could with honour.
> But I shall come back afterwards the wiser and the stronger for my gamble. And then we will think of other and wider spheres of action.[6]

After the charge, he confided to her that he had wanted to lead his men back into the fray:

> I told my troop they were the finest men in the world and I am sure they would have followed me as far as I would have gone and that I may tell you and you only – was a very long way – for my soul becomes very high in such moments.[7]

This spirit never left Churchill. As war-time Prime Minister he was still playing to the gallery, and was at his happiest when he was closest to the skirmish line or inspiring his troops. Here was a leader who was

---

[4] Sarah Churchill, 'A Thread in the Tapestry', pp.99-102.
[5] CAC, Churchill Papers, CHAR 28/25/32.
[6] CAC, Churchill Papers, CHAR 28/25/36.
[7] CAC, Churchill Papers, CHAR 28/25/44.

prepared to gamble, and to take calculated risks in order to open 'other and wider spheres of action'.

The key to understanding how Winston waged war lies in appreciating why. He was motivated by a sense of destiny and self-belief, a hatred of tyranny, and a desire to achieve victory and preserve the status quo. Complicated war aims, or utopian ideals, or dreams of territorial conquest were not for him. It is true that he embraced the declaration of the Atlantic Charter and the principle of unconditional surrender, but he did so more out of necessity than strongly-held conviction, hoping that they would help him in the moment. The former was to become a source of pride; the latter perhaps of regret. His approach to the future was driven by more practical considerations: the need for an understanding with Stalin; and the importance of the continuation of the special relationship with the United States to help preserve the peace and constrain the Soviet Union should that understanding with Moscow fail. He is considered an architect of the United Nations, but he was prepared to leave the detail to others. It was the same story on the British Home Front. His focus remained firmly on the war effort, on managing strategy, politics and international relations. It was a practical approach, fixed on achieving immediate results.

Churchill saw himself standing in the historical tradition of Drake, Marlborough, Nelson and Wellington. He quoted Cromwell and Napoleon, drawing inspiration from the past and channelling it for the benefit of the histories of the future, including his own. His language, in public and private, was often deliberately archaic. National honour was invoked, troops were ordered to fight to the death, even if these orders could not be enforced, and great weight was put on the quantity and quality of British frontline fighting troops. As Brooke noted, it was about winning laurels. He wanted to live his life on an historic plane, but that did not mean he would not immerse himself in minutiae should an issue attract his attention. The contradictions in this most complex character abound. He was a patron for independent innovators and new weaponry, but did not always seem to appreciate the logistics and support services required to move, service and maintain a modern army. But in a sense that did not matter. One of his key roles was as a prod, constantly questioning and goading his military commanders. His focus was on the here and now, even if it was presented in the language of the past, and motivated by a desire to prove himself 'superior even to time' – a phrase he had once used to describe his hero, Napoleon.[8]

---

[8] CAC, Churchill Papers, CHAR8/540.

He was at his best in the moment, in the heat of a crisis, and at his worst during periods of inactivity and waiting. It is revealing that in his war memoirs he admitted that when faced with the U-boat stranglehold, he would have willingly 'exchanged a full-scale attempt at invasion for this shapeless, measureless peril, expressed in charts, curves and statistics!'[9] The overseas travel, though increasingly gruelling, provided an escape from the confines of Whitehall and he relished the stimulus provided by face-to-face diplomacy with Roosevelt and Stalin, or by proximity to danger. Such trips allowed him to assert his independence and exercise some executive authority, sacking Auchinleck or brokering a truce in Athens. They also reinforced the image, so carefully cultivated in public, of an active commander in chief, even if behind the scenes he was more consultative and often more pragmatic.

The Victorian subaltern had been tempered by years of political experience, including periods of setback and disappointment, learning valuable lessons about the limitations and exercise of personal power. Churchill placed himself at the heart of the war machine, but he did not try and subvert the system. He may have worked most closely with the Chiefs of Staff and a select group of key advisers and ministers, but he took pains to consult the War Cabinet on all major decisions and remained keenly responsive to the mood of parliament and the opinions of the press. Much of his time was spent on communication by minute and telegram with generals, politicians, dominion leaders and allies. This was government by conference, conciliation and compromise, not dictatorship. He knew he was leading a coalition at home, and working with allies abroad. Churchill may have waged war from the front, but he went to great lengths to take others with him, and showed himself adept at political management and manoeuvring. It is that crucial backroom role which has been somewhat obscured by his own oratory and by the creation of his image as the roaring lion.

At the beginning of the war he was reacting to events, but also shaping and influencing them. As the conflict developed and widened, his influence declined as that of the United States and Soviet Union grew, but he continued to look for ways of promoting a British policy and acting independently. His political position at home, though never seriously challenged, was not as strong as Roosevelt's or Stalin's, and he was forced to navigate the fallout of successive military defeats and re-emerging domestic political divisions. The effect of waging war at the highest level took its inevitable toll on his health, and the number

---

[9] Churchill, *The Second World War*, Vol. III, pp.100-101. Cited by Pawle, *The War & Colonel Warden*, p.99.

of problems and frustrations facing the Prime Minister intensified as events moved towards the 'hideous aftermath'. He was not as decisive towards the end of the conflict, when faced with the bombing of the French railways or the crisis in Greece, but once roused he could still summon the energy, charisma and the personal influence to fight his corner, though it was clearly getting harder. It was far easier to keep the country focused and united when it was directly threatened, not least because his conservative vision of the future often conflicted with that of the Labour Party, the White House and the Kremlin.

Faced with all these challenges, Churchill could not always make the right decisions. Of course, in many cases there were no right decisions, only different outcomes, all potentially difficult and damaging. He was often playing a weak hand with few resources. His preferred response was to live in the moment: to prioritise, debate and then act upon the evidence in front of him. Whether sinking the French fleet, attacking in the Mediterranean, promoting the Atlantic Charter, accepting the Russian alliance, adopting unconditional surrender, or flying to Athens, time and again he chose not to worry about the possible long-term implications, but to win the immediate battle. Many of those who worked most closely with him spoke about his ability to find and focus on what was most important. Norman Brook of his War Cabinet secretariat noted that he had 'a remarkable intuitive capacity for picking out the questions on which he could most usefully concentrate his effort', while Colville recalled his ability to turn 'the searchlight of his mind' on any major problem, 'neglecting all else in the fervour of his concentration'.[10] Lord Moran recalled Clementine telling him that Winston always saw things in blinkers: 'His eyes are focused on the point he is determined to attain. He sees nothing outside that beam'.[11] Churchill gambled that one success would lead to another. This was about seizing the moment. The key to victory was to keep moving forward.

One battle at a time. That was how Winston waged war. Nor did he pretend it was otherwise. Speaking to the Commons on 27 February 1945, in the aftermath of the Yalta Conference, he reflected on his role:

> In 1940-41, when we in this island were all alone, and invasion was so near, the actual steps we ought to take seemed plain and simple. If a man is coming across the sea to kill you, you do everything in your power to make sure that he dies before he finishes his journey. That may be

---

10 Wheeler Bennett (ed), *Action This Day*, p.21 & p.51.
11 Moran, *Struggle for Survival*, p.247.

difficult and painful, but it is at least simple. Now we enter into a world of imponderables, and at every stage occasions for self-questioning arise. It is a mistake to look too far ahead. Only one link in the chain of destiny can be handled at a time.[12]

It was by keeping his eyes fixed on strengthening the individual links, that Churchill helped to forge the chain which led to victory.

---

[12] CAC, Churchill Papers, CHAR 9/167/168-169.

Select Bibliography

Primary sources
The National Archives (TNA)
CAB 65, War Cabinet & Cabinet Minutes
CAB 66, War Cabinet & Cabinet Memoranda
CAB 69, Defence Committee (Operations): Minutes & papers
CAB 80, Chiefs of Staff Committee Memoranda
CAB 99, Commonwealth & International Conferences: Minutes & papers
CAB 121, Cabinet Office Special Secret Information Centre
PREM 3, Prime Minister's Office: Operational correspondence & papers
PREM 4, Prime Minister's Office: Confidential correspondence & papers

The Churchill Archives Centre (CAC)
CHAR   Personal papers of Sir Winston Churchill (pre-1945)
CHUR   Personal papers of Sir Winston Churchill (post-1945)
AMEL   Personal papers of Leo Amery
ATLE   Personal papers of Lord Attlee
BRDW   The Broadwater Collection of Churchill family photographs & newspaper
        cuttings
BRNT   Personal papers of Correlli Barnett
CHPC   The Churchill Press Cuttings Series
CLVL   Personal papers of Sir John ('Jock') Colville
CSCT   Personal papers of Baroness (Clementine) Spencer-Churchill
DEKE   Personal papers of Denis Kelly
DUFC   Personal papers of Viscount Norwich (Duff Cooper)
HNKY   Personal papers of Lord Hankey
JACB   Personal papers of Sir Ian Jacob
KNNA   Personal papers of Patrick Kinna
LKEN   Personal papers of Leo Kennedy
LWFD   Personal papers of Valentine Lawford
MART   Personal papers of Sir John Martin
SCHL   Personal papers of Sarah Churchill
WCHL   The Churchill Additional Collection

Other Archives
Cherwell Papers, Nuffield College, Oxford
Hansard
Royal Archives, Windsor
The Times Digital Archive 1785-2011 (Gale-Thomson)

Secondary Sources (including published editions of diaries and papers)

Addison, P., *Winston Churchill*, (Oxford, Oxford University Press, 2007)

Barker, E., *Churchill and Eden at War*, (London, Macmillan, 1978)

Barnett, C., *The Desert Generals*, (London, Allen & Unwin, 1983)

Bennett, G., *Churchill's Man of Mystery*, (London, Routledge, 2007)

Best, G., *Churchill: A Study in Greatness*, (London, Hambledon & London, 2001)

Brendon, P., *Winston Churchill: A Brief Life*, (London, Pimlico, 2001)

Brooke, S., 'The Labour Party and the 1945 General Election', *Contemporary Record*, (Vol. 9, 1995)

Butler, J., *Grand Strategy*, Vol. 2, 'September 1939-June 1941', (London, HM Stationery Office, 1957)

Calder, A., *The Myth of the Blitz*, (London, Jonathan Cape, 1991)

Charmley, J., *Churchill: The End of Glory*, (London, Hodder & Stoughton, 1993)

Churchill, S., *A Thread in the Tapestry*, (London, Deutsch, 1967)

Churchill, W.S.,   *The World Crisis*, 6 vols (London, Thornton Butterworth, 1923-1931)

_____, *Arms and the Covenant* (London, Harrap, 1938)

_____, *The Second World War*, 6 vols (London, Cassell, 1948-1954)

_____, *The Dream*, (2nd edn, International Churchill Society, 1994)

Churchill, W., (grandson of Sir Winston) *His Father's Son*, (London, Weidenfeld & Nicolson, 1996)

_____, (ed.) *The Great Republic*, (London, Cassell, 2002)

Colville, J., *The Fringes of Power. Downing Street Diaries 1939-1955*, (London, Hodder & Stoughton, 1985)

Corbett, H., *Churchill the defender of Polish independence: The war of 1919-21 and its repercussions*, (unpublished MPhil dissertation, University of Cambridge, 2017)

Crang, J. & Addison P. (eds), *Listening to Britain*, (London, Bodley Head, 2010)

Danchev, A. & Todman D. (eds), *War Diaries 1939-1945. Field Marshal Lord Alanbrooke*, (London, Weidenfeld & Nicolson, 2001)

Day, D., *The Great Betrayal*, (Oxford, Oxford University Press, paperback edition, 1992)

Eden, A., *The Eden Memoirs, The Reckoning*, (London, Cassell, 1965)

De Gaulle, C., *War Memoirs*, Vol II, 'Unity', Richard Harwood (trans), (London, Weidenfeld & Nicolson, 1959)

Dilks, D. (ed), *The Diaries of Sir Alexander Cadogan*, (London, Cassell, 1971)

Eade, C., (ed.) *Churchill by his Contemporaries*, (London, Hutchinson, 1953)

Eisenhower, D., *Crusade in Europe*, (London, Heinemann, 1948)

Farrell, B. (ed) 'Churchill and the Lion City: Shaping Modern Singapore', (National University of Singapore, 2011)

Gilbert, M., *Winston S. Churchill*, Vol VI, 'Finest Hour', (London, Heinemann, 1983)

_____, *Winston S. Churchill*, Vol VII, 'Road to Victory', (London, Heinemann, 1986)

_____, *Churchill: A Life*, (London, Heinemann, 1991)

_____, *In Search of Churchill*, (London, Harper Collins, 1994)

_____, *Churchill and America*, (New York, The Free Press, 2005)

_____, *Churchill and the Jews*, (London, Simon & Schuster, 2007)

_____, *The Churchill Documents*, Vol 17, 'Testing Times 1942', (Hillsdale College Press, 2014)

Gorodetsky, G. (ed), *The Maisky Diaries. Red Ambassador to the Court of St James's 1932-1943*, (New Haven, Yale University Press, 2015)

Harvey, J. (ed), *The Diplomatic Diaries of Oliver Harvey, 1937-1940*, (London, Collins, 1970)

Ismay, H., *The Memoirs of General the Lord Ismay*, (London, Heinemann, 1960)

Jenkins, R., *Churchill*, (London, Macmillan, 2001)

Kandiah, M., 'The Conservative Party and the 1945 General Election', *Contemporary Record*, (Vol 9, 1995)

Keegan, J. (ed), *Churchill's Generals*, (London, Weidenfeld & Nicholson, 1991)

Kennedy, P., *The Engineers of Victory*, (London, Allen Lane, 2013)

Kimball, W., *Churchill and Roosevelt. The Complete Correspondence*, Vol I, 'Alliance Emerging October 1933 – November 1942', (Princeton New Jersey, Princeton, 1984)

_____, *Forged in War*, (London, Harper Collins, 1997)

Lawlor, S., *Churchill and the Politics of War, 1940-1941*, (Cambridge, Cambridge University Press, 1994)

Love, R. & Major, J. (eds), *The Year of D-day: The 1944 Diary of Admiral Sir Bertram Ramsay*, (Hull, Hull University Press, 1994)

Lukacs, J., *Five Days in London, May 1940*, (New Haven, Yale Nota Bene, 2001)

MacDougall, D., *Don and Mandarin. Memoirs of an Economist*, (London, John Murray, 1987)

Macleod, R. & Kelly, D. (eds), *The Ironside Diaries, 1937-1940* (London, Constable, 1962)

Macmillan, M., *War Diaries: Politics and War in the Mediterranean 1943-1945*, (London, Macmillan, 1984),

Macrae, S., *Winston Churchill's Toyshop*, (2nd edn, Stroud, Amberley, 2010)

Mace, M. & Grehan, J. (eds), *Despatches from the Front. The Commanding Officers' Reports from the Field and at Sea. Disaster in the Far East 1940-1942. The Defence of Malaya, Japanese Capture of Hong Kong, and the Fall of Singapore*, (Barnsley, Pen & Sword, 2015)

Milton, G., *The Ministry of Ungentlemanly Warfare*, (London, John Murray, 2016)

Montgomery of El Alamein, *The Memoirs of Field-Marshal the Viscount Montgomery of El Alamein*, (London, Collins, 1958)

Moran, Lord., *Winston Churchill: The Struggle for survival 1940-1965*, (London, Constable, 1966)

Morton, H., *Atlantic Meeting*, (London, Methuen, 1943)

Nel, E., *Mr Churchill's Secretary*, (London, Hodder & Stoughton, 1958)

Olson, S. (ed), *Harold Nicolson, Diaries and Letters 1930-1964*, (Penguin, 1984)

Overy, R., *The Bombing War*, (London, Penguin Books, 2014)

Pawle, G., *The War and Colonel Warden* (London, Harrap, 1963)

Playfair, I., *The Mediterranean and the Middle East*, Vol I (London, HM Stationery Office, 1954)

Reynolds, D., *The Creation of the Anglo-American Alliance 1937-41*, (Chapel Hill, The University of North Carolina Press, 1982)

_____, *In Command of History*, (London, Allen Lane, 2004),

Rhodes James, R. (ed), *Winston Churchill: His Complete Speeches*, 8 vols., (New York, Chelsea House, 1974)

Roberts, A., *Masters and Commanders*, (London, Allen Lane, 2008)

Roosevelt, E., *As He Saw It*, (New York, Duell, Sloan and Pearce, 1946)

Roskill, S., *The War at Sea*, Vol I (London, HM Stationery Office, 1954)

_____, *Churchill and the Admirals*, (London, Collins, 1977)

Schneer, J., *Ministers at War*, (Richmond, Oneworld, 2015),

Self, R. (ed) *The Neville Chamberlain Diary Letters*, Vol IV (Aldershot, Ashgate, 2005)

Shakespeare, N., *Six Minutes in May*, (London, Harvill Secker, 2017)

Soames, M., *Clementine Churchill*, (revised edition, London, Doubleday, 2002)

_____, *Speaking For Themselves*, (London, Doubleday, 1998)

_____, *A Daughter's Tale*, (London, Doubleday, 2011)

Spears, E., *Assignment to Catastrophe*, 2 vols., (London, Heinemann, 1954)

Stuart, J., *Within The Fringe*, (London, Bodley Head, 1967)

Tamkin, N., 'Britain, the Middle East and the "Northern Front", 1941-1942', *War in History*, (Vol. 15, No.3, 2008)

Taylor, A., *Beaverbrook*, (London, Hamish Hamilton, 1972)

Toye, R., *Churchill's Empire*, (London, Macmillan, 2010)

_____, *The Roar of the Lion*, (Oxford, Oxford University Press, 2013)

Vale, J. & Scadding, J., 'In Carthage ruins: the illness of Sir Winston Churchill at Carthage, December 1943', *Journal of the Royal College of Physicians Edinburgh*, (Vol. 47, 2017)

Wheeler-Bennett, J. (ed), *Action This Day* (London, Macmillan, 1968)

Woodward, L., *British Foreign Policy in the Second World War*, Vol. I (London, HM Stationery Office, 1970)

Index